IMAGES
of America

TIOGA COUNTY
NEW YORK

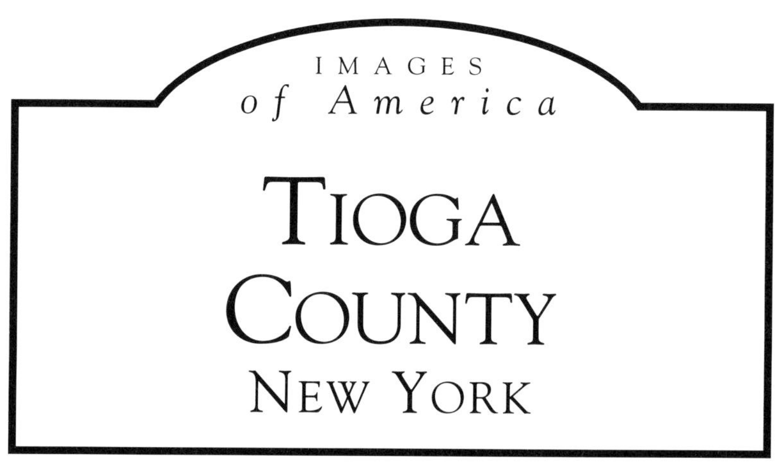

IMAGES
of America

TIOGA COUNTY NEW YORK

Richard Quest
Tioga County Historical Society

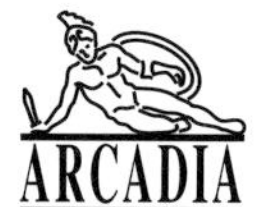

ISBN 0-7385-0287-1

Published by Arcadia Publishing,
an imprint of Tempus Publishing, Inc.
2 Cumberland Street
Charleston, SC 29401

Printed in Great Britain.

Library of Congress Catalog Card Number applied for.

For all general information contact Arcadia Publishing at:
Telephone 843-853-2070
Fax 843-853-0044
E-Mail arcadia@charleston.net

For customer service and orders:
Toll-Free 1-888-313-BOOK

Visit us on the internet at http://www.arcadiaimages.com

Contents

Acknowledgments 6

Introduction 7

1. Good Times 9

2. Making a Living 27

3. Picking Up the Pieces 55

4. Over the River and Through the Woods 67

5. Friends and Neighbors 79

6. Town and Country 101

ACKNOWLEDGMENTS

It would be impossible for me to create such a book alone, and so it is very important to me to be able to thank those who have been so very helpful. I would like to thank the Tioga County Historical Society for allowing me to undertake this exciting project. Thanks go to Emma Sedore for her confidence in me and her understanding. The wonderful photographs presented here came from many generous people including William Caloroso, Shirley Callahan, Joan Shaver, the Lena Bushnell collection, the Julian A. Campbell collection, Jean Alve and the Spencer Historical Society, Carol Henry, and Clarence and Mary Lacey. Your generosity, time, and insight have been invaluable. Thank you to Kathleen Tomosky for typing, typing, and typing some more. Special thanks go to Joann Llewellyn, the director of collections at Tioga County Historical Society who allowed me unfettered access to the society's fantastic collection of photographs, for her unlimited patience and willingness to listen. Very special thanks go to my wife, Patti, and children, Crystal and Ricky, for their unwavering support, help, patience, and love throughout this project and always.

—Richard E. Quest
Candor, New York

INTRODUCTION

This brief photographic history of Tioga County, New York, includes scenes from each of its nine towns: Barton, Berkshire, Candor, Newark Valley, Nichols, Owego, Richford, Spencer, and Tioga.

For more than 5,000 years, Tioga County has been a home to people. The historic period essentially began here in Tioga County as the Continental Army, under the leadership of Gen. George Washington, attempted to deal a severe blow to the British and their Iroquois allies. The patriots fighting under Generals John Sullivan and James Clinton marched through *Ah-Wa-Ga* (Owego) in August 1779. There they burned the Iroquois homes and destroyed the crops destined for British stomachs. As the soldiers traveled through the area, they noted in their diaries the beauty and richness of the land. With the end of the Revolutionary War, people yearned for a new beginning, and so began the movement toward the western frontier in New York and the creation of Tioga County.

During the post–Revolutionary War period, many veterans returned to this region to purchase land and to raise families. The Browns, the Parks, the Bements, the Harts, the McMasters, the Drapers, and the Gridleys settled the county. These people and others walked the entire distance from Connecticut and the Berkshire Mountains in Massachusetts to this area with a team of oxen pulling sleds and carts full of possessions. Slowly the pioneers carved a homestead out of the wilderness.

As the 18th century gave way to the 19th century, small farming communities began to dot the countryside. Early industry started to capitalize on the abundant mature forest, and lumbering became a way of life for many. The creeks, streams, and rivers not only served as the early highways, but also provided the power for gristmills and sawmills. The cut lumber was then hauled to the banks of the Susquehanna River, tied into rafts, and floated south to Harrisburg, Pennsylvania, and to the Chesapeake River.

Slowly, decade after decade, change became inevitable. As the age of the homespun drifted from living memory, another terrible war pitting brother against brother attempted to tear the country apart. Tioga County and its residents quickly answered President Abraham Lincoln's call for "300,000 more" troops. Men from all walks of life, such as New York state assemblyman Benjamin F. Tracy and lawyer, Isaac Catlin, volunteered to serve in the 109th and 137th New York State Volunteers. They went on to prove their courage at Gettysburg, the Wilderness, and Petersburg. Too many of them never returned.

After the war, Reconstruction fell to the politicians, such as U.S. Senator Thomas Collier

Platt from Owego, and the wealthy captains of industry, such as multimillionaire John D. Rockefeller from Richford. Women began to be vocal about equal rights. One woman, Esther McQuigg Morris from Spencer, quietly and adeptly carried out the duties given to her as the first female justice of the peace appointed in the United States.

Again, America and Tioga County respond with valor as young men and women resolutely volunteered for service in the Spanish-American War, World War I, and World War II. All too often as is the case in war, young men made the supreme sacrifice, as did Hiram Saddlemire of Newark Valley. There are but few happy endings under such tragic circumstances, but Margaret Hastings of Owego and her rescue from the jungles of New Guinea in World War II serves as one of inspiration.

Events from the 1860s to the 1950s have been captured on ambrotypes, tintypes, and film. They serve as a reminder to us as to who we are, where we come from, and how we arrived here. So, stroll through years gone by, enjoy the good times, work hard in making a living, travel the roads, and visit with friends and neighbors. Sit back and reminisce, and then prepare to celebrate the next century and new millennium—and don't forget to keep those cameras close by.

—Richard E. Quest

One
Good Times

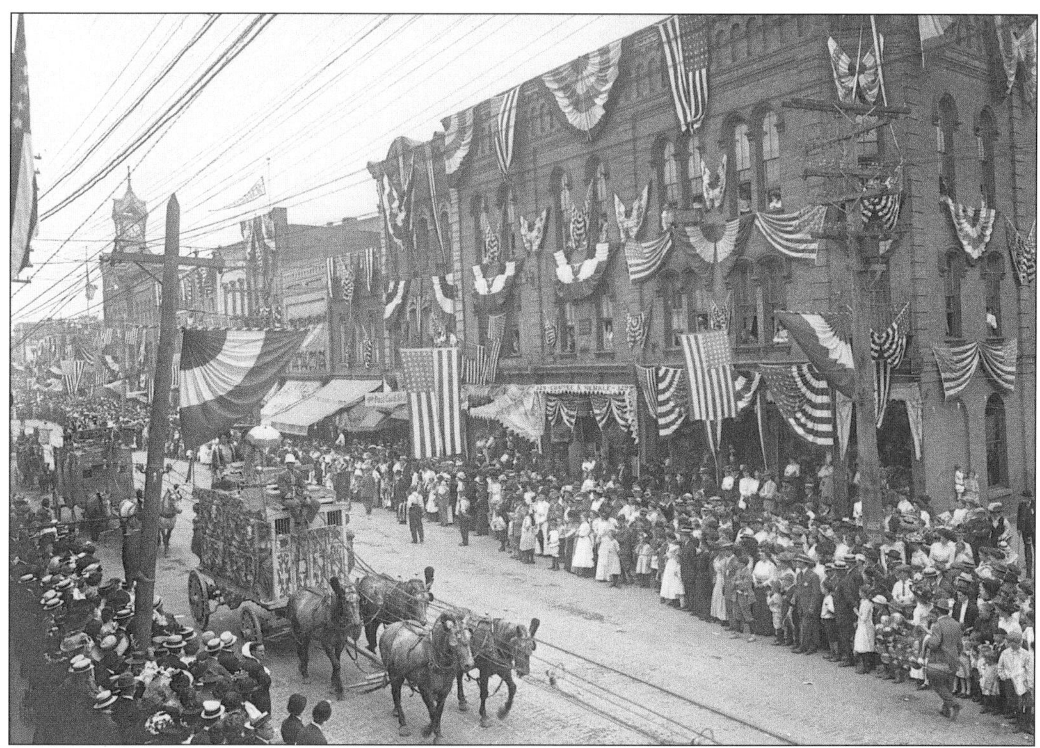

This photograph shows a brightly decorated Broad Street in Waverly during the Old Home Day celebration in 1910.

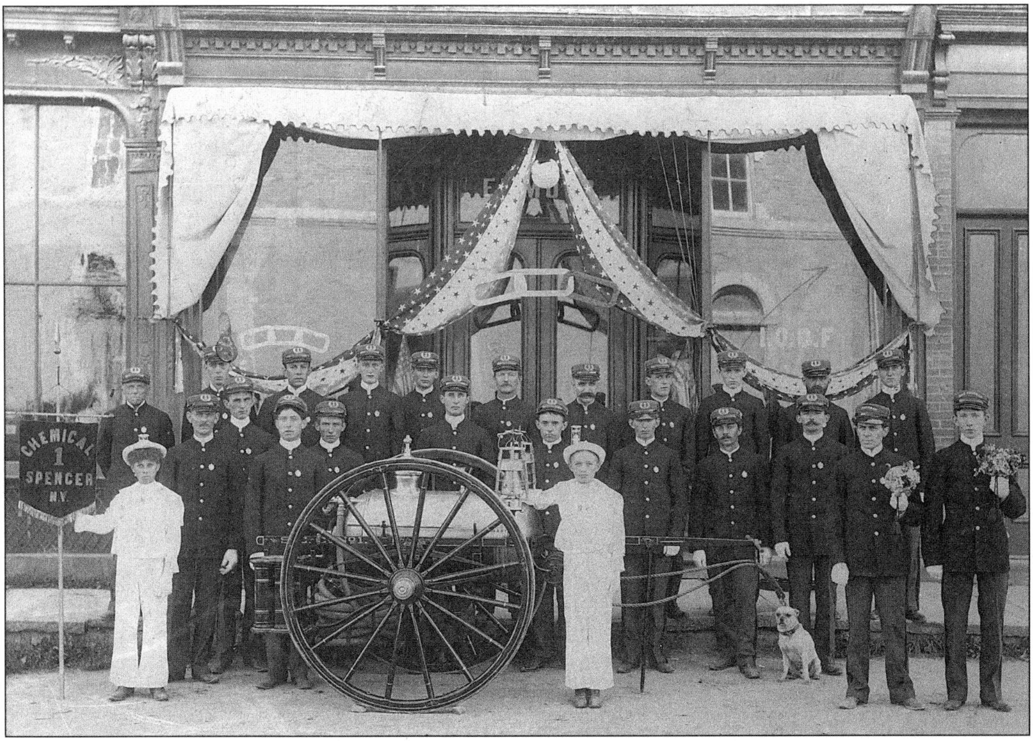

Spencer Chemical No. 1 was organized in October 1896. This was the first organized fire department in Spencer other than the earlier bucket brigades. This chemical engine was the pride of the community and was often displayed during parades and celebrations as seen here.

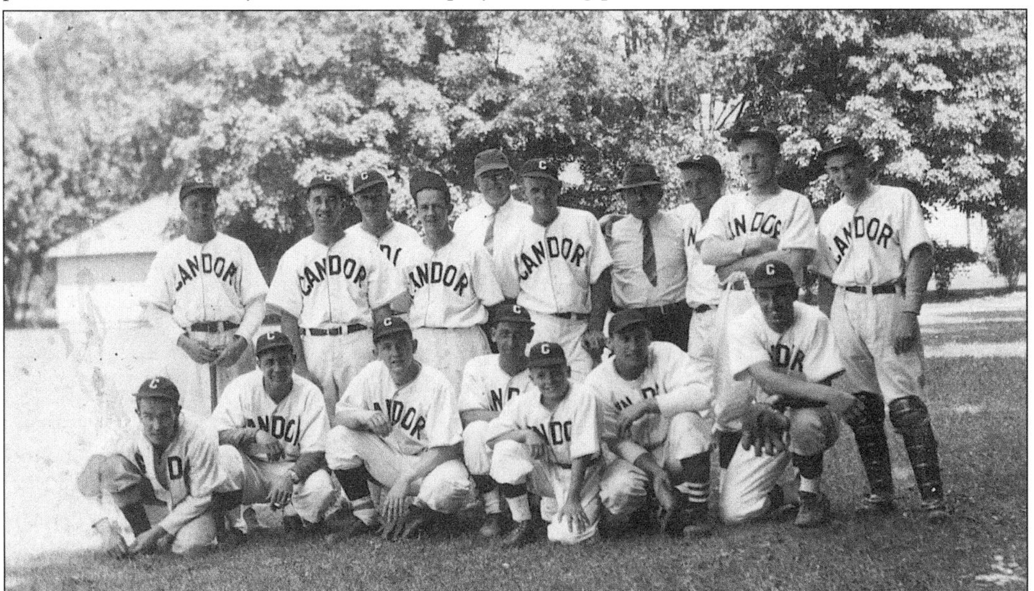

Here is the Candor town baseball team in 1938. Pictured, from left to right, are the following: (front row) Dave Birch, Andy Consalvi, Bob Brown, Chink Pichany, Iggy Craig, Alex Osovski, and Joe Luciani; (back row) Vic Osovski, Kicky Luciani, Bill Jordan, Bud Manning, Deforest Doane, Marv Birch, Jimmy Luciani, Joe Czerniecki, Tony Czerniecki, and John Robinson.

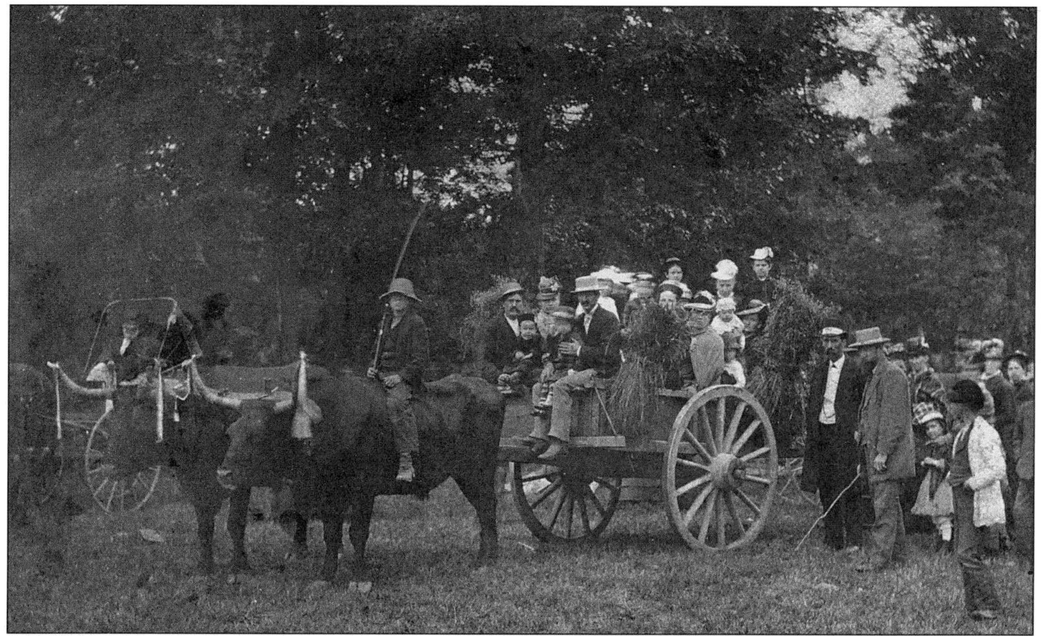

The first annual Newark Valley Fair was held September 15 and 16, 1880. The fair was originally organized as the Newark Valley Agricultural Society. No admission was charged. Among the events were ox rides, as pictured here; a baby contest, with a first prize of $5; a competition for the best tub of butter, with a first prize of a silver-plated butter dish; and a contest for the best loaf of bread made by a girl under 16, with a prize of a set of silver-plated knives and forks.

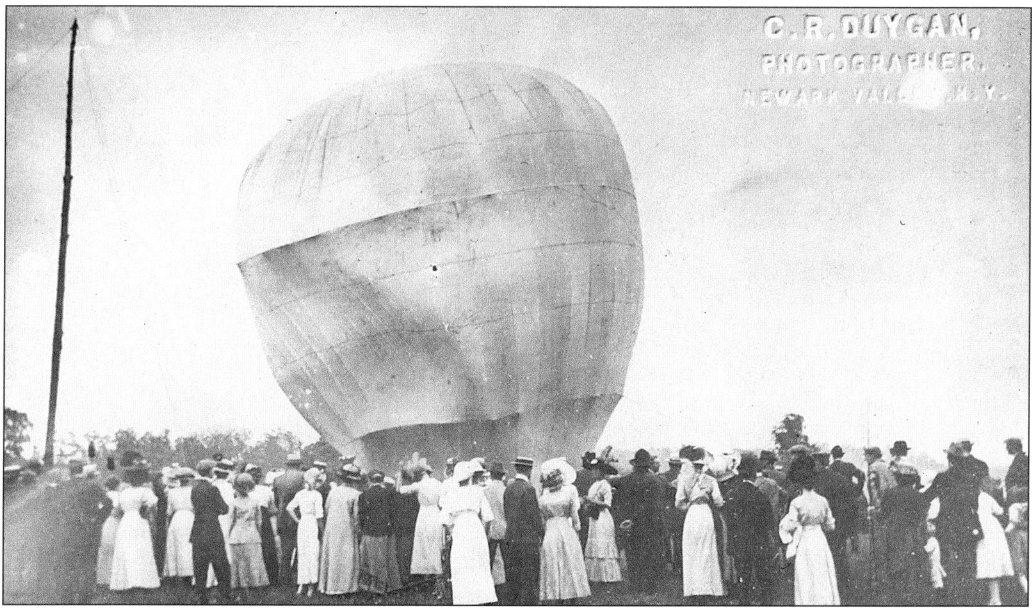

This hot-air balloon is about to ascend at the Newark Valley Fair on August 8, 1912. After the balloon went up, Jack Fanning was to perform a stunt by jumping out of the balloon, opening two separate parachutes, and gliding safely to earth. However, the second parachute failed to open properly, and Fanning fell the last 40 feet. He died from internal injuries.

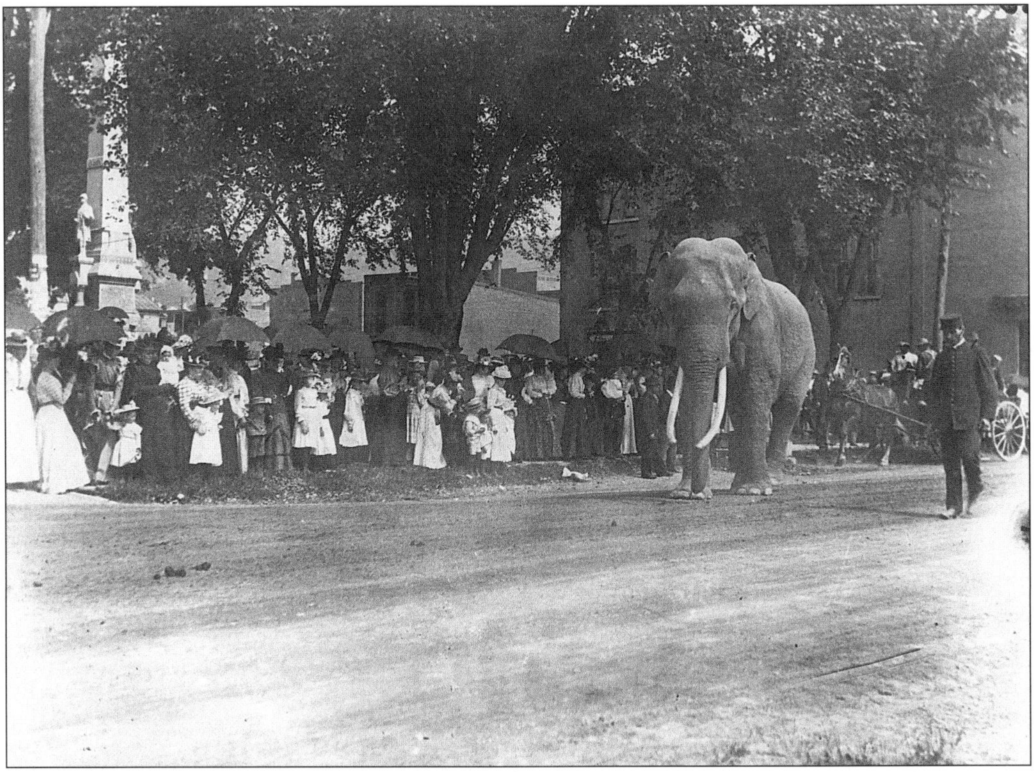

An elephant walks down Court Street in Owego during a celebration and parade *c.* 1900. Notice the Civil War Soldiers and Sailors Monument in the background.

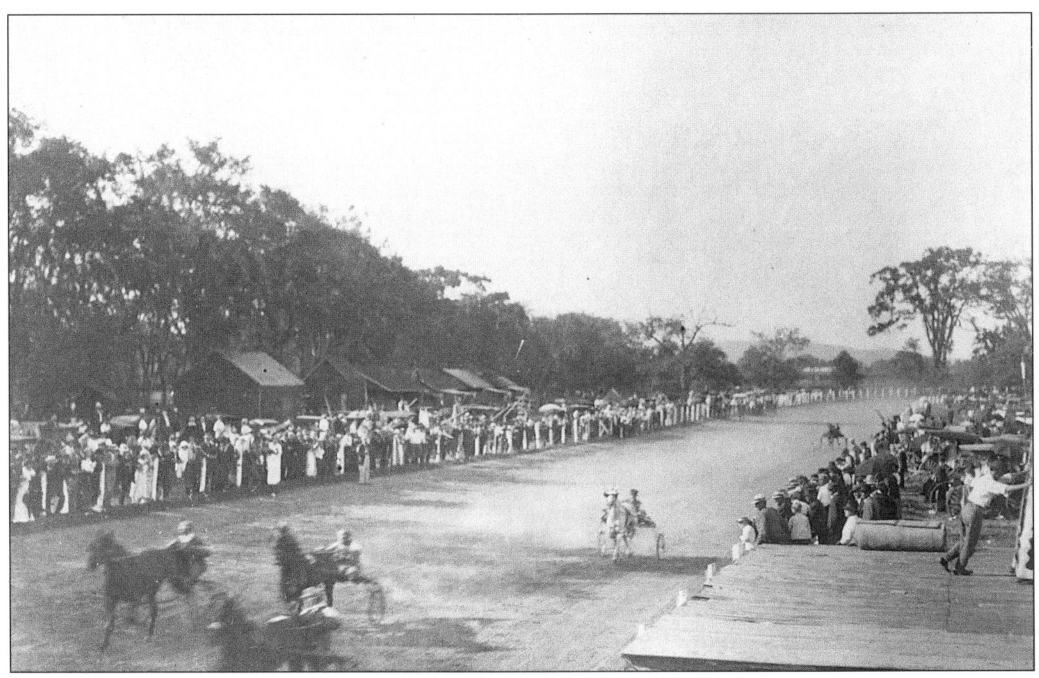

This photograph shows a horse racing event at the Newark Valley Fair.

Fritz Schwalbach became a member of the Kirby Band c. the World War I years. A professional musician, he posed for this photograph in 1961.

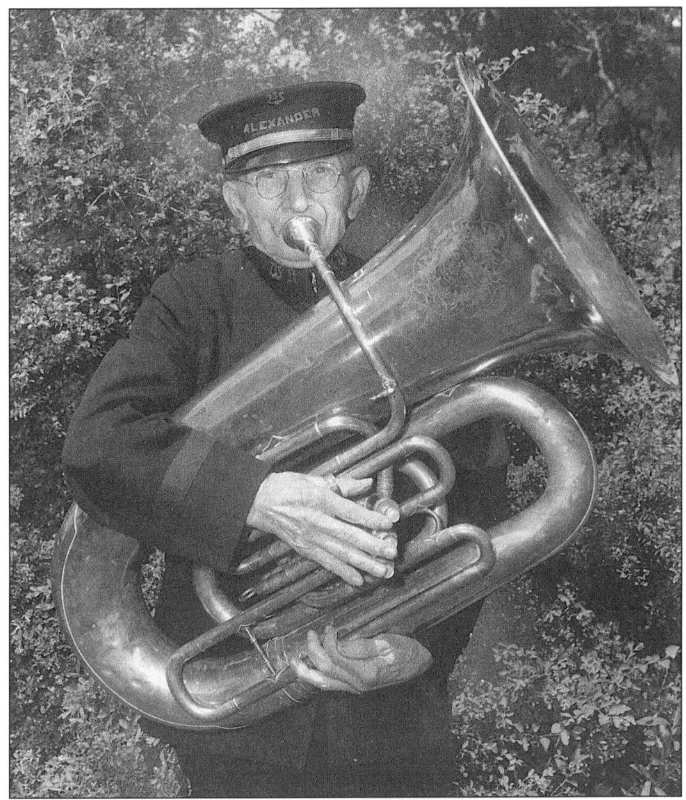

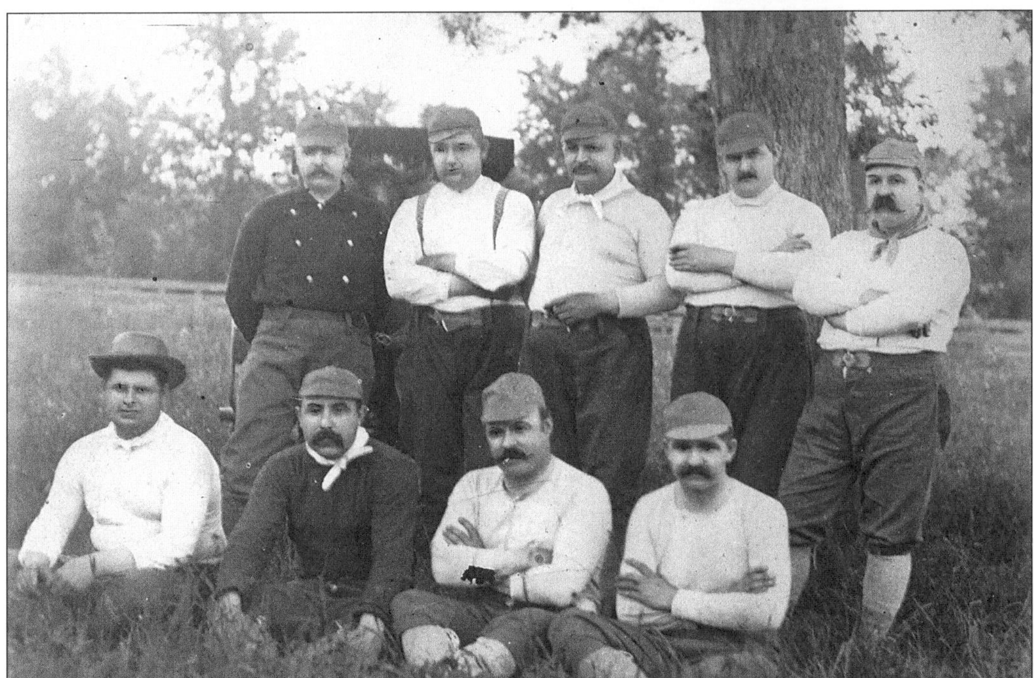

This photograph shows the Owego baseball team c. 1886. Members include, bottom row left, A.W. Parmelee, "Cat" Thompson, and Mike Murray.

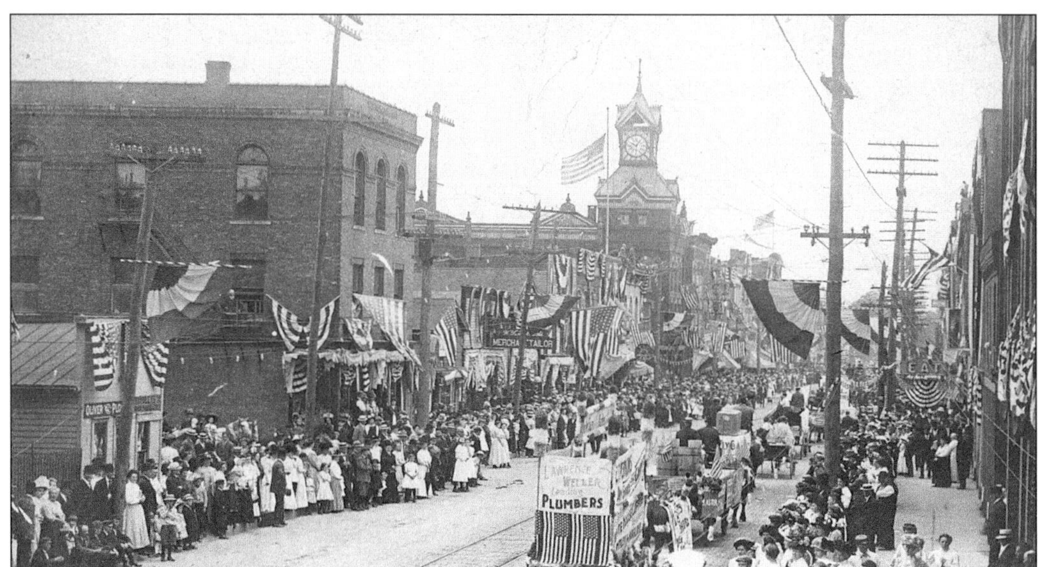

This festive celebration occurred during Old Home Week in Waverly in 1910.

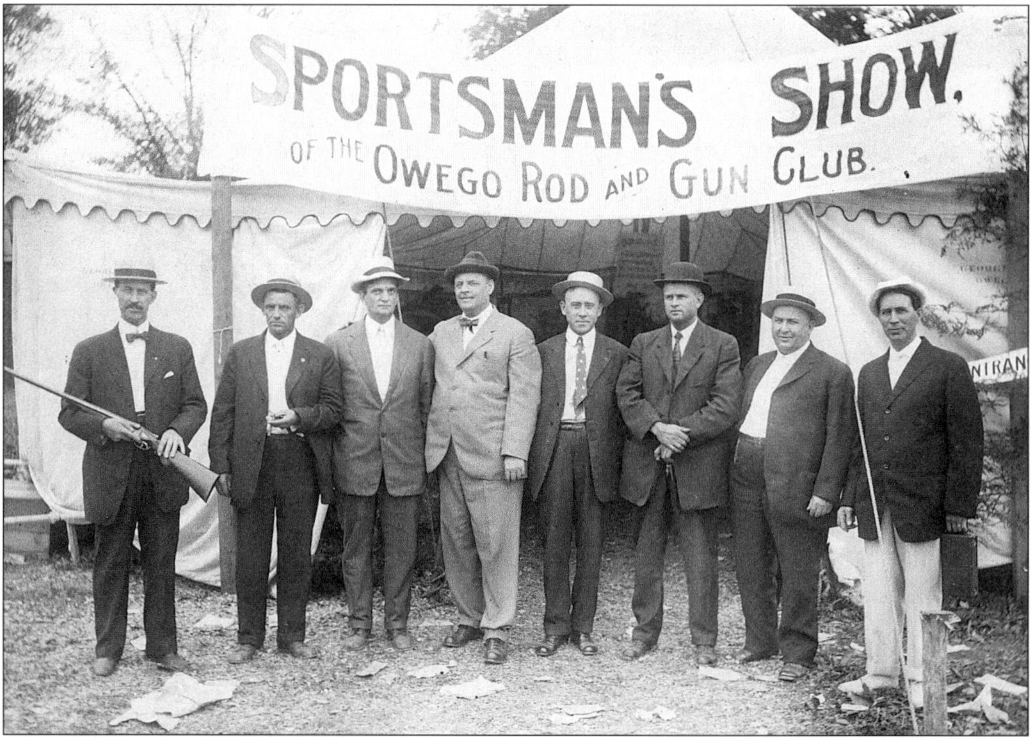

The Owego Rod and Gun Club was founded by Fred J. Davis. It was the first such club organized in Tioga County. The club was politically active in promoting early fish-and-game laws and conservation. This photograph was taken *c.* 1920.

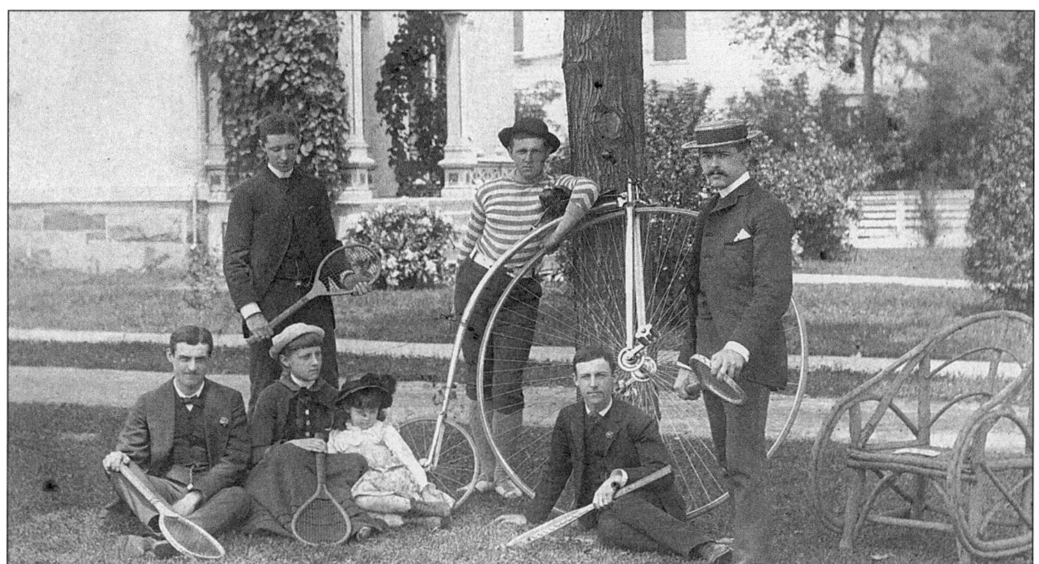

With tennis rackets in hand and a "penny farthing" bicycle as transportation, a group of young people prepare to enjoy a summer's day *c.* 1895.

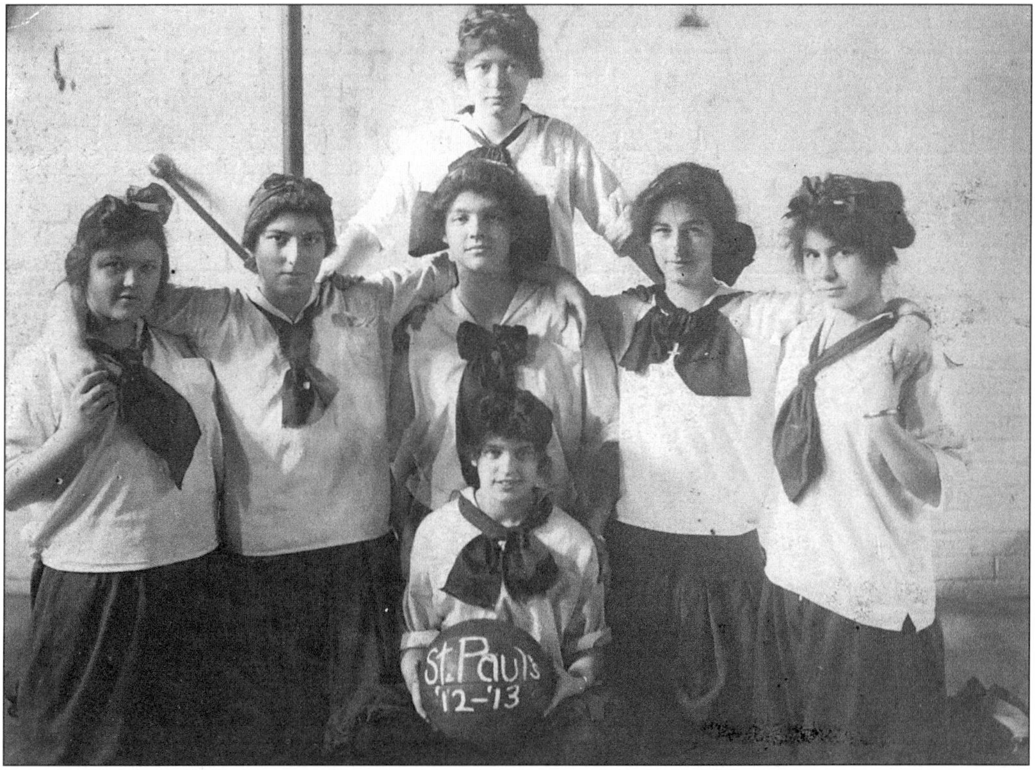

Members of the 1912–13 St. Paul's girls' basketball team pose for a photograph. The Episcopal church was first organized in Owego on February 10, 1834. The stone church that now stands on the corner of Main and Liberty Streets was built in 1893. Pictured are, from left to right, the following: (standing) Mildred Stone; (kneeling) Dorothy Strong, Alma Myers, Constance Storrs, Lucille Baldwin, and Elfrida Sporer; (sitting) Cornelia Hubbard.

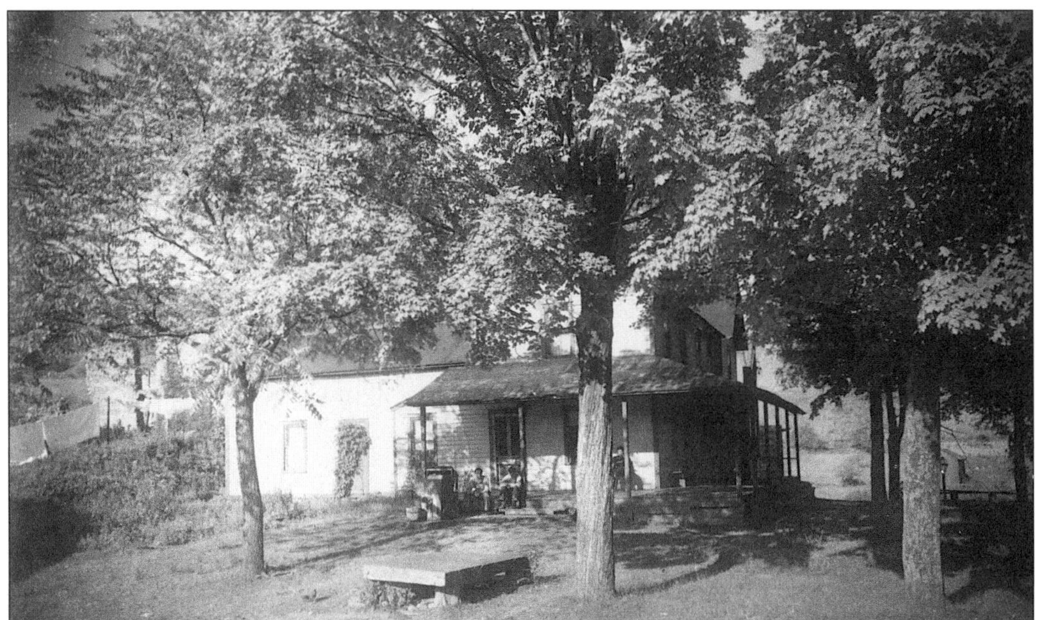

This *c.* 1910 photograph shows a Spencer Lake house, located in the area known in early times as Huggtown. Fed by various springs, Spencer Lake was a popular fishing, picnicking, and boating area. The lower portion of the lake was created when a dam was built near the lake house. The dam provided waterpower to turn one of the area's first gristmills.

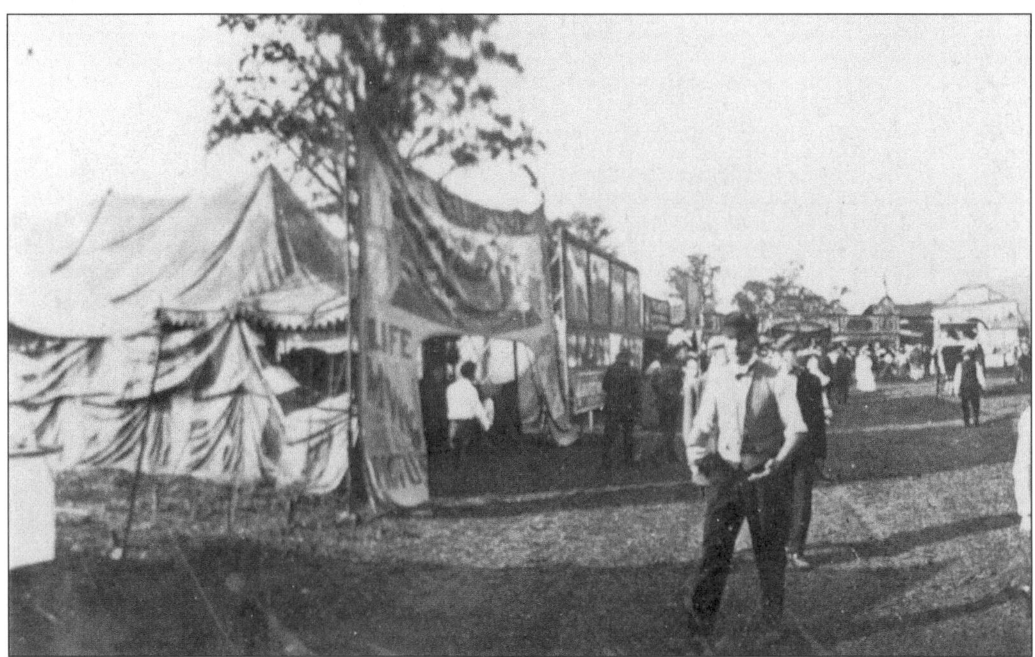

The Tioga County Agricultural Society held its first county fair in Spencer in 1859. This photograph shows the midway of the Tioga County Fair held September 14–18, 1909.

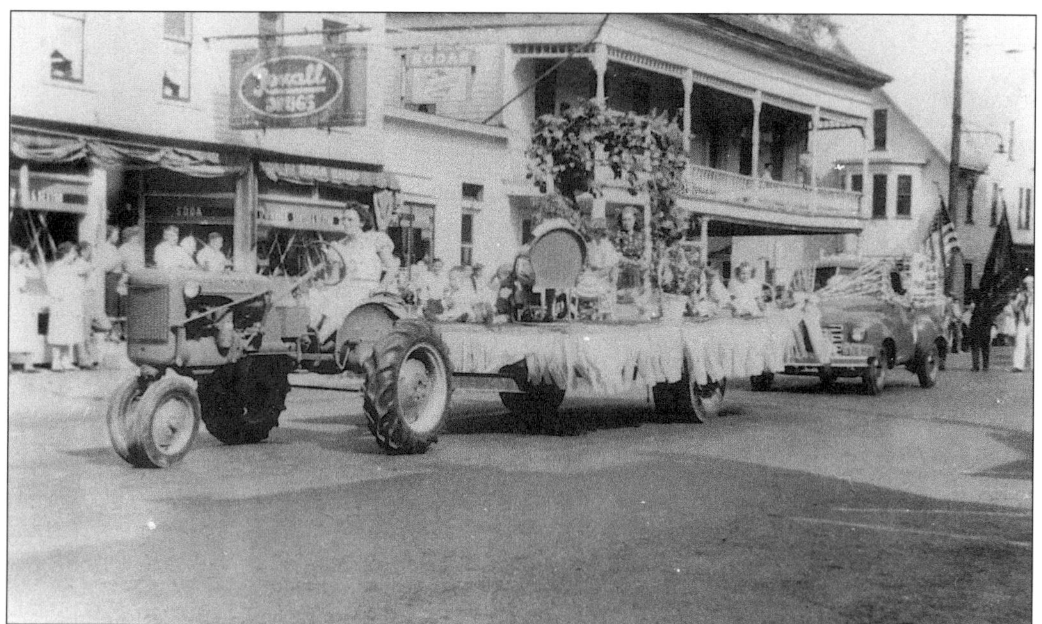

This photograph shows the 1949 Old Home Day Parade in Nichols. The Rexall drugstore building is currently a diner. The hotel at right was torn down in 1959.

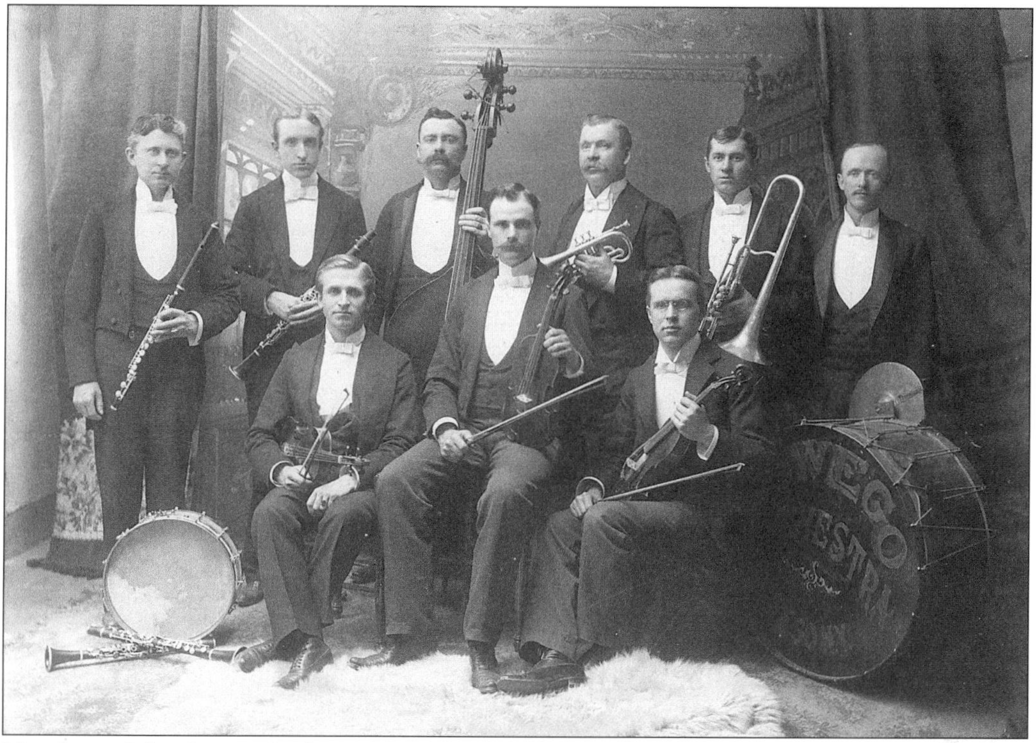

Members of the Owego Orchestra *c.* 1915 were, from left to right, as follows: (front row) Prof. G. Pultz, director; Edwin P. Brooks, first violin; and N. Frank Mead, second violin; (back row) J.E. Catlin, flute and piccolo; Charles N. Forsythe, clarinet; L.J. Putnam, double bass; F.J. Putnam, cornet; B.W. Case, trombone; and N.W. Adams, drums and traps.

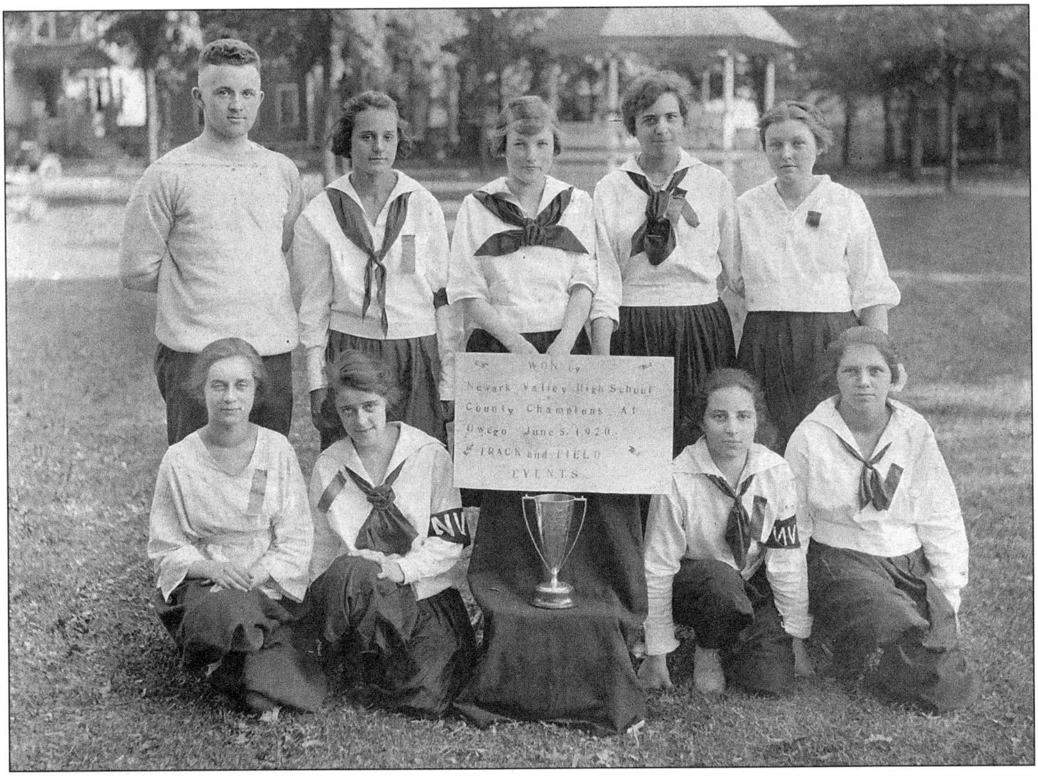

Members of the Newark Valley girls' track and field team are pictured here on June 5, 1920, from left to right, as follows: (front row) Elizabeth Ives, Marguarite VanDeVort, Mildred Graham, and Mabel Thompson (Baird); (back row) Lester Knapp, Marjorie Barber, Blanche Stoughton (Pulling), Wilma Wright, and Georgia Stoughton (Curkendall).

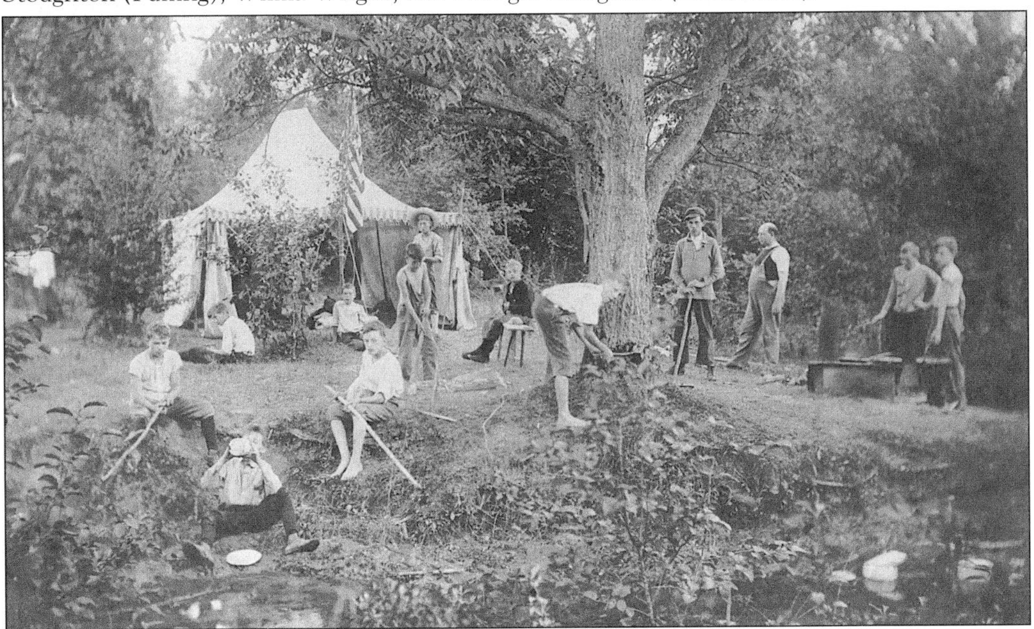

This 1906 view shows a camping spot along the Catatonk Creek.

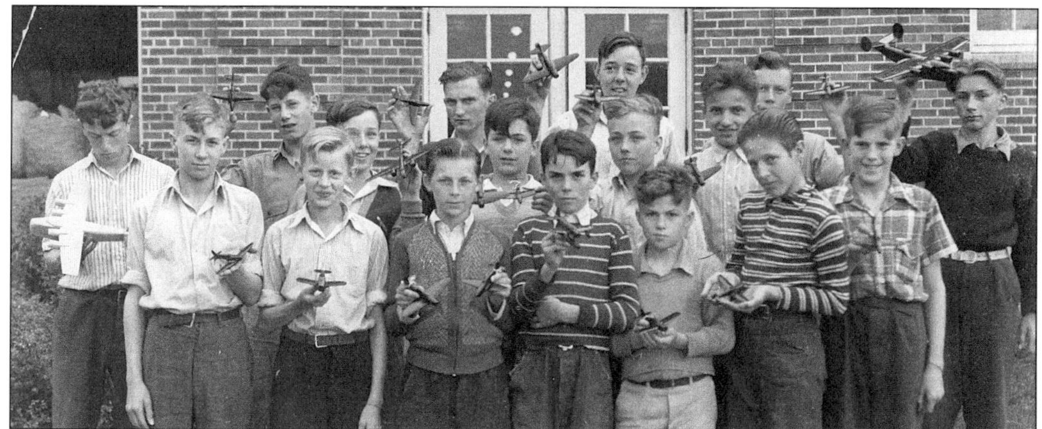

This photograph shows the Spencer School Airplane Club of 1942. The club made model World War II aircraft for purposes of identification. Members are, from left to right, as follows: (front row) Perry Williams, David Kroplin, Jimmy Westbrook, Pete Riker Jr., Jimmy Butts, and Louis Riker; (middle row) Arnold Redsicker, Edwin Redsicker, Charles Ritzler, Michael Labosky, and Charles Cotton; (back row) Charles Snyder, Glenn Ahart, Richard Rumsey, Raymond Redsicker, Taisto Kumpula, and Terry Gibbs.

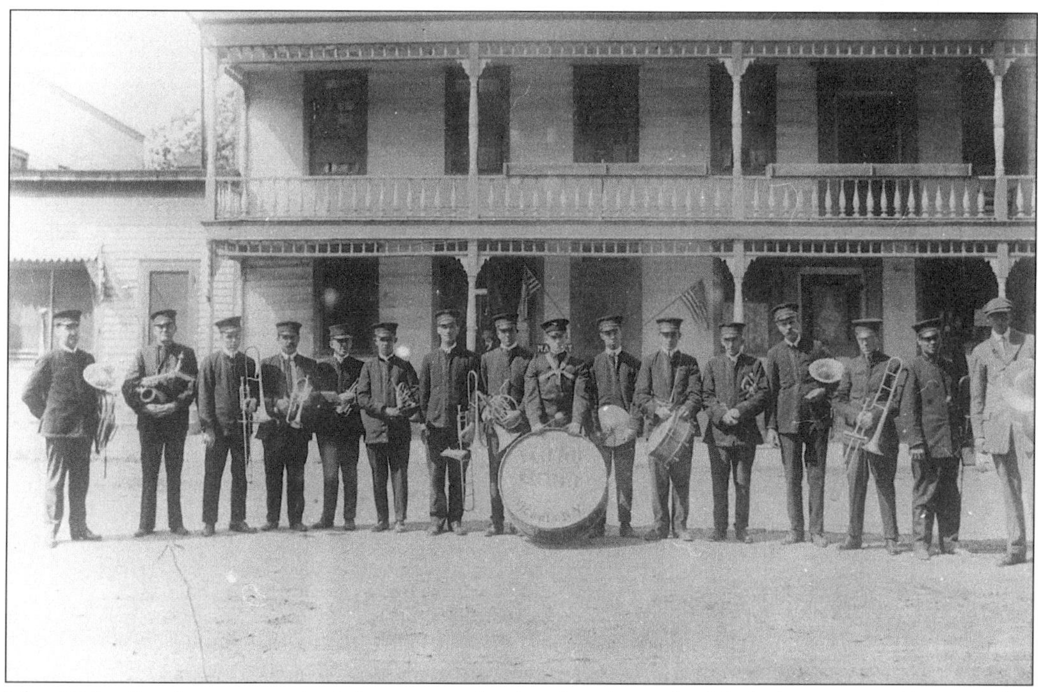

The Kirby Band was organized from several other bands in the Nichols vicinity. Some of the earliest components of the band date to 1835. The actual Kirby Band was organized in 1876 by J.W. Pecket. However, due to Pecket's untimely death, Allen Kirby became the bandleader. Kirby directed the band for nearly 70 years. This photograph shows the Kirby Band in 1916 on Main Street in Nichols.

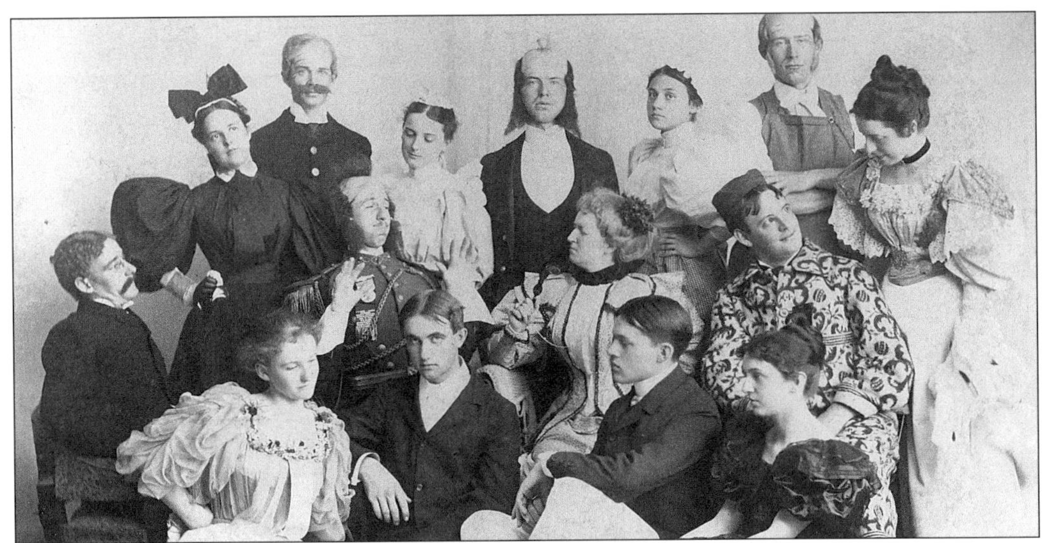

The Casino Club was a local theater group. In costume *c.* 1895 for the show *Everybody's Friend* were the following, from left to right: (front row) Minnie Renwick, Merle Downs, Charlie Storrs, and S.C.M.; (seated) Fred Gladden, John Parker, May Harrison, and Fred Harris; (standing) Elsie Smull, Will Truman, Ms. Bassett, Jim Truman, Bessie Gere, Storrs Hunsell, and Laura Ayer.

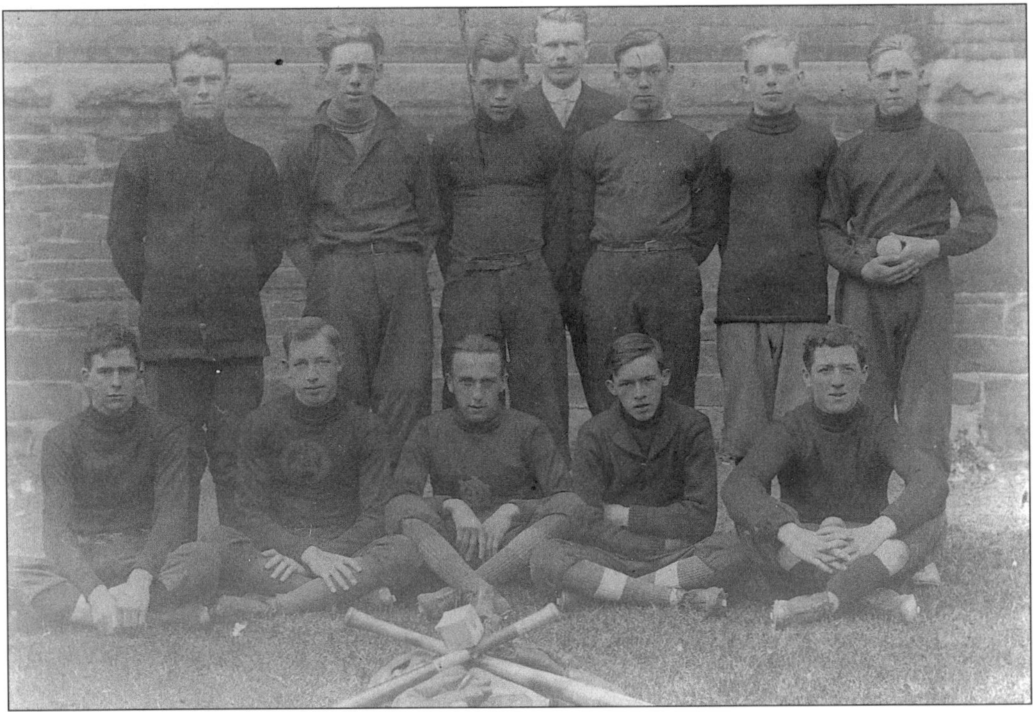

Members of the Owego Free Academy baseball team *c.* 1915 include the following, from left to right: (front row) Campbell, left field; Cook, pitcher; Ingersoll, catcher; Relihan, shortstop; and Collins, first base; (back row) VanGorder, pitcher and second base; Comstock, right field; Tayler, center field; Professor Hays; Rockwell, shortstop and second base; Bensley, third base; and DeGaramo, second base.

These boys appear to be enjoying some refreshments from the Thomas and Snyder Bottling Works in Owego *c*. 1900.

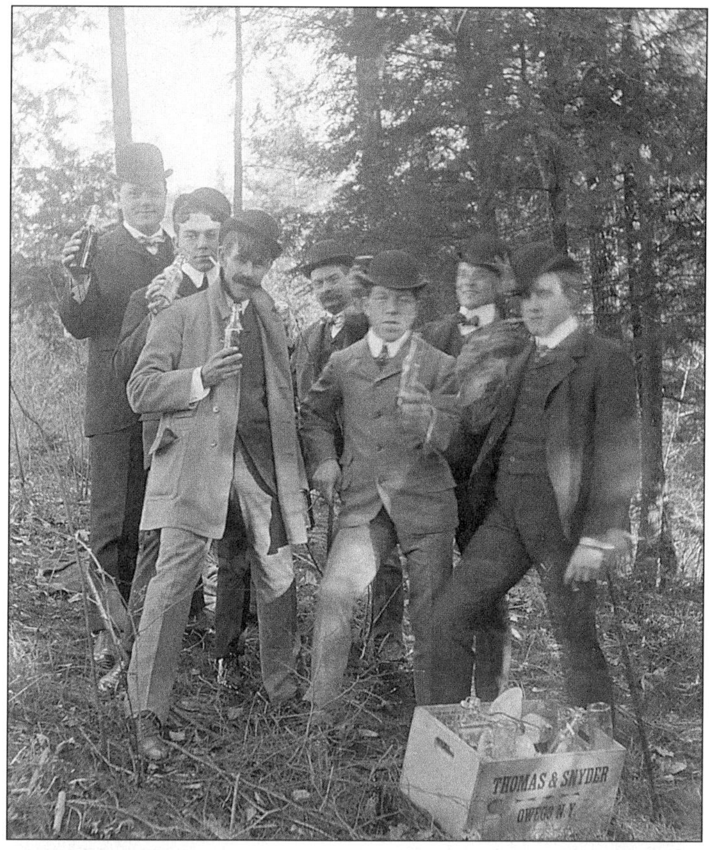

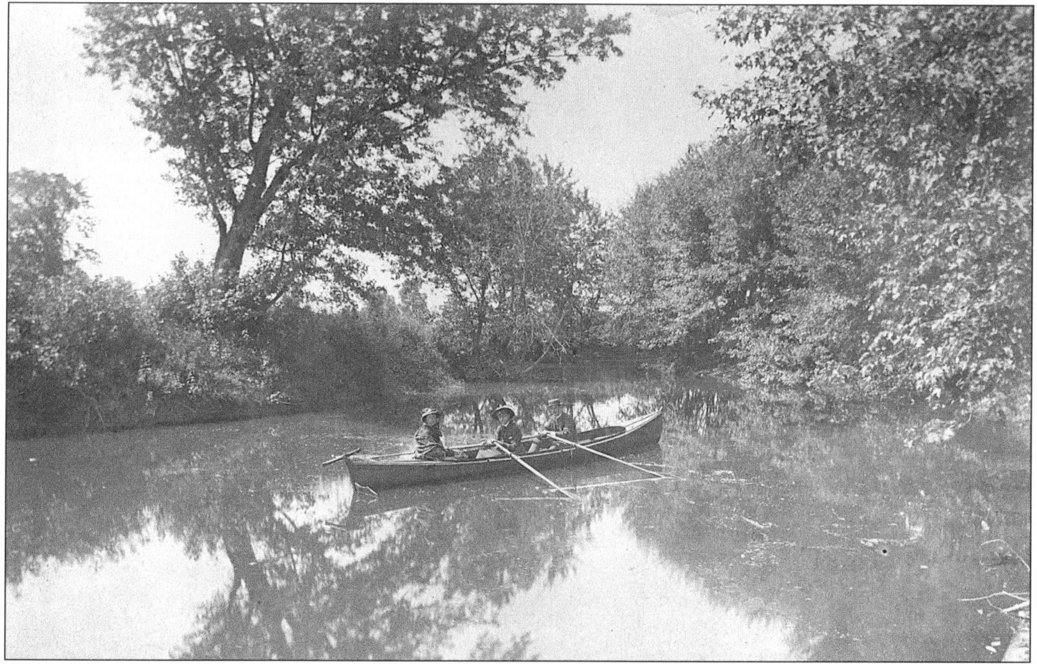

Dora Stanbrough and two companions enjoy an afternoon on the water *c*. 1880.

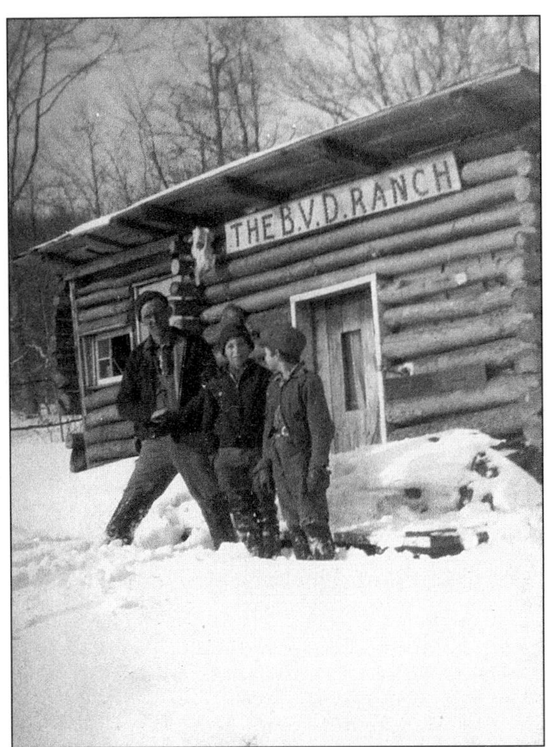

This cabin, known as the BVD Ranch, was constructed of basswood *c.* 1929. Elwin Satterly, Bud Nixon, Don Allen, and Clarence Lacey built it and camped here during the summers and school vacations. It was named after the trademarked underwear because in the winter the cabin was kept so hot that everyone wore only their BVDs. Pictured are Elwin Satterly, Web Lacey, and Pete Lacey.

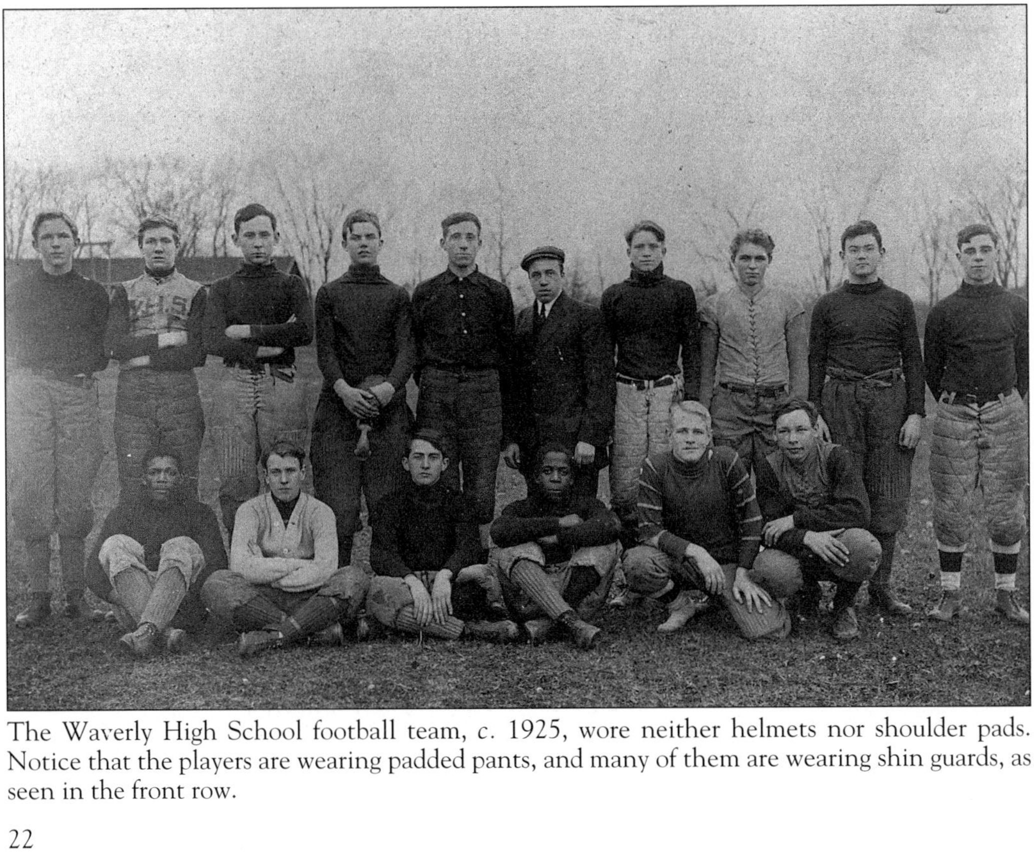

The Waverly High School football team, *c.* 1925, wore neither helmets nor shoulder pads. Notice that the players are wearing padded pants, and many of them are wearing shin guards, as seen in the front row.

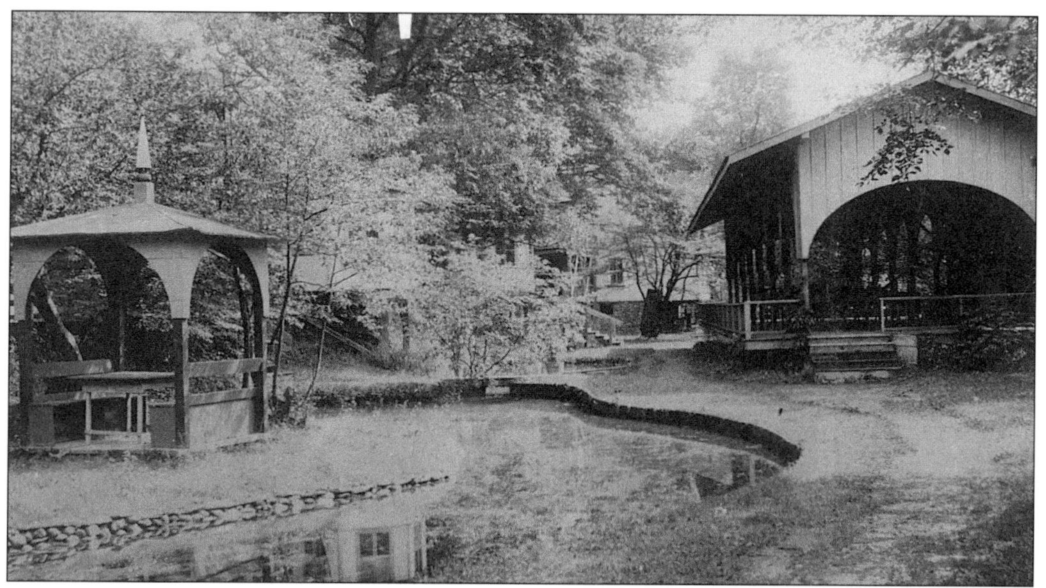

This 1909 view shows the Trout Ponds of Newark Valley.

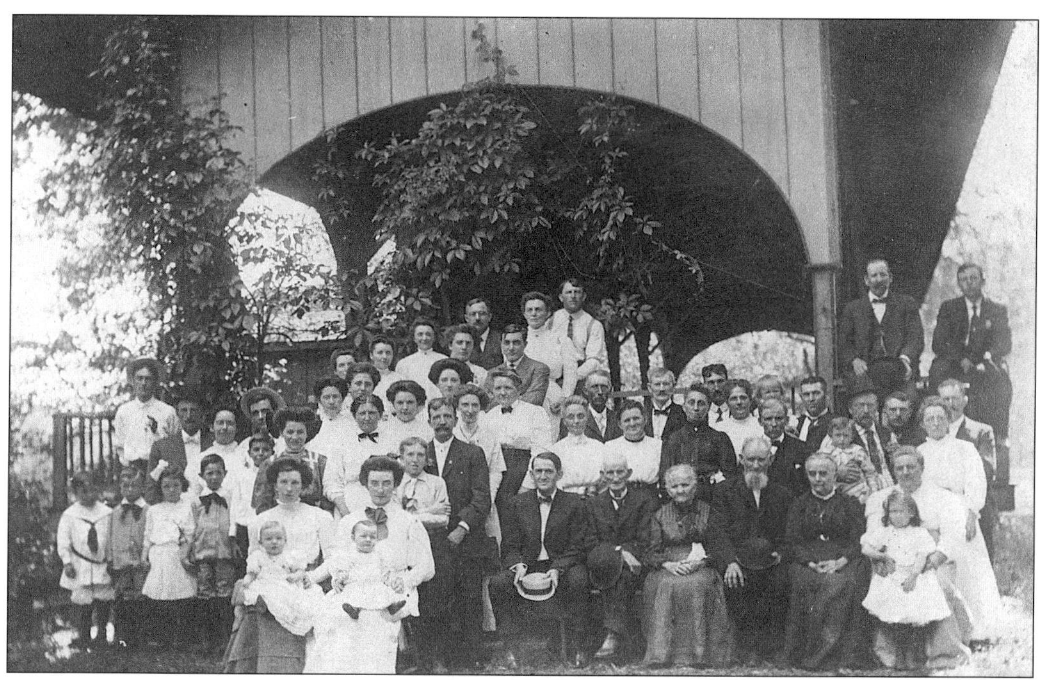

The Reed family reunion was held *c.* 1908 at the Trout Ponds in Newark Valley.

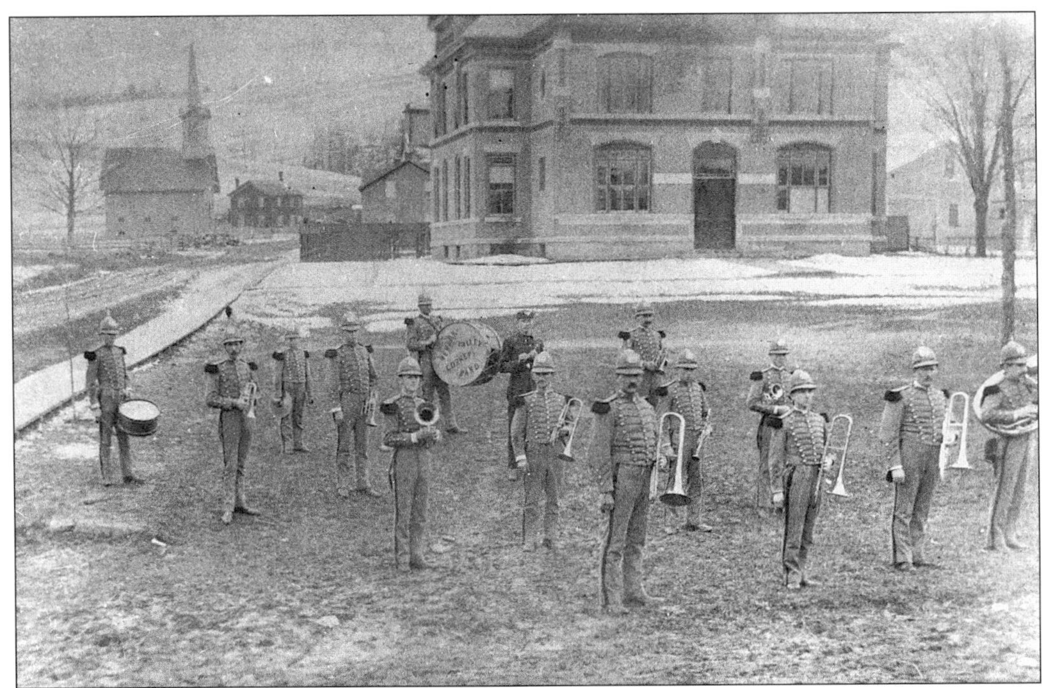

Members of the Newark Valley Cornet Band *c.* 1890 included J.D. Joslin, Fred Moses, C.G. Lyman, Addison G. Butler, and Edgar F. Belden. Note the new District No. 2 school directly behind the band. The Catholic church in the background was dedicated on January 8, 1881.

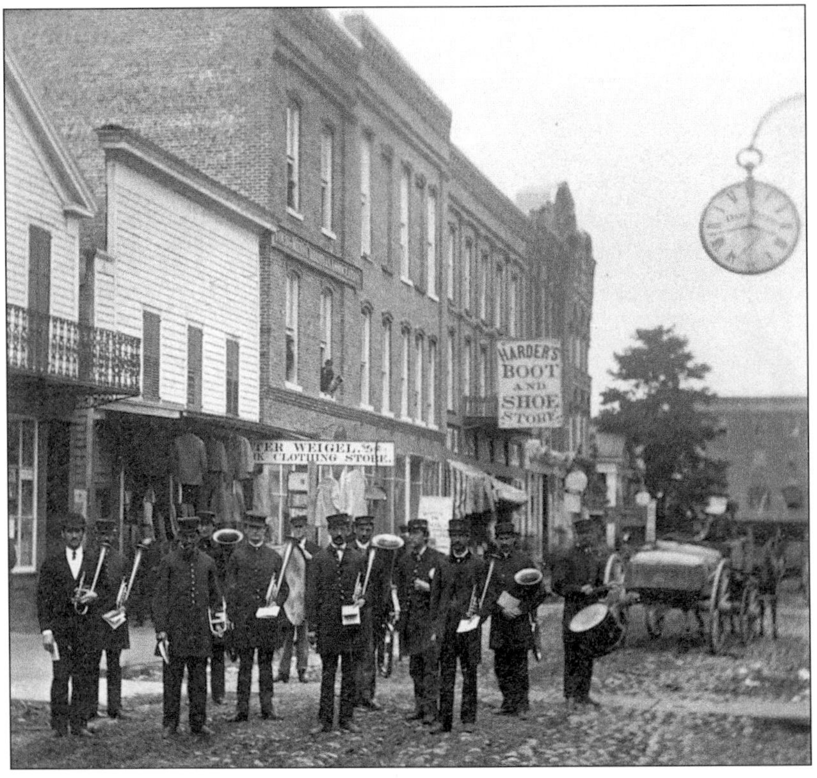

This photograph shows the Owego Brass Band *c.* 1872.

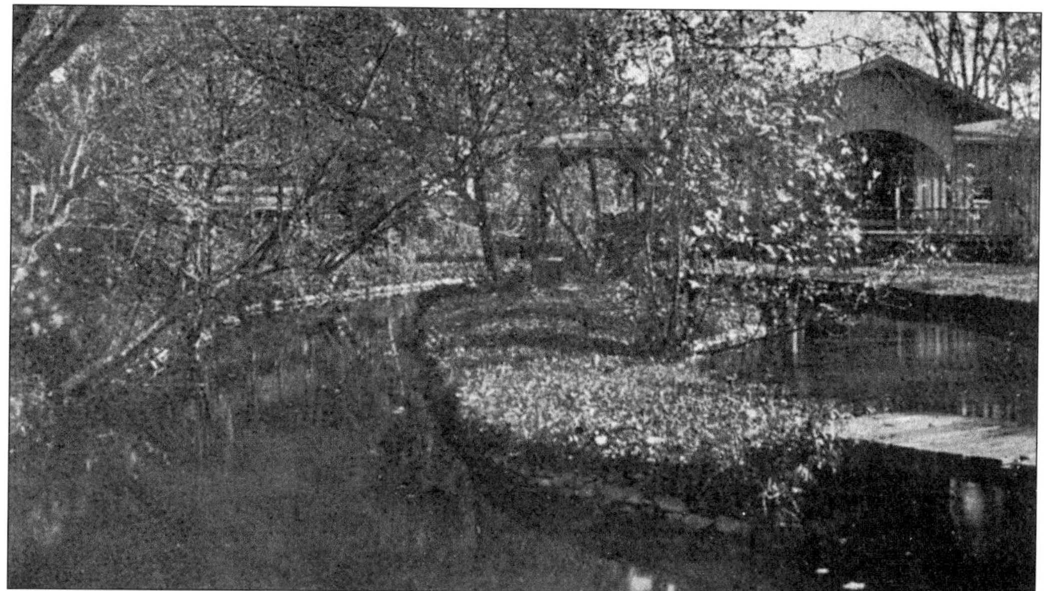

This view shows Squash Island at the Trout Ponds in Newark Valley c. 1900. The ponds have been a favorite gathering place for generations. Originally, they were filled with large brook trout. Surrounding the ponds were myriad seats, arbors, tables, bowling alleys, and a dance hall. Many family gatherings and reunions took place here.

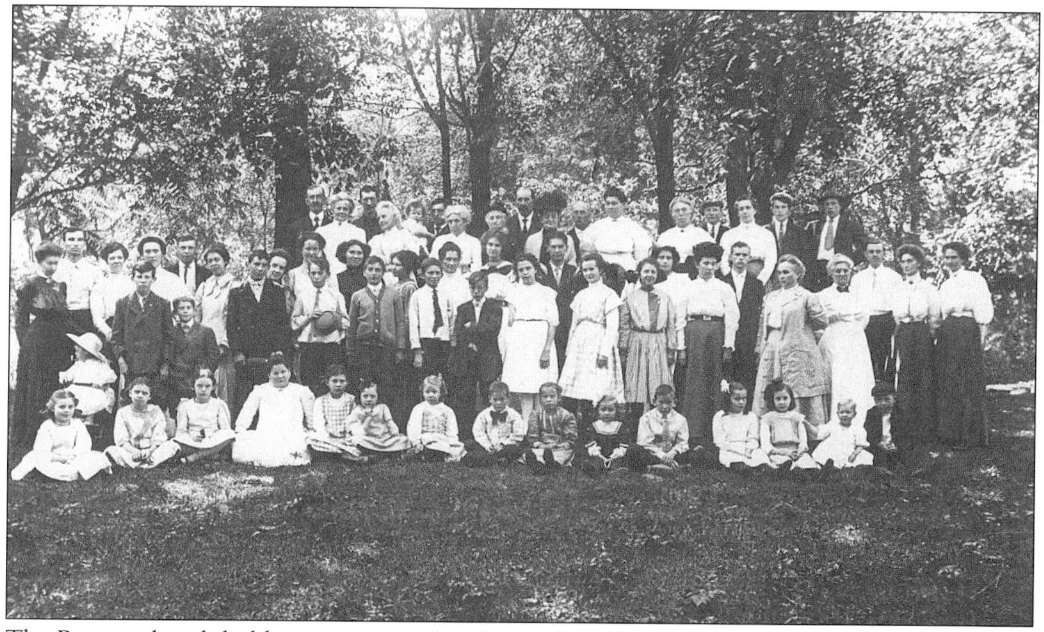

The Baptist church held a picnic near the Maple Grove Cemetery in Candor in 1912.

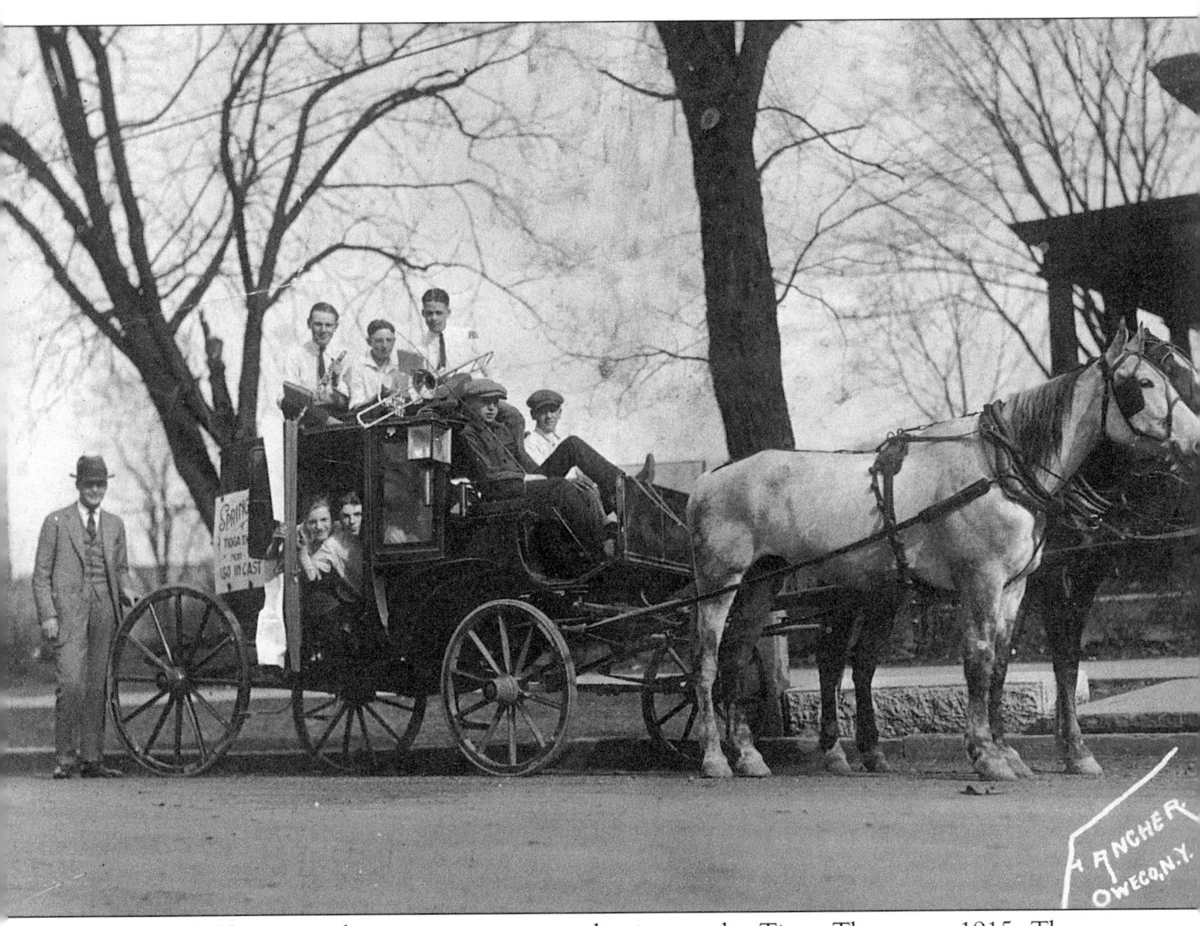

These children are advertising a spring production at the Tioga Theater *c.* 1915. They are posing alongside Draper Park in Owego.

Two

Making a Living

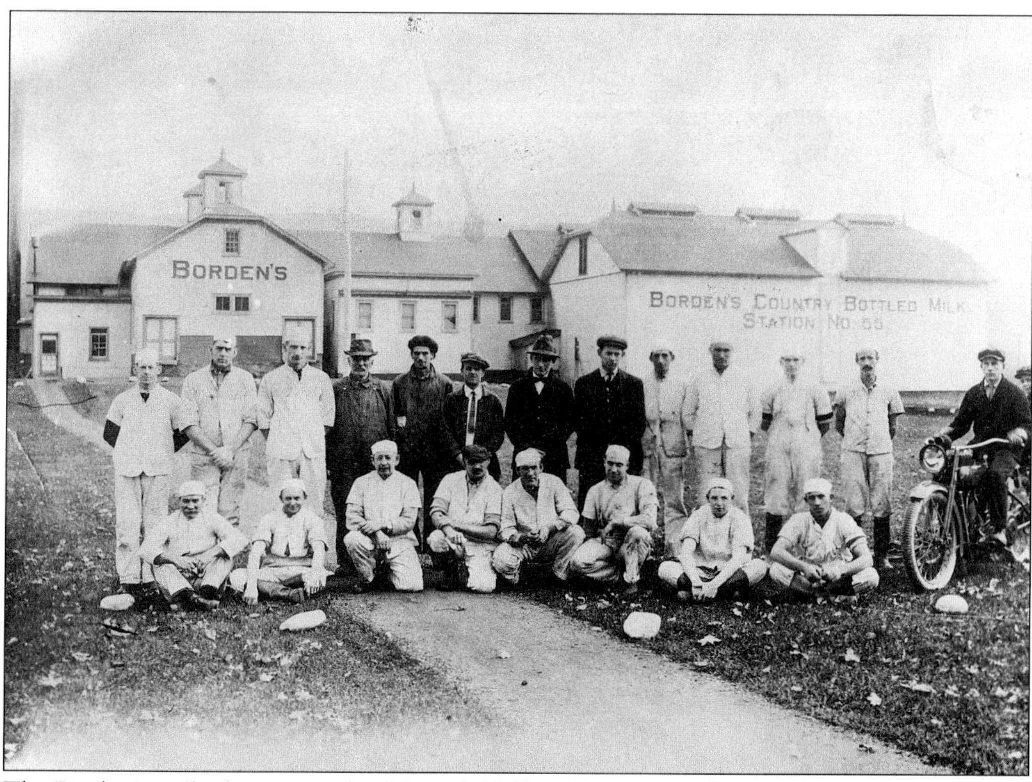

The Borden's milk plant opened in Newark Valley *c.* 1906 on Whig Street next to the railroad tracks. At one point, 65 men were employed there and handled over 20 tons of milk a day. The plant closed in 1962.

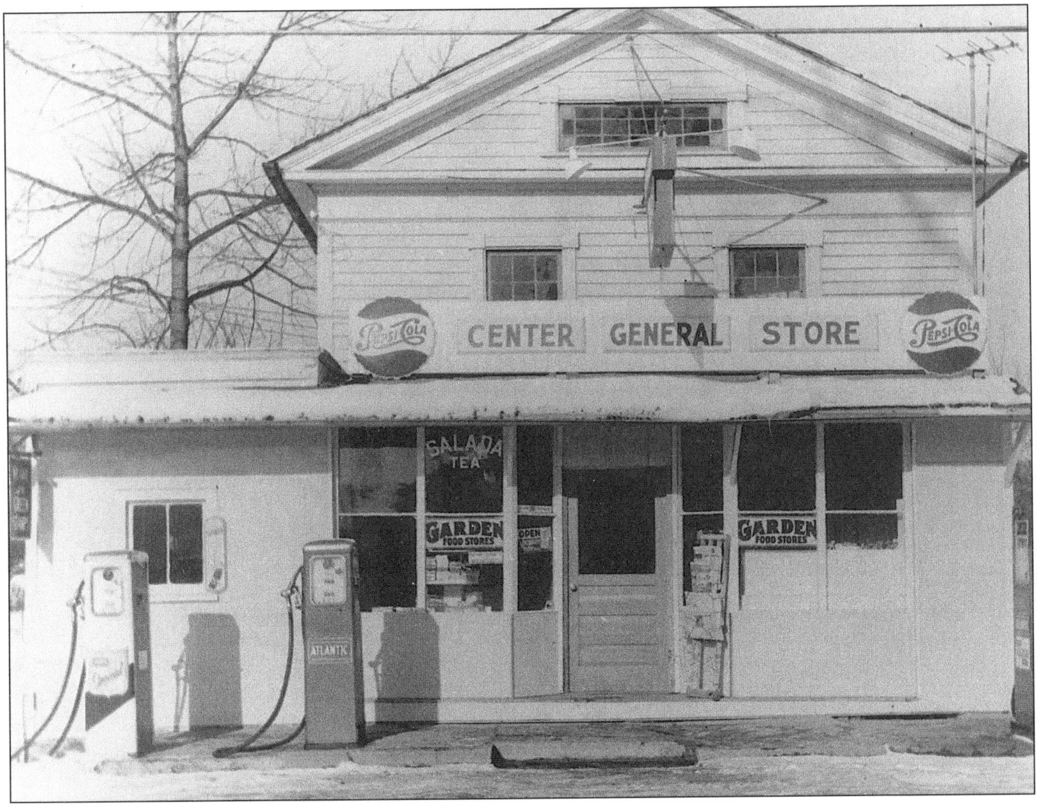

This photograph shows the Tioga Center General Store.

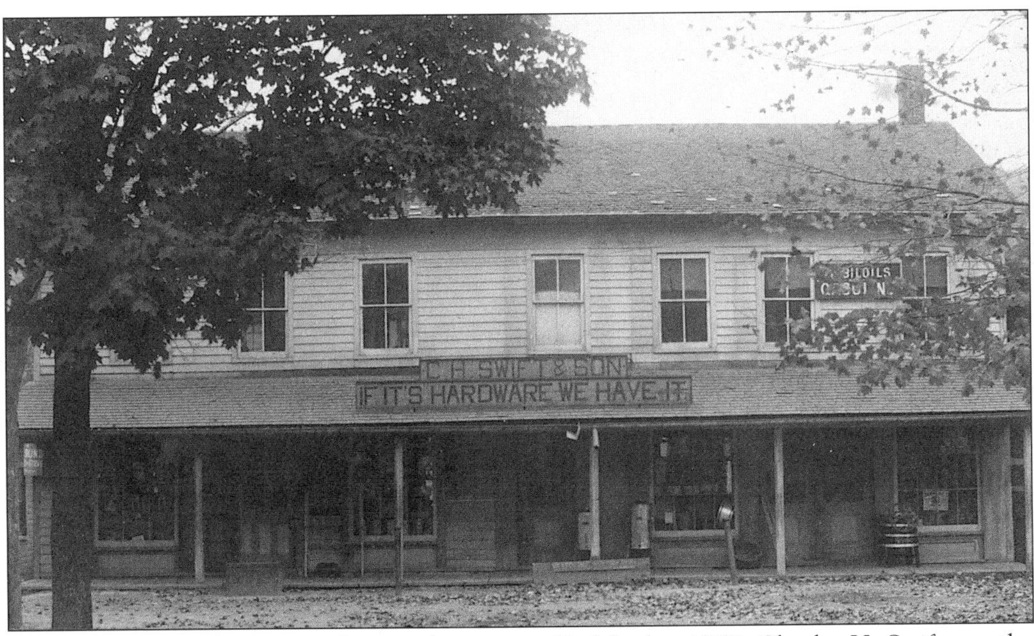

Swift's Hardware Shop was a thriving business in Richford *c.* 1900. Charles H. Swift was the owner. His store slogan, seen here, sums up his business demeanor.

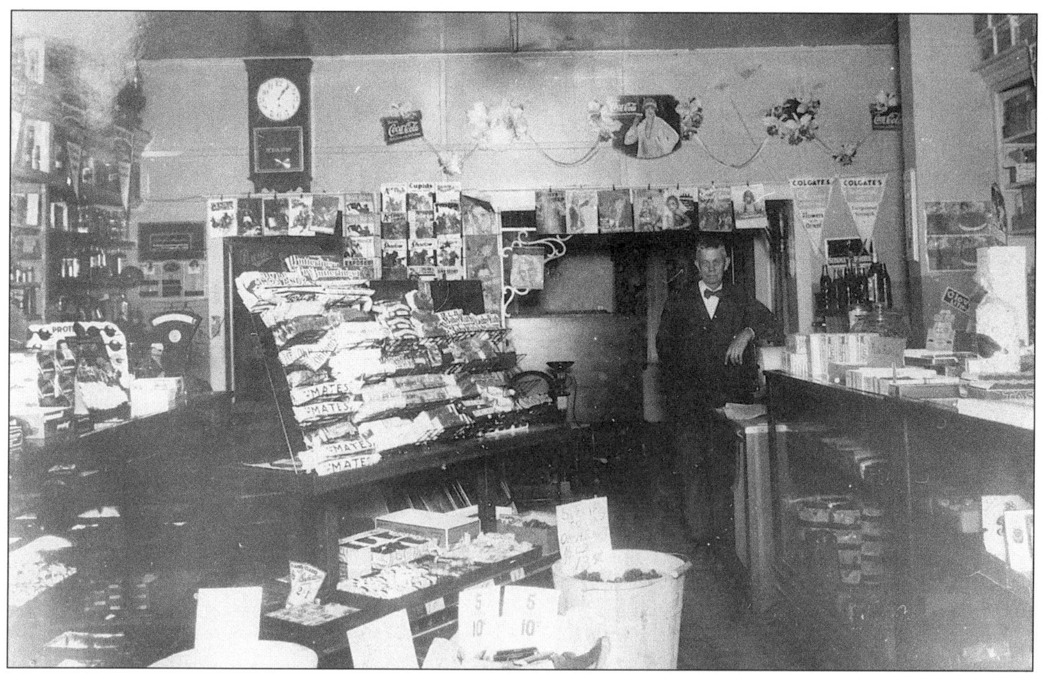

This photograph shows Sidney Duke inside his store in Nichols *c.* 1932.

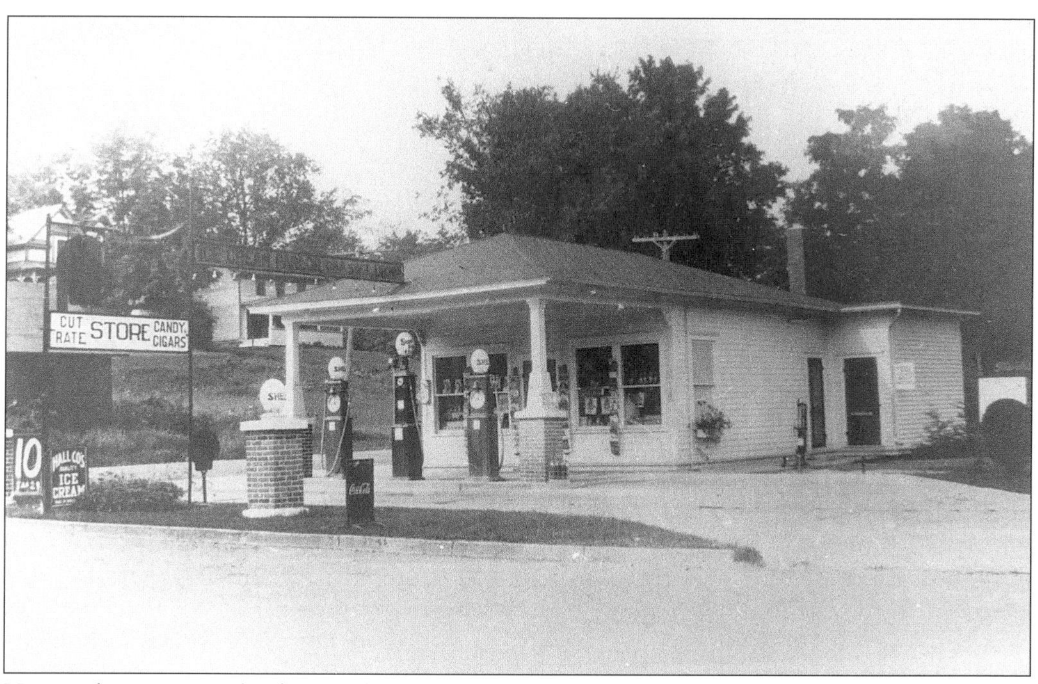

Here is the exterior of Sidney Duke's store *c.* 1930. The store closed on December 31, 1998.

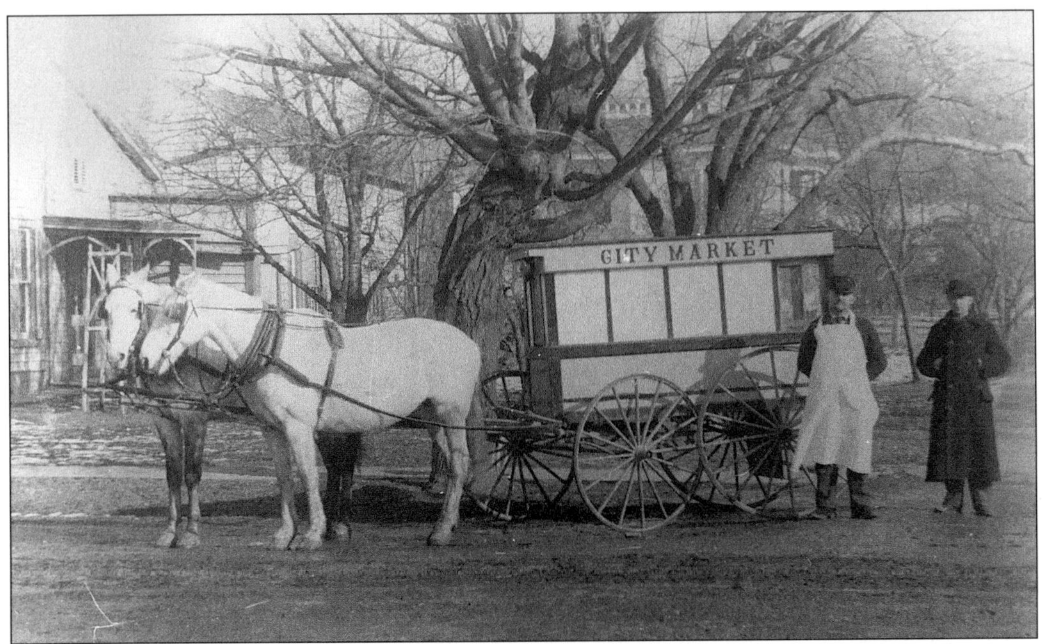

This *c.* 1896 view shows the City Market carriage delivering meat in Nichols. The gentleman on the left is Charlie Rogers, and the one on the right is Frank Leasure.

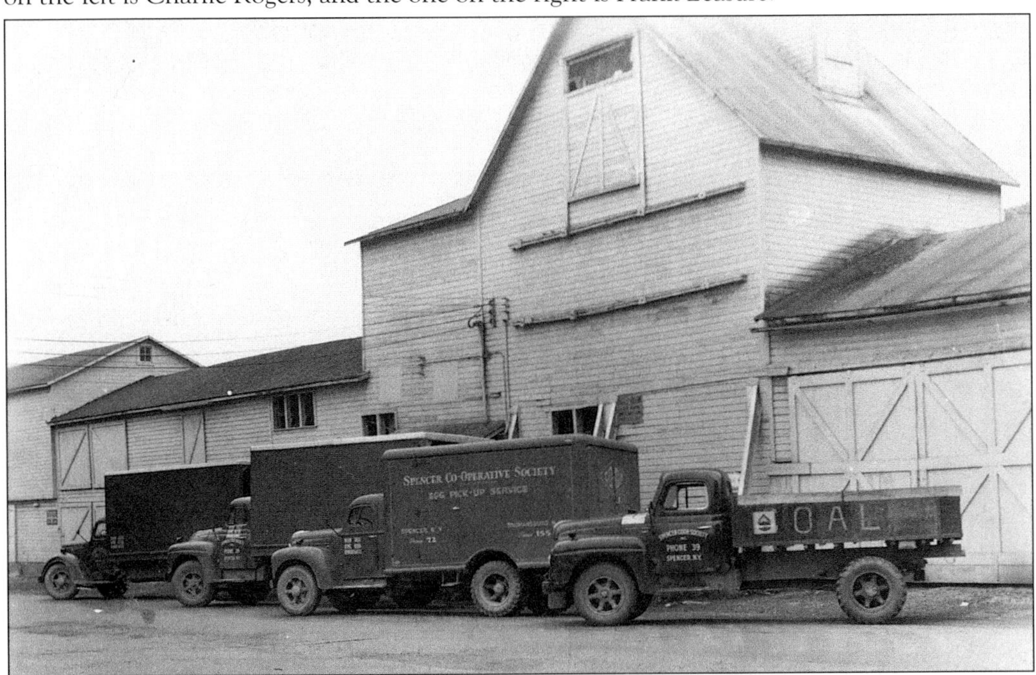

The Spencer Cooperative Society was formed in 1928 on Railroad Avenue. Early Finnish immigrants came to the Spencer area in 1908 to purchase inexpensive farmland, which had been advertised in major newspapers around the country. Finding that the land and the farms needed tremendous work to be productive, they formed a cooperative to purchase needed materials, stock, and feed directly from wholesalers in order to save money. This photograph dates from *c.* 1938.

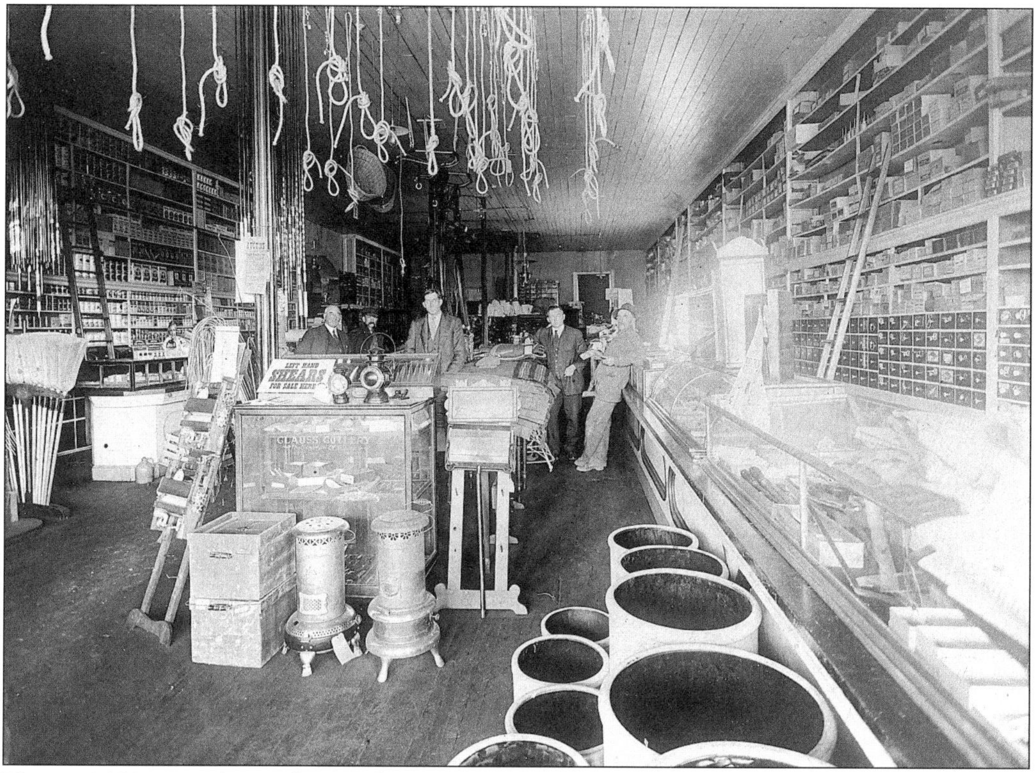

This c. 1900 view shows the inside of Marvin D. Fisher's hardware store located in Spencer. Fisher, who built the store c. 1895, is on the far left, and his son, Henry Fisher, is fourth from the left.

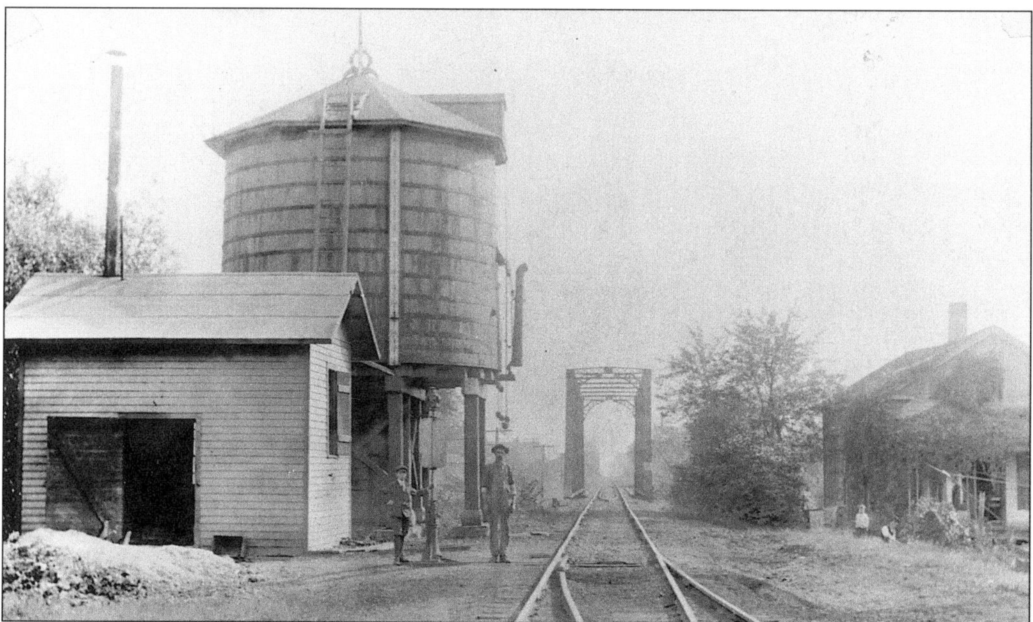

Engines of the Lehigh Valley Railroad refilled at this water tank. Pictured at the tank c. 1905 is Dennis Murray, a track worker and caretaker of the tank.

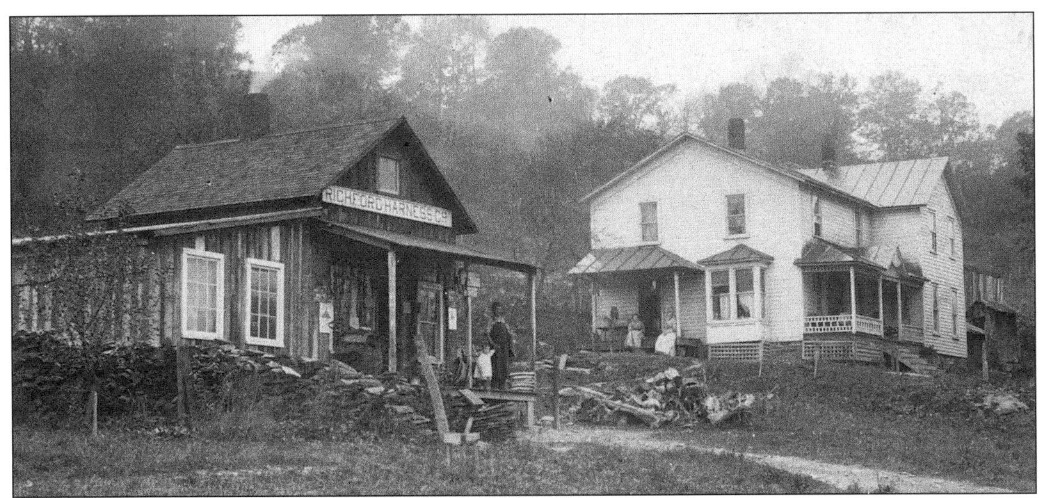

This *c.* 1911 photograph shows the Richford Harness Company. The gentleman standing on the porch of the shop is the proprietor, Arba Barnes.

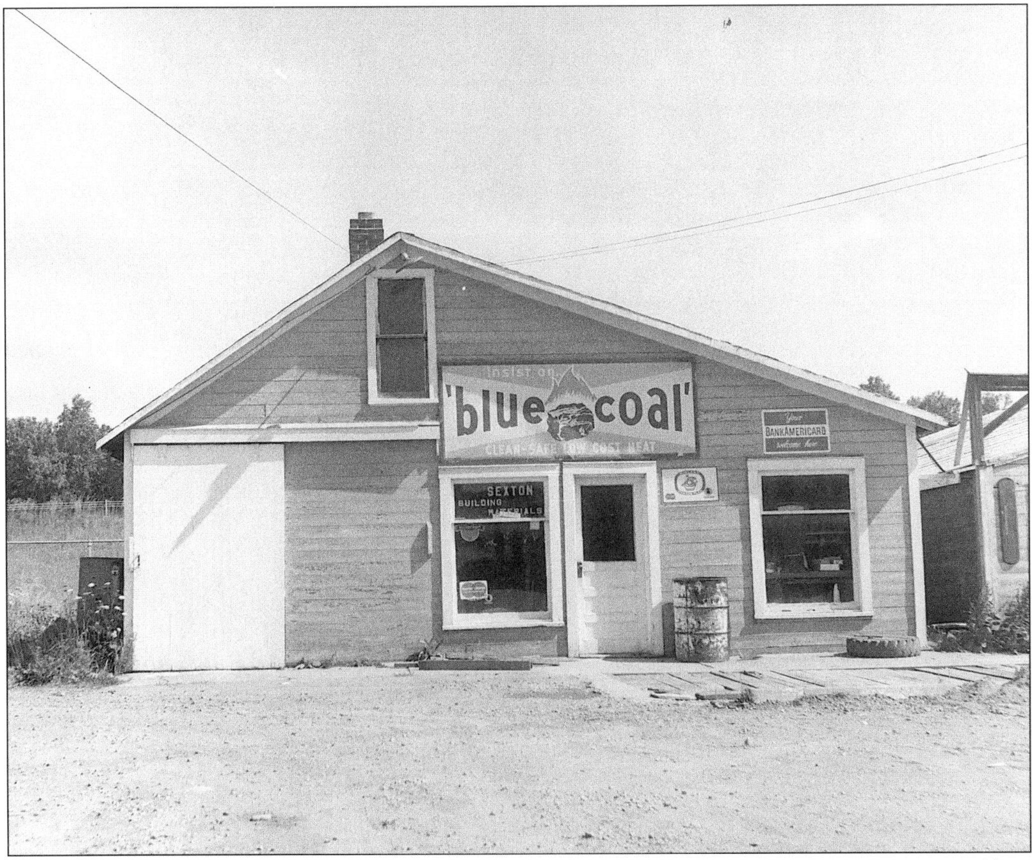

During the 1930s, Raymond Sexton entered business with his father, Lewis Sexton, selling cement products. After his father died in the late 1930s, Sexton expanded the business to include coal and lumber. He continued in business until 1964, when he sold the Sexton Lumber Company.

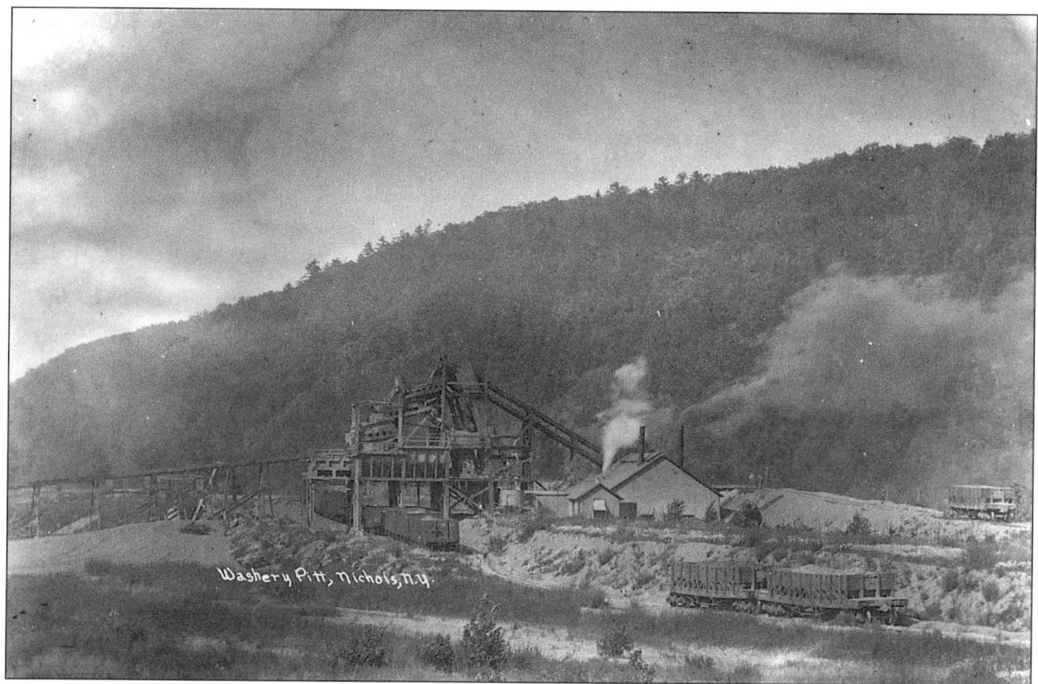

This *c.* 1917 view shows the washery pit in Nichols. Built *c.* 1880, the washery pit was used by the Lackawanna Railroad, which shipped gravel and sand throughout the region for use in construction projects. By the end of the 1920s, the sand played out, and the pit was abandoned.

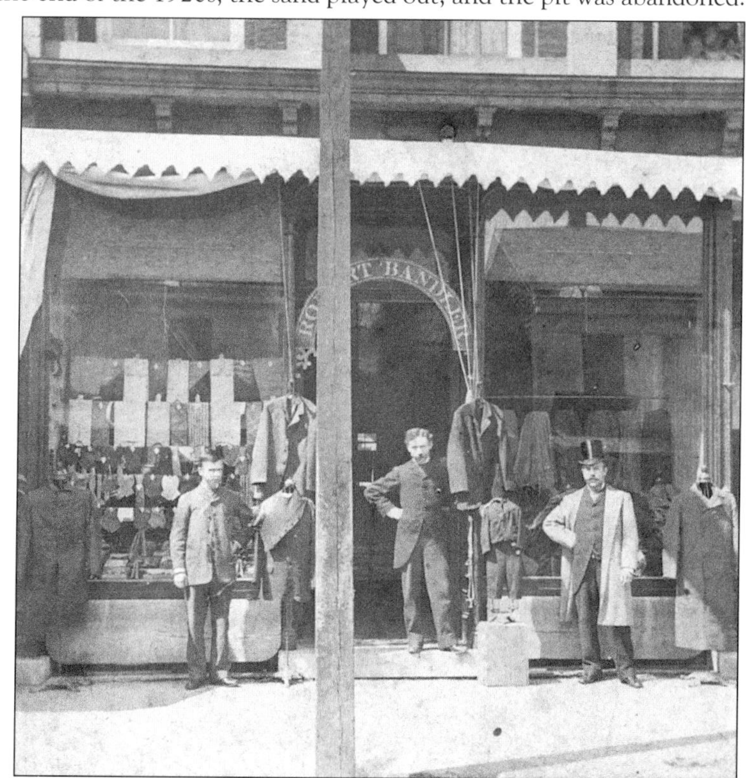

Robert Bandler arrived in Owego in 1865 from New York City and established a clothier. Today known as Bandler, Stiles, and Keyes, the clothier is the oldest retail business still operating in Tioga County. This photograph, taken *c.* 1875, shows A.J. Klem on the left and Robert Bandler on the right. Notice the children peeking from the upper right window.

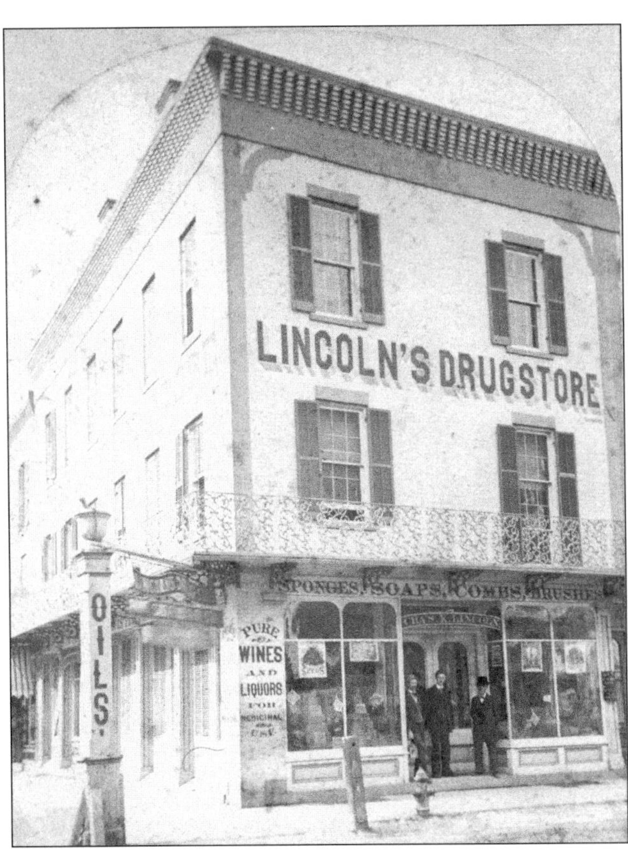

This c. 1870 photograph shows Lincoln's Drug Store in Owego. Charles K. Lincoln is on the right.

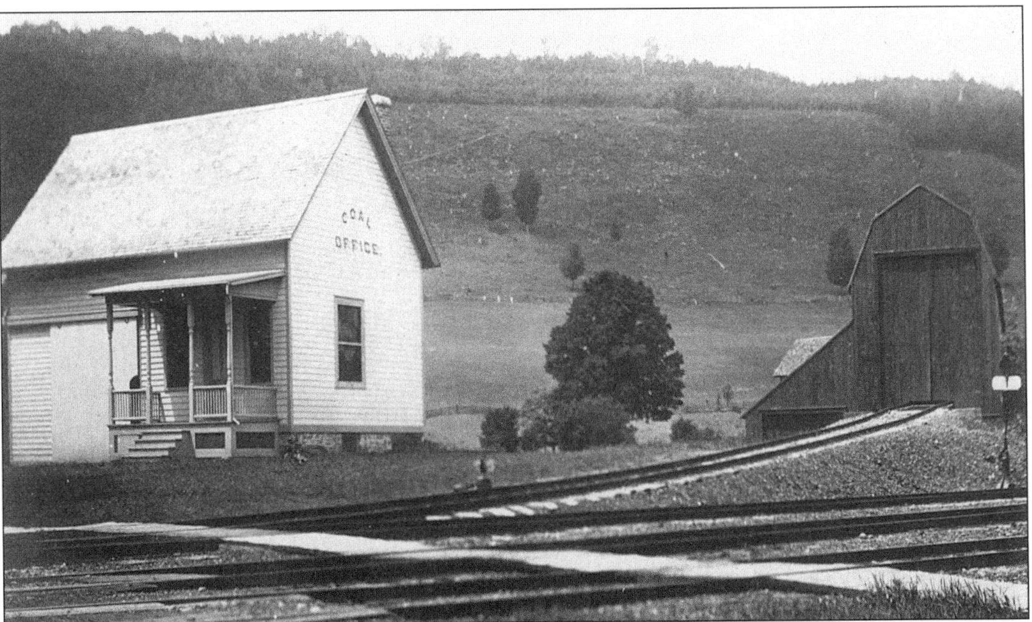

Heath's Coal Office and storage facility, on the right, were built in Candor in 1907. This photograph dates from c. 1910. Today, the office is a residence, and the barn has been used as an auction facility. Note the cleared fields in the background; today, they are a forest.

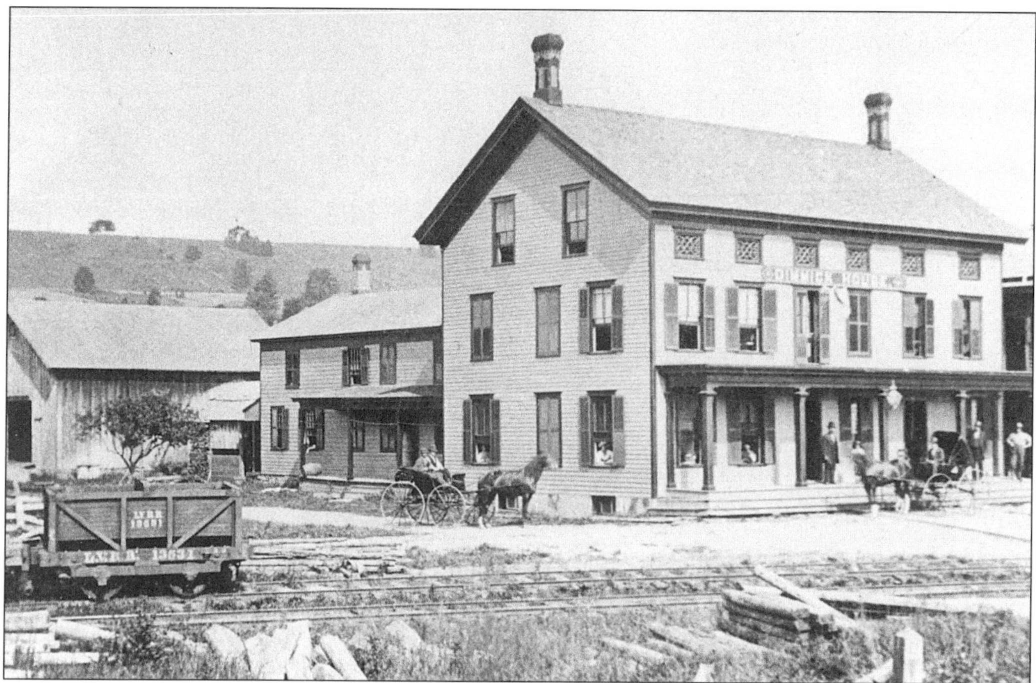

The Dimmick Hotel was built in Newark Valley in 1871 by Ossian Dimmick and his father-in-law, Hiram Young. This building burned in 1879, along with the two adjacent structures. The following year the hotel was rebuilt, this time of brick. Between 1926 and 1928, during Prohibition, the hotel was raided four times. During the fourth time, the proprietor was heard to say that he was going to go back to the baking business. The hotel was taken down in 1963.

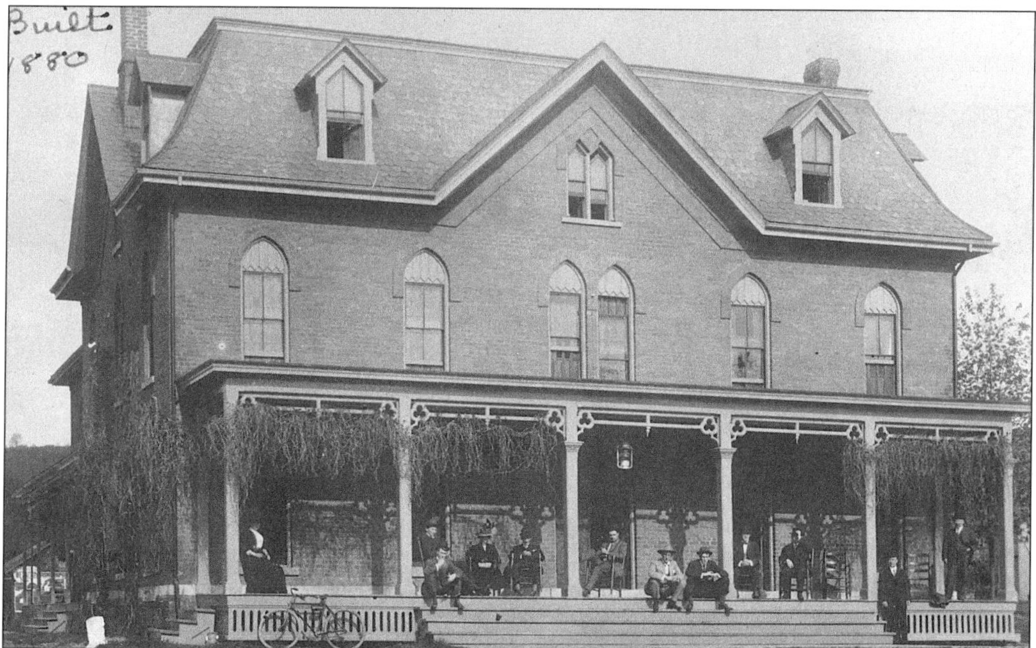

The Dimmick Hotel was rebuilt in 1880 at its Newark Valley site, following the 1879 fire that destroyed the original structure.

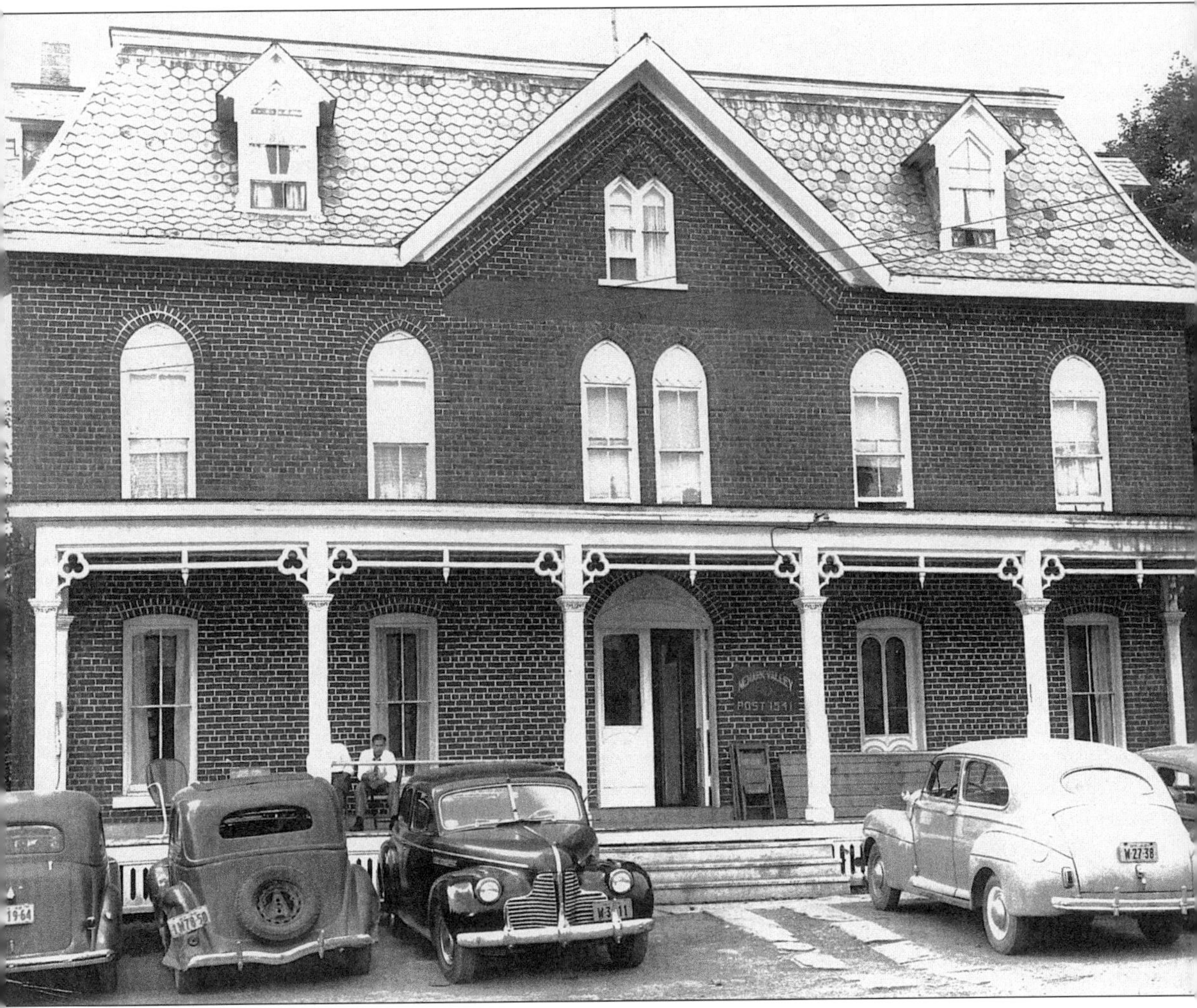

This photograph shows the Dimmick Hotel in Newark Valley c. 1950.

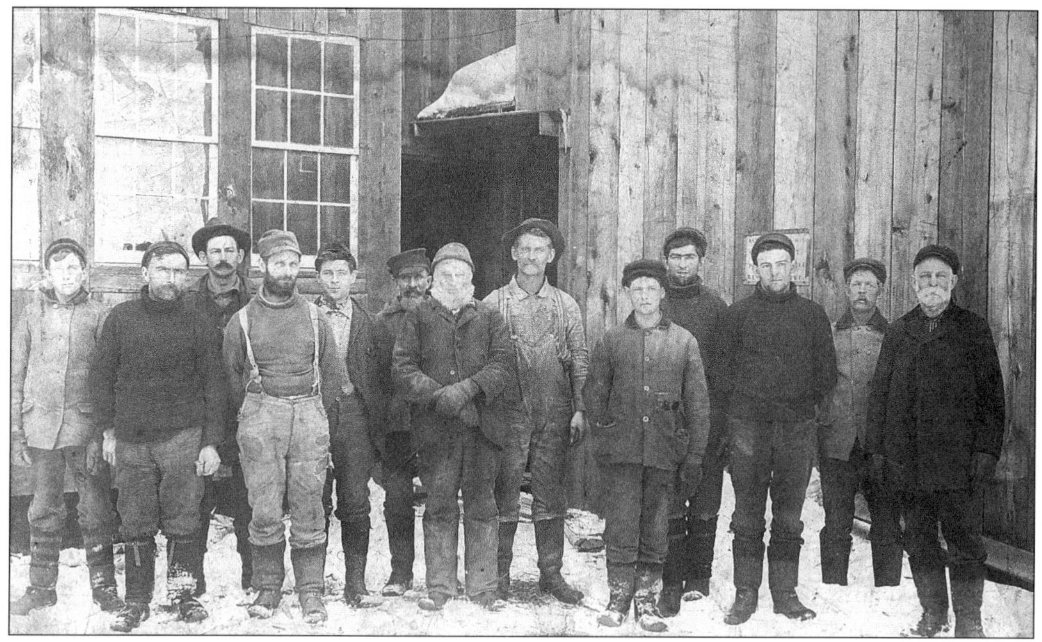

This 1902 photograph show the employees of Clarence Finch's Sawmill in Richford. They are, from left to right, George Rice, Dudley Hayes, Bert Cox, Wilson Marshall, George J. Clark, Frank Holland, Wallace Livermore, Joe Ayers, Floyd Marshall, Leon Tarbox, Leon Polley, George Slater, and Clarence Finch.

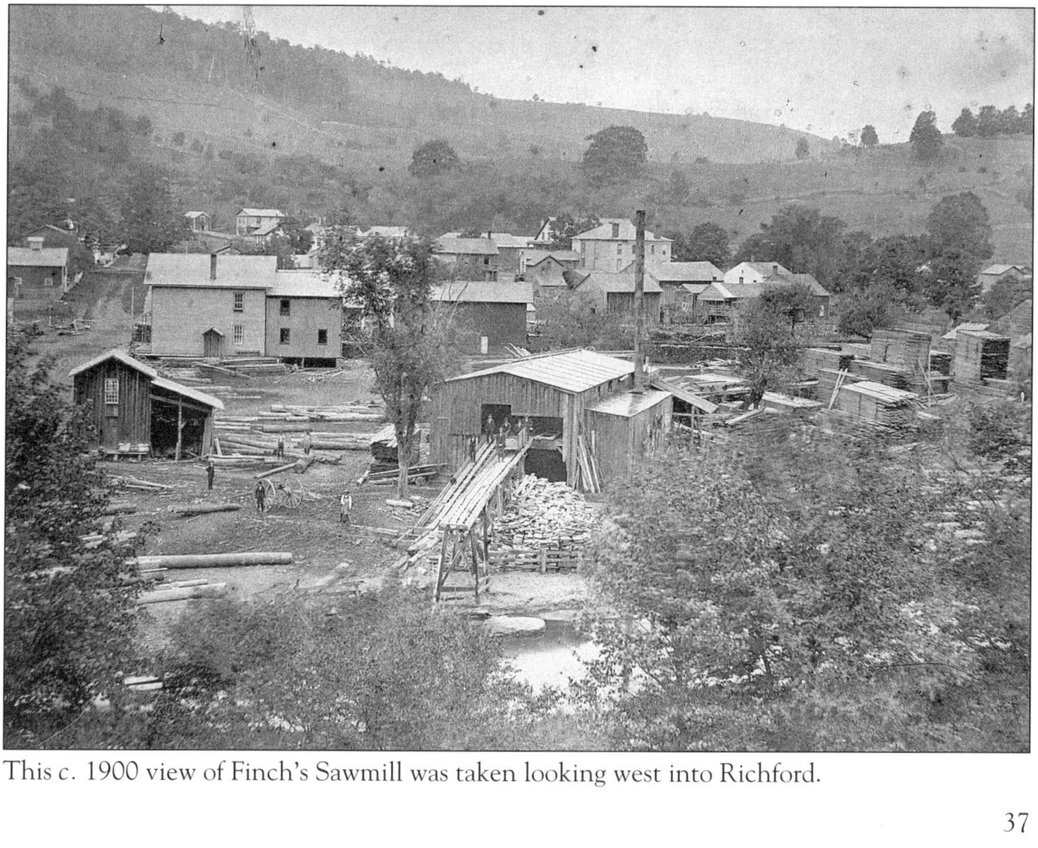

This *c.* 1900 view of Finch's Sawmill was taken looking west into Richford.

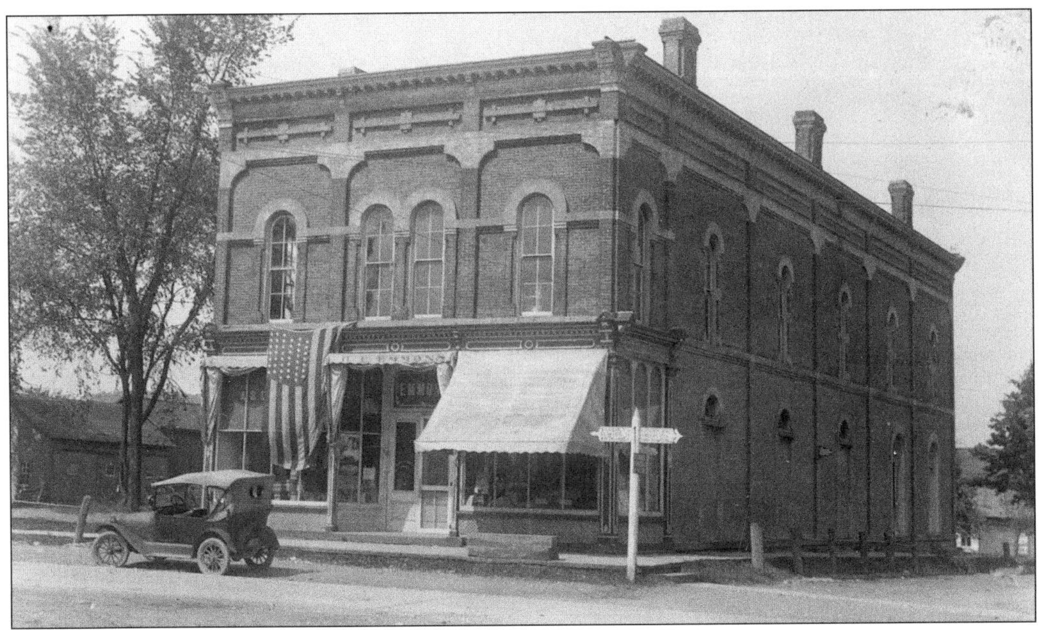

Located at the four corners in Spencer was Emmons Store. The brick building was constructed in the late 1870s. The store was the exclusive producer of the Electro-Silicon Liniment and of Dr. Shorey's Investigator remedies. This photograph was taken *c.* 1915.

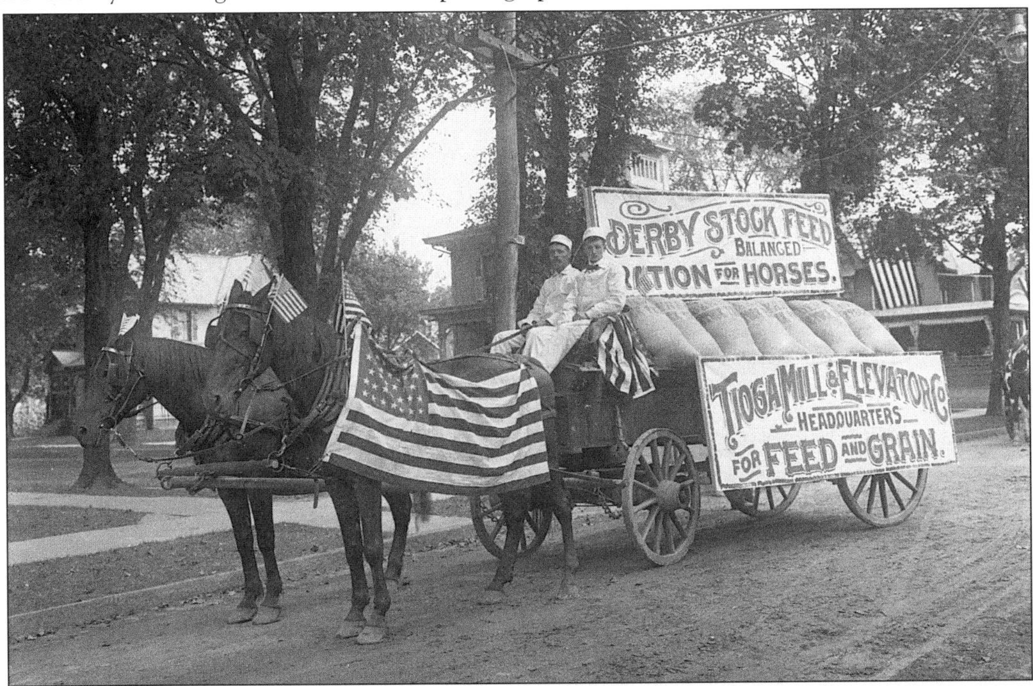

Tioga Mills was founded in 1908 by Arthur C. Palmer. The town of Barton proved to be a prime location for the business, due to the presence of three railroads nearby. The business supplied feed to much of eastern New York and Pennsylvania. The plant prospered through most of this century before it closed in 1973. This photograph was taken in 1910 in Waverly during the Old Home Day celebration.

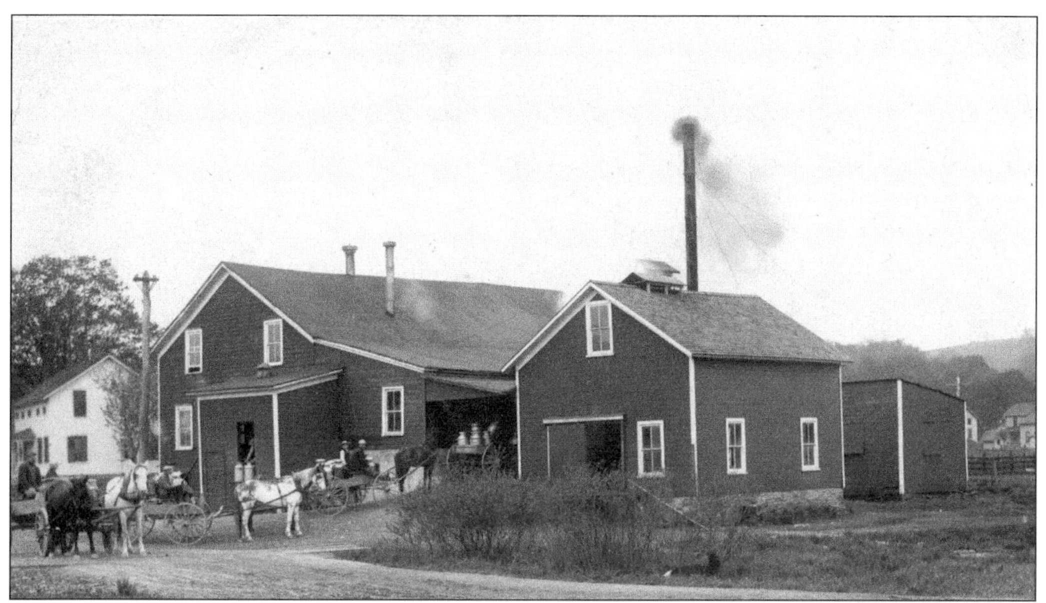
The Creamery was located in Berkshire. This photo was taken *c*. 1900.

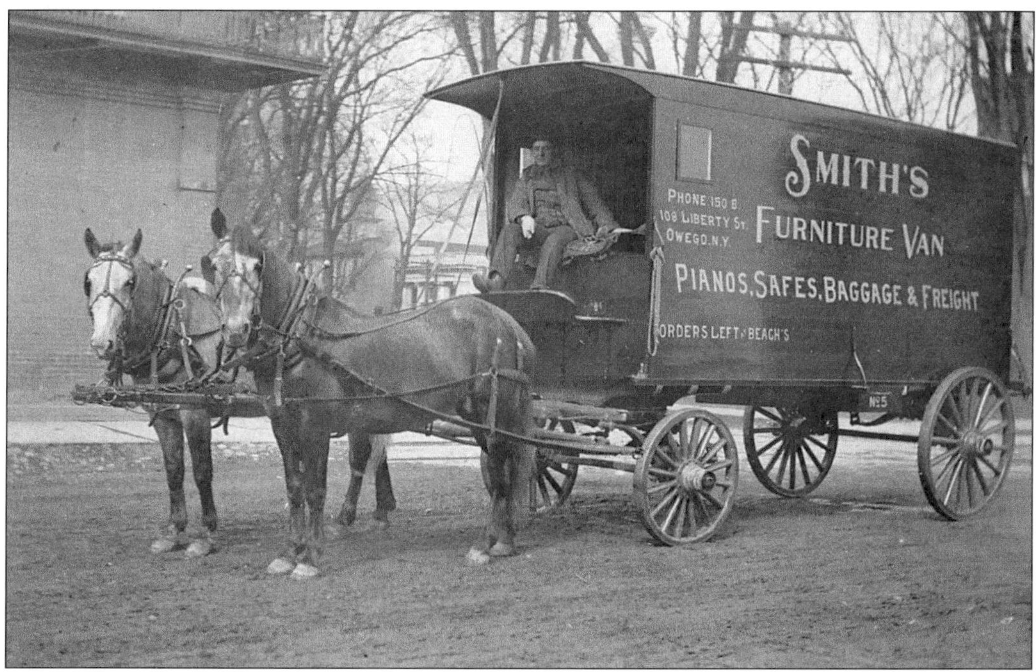

This *c*. 1900 view shows Smith's Furniture Van of Owego, one of the early moving companies in the area.

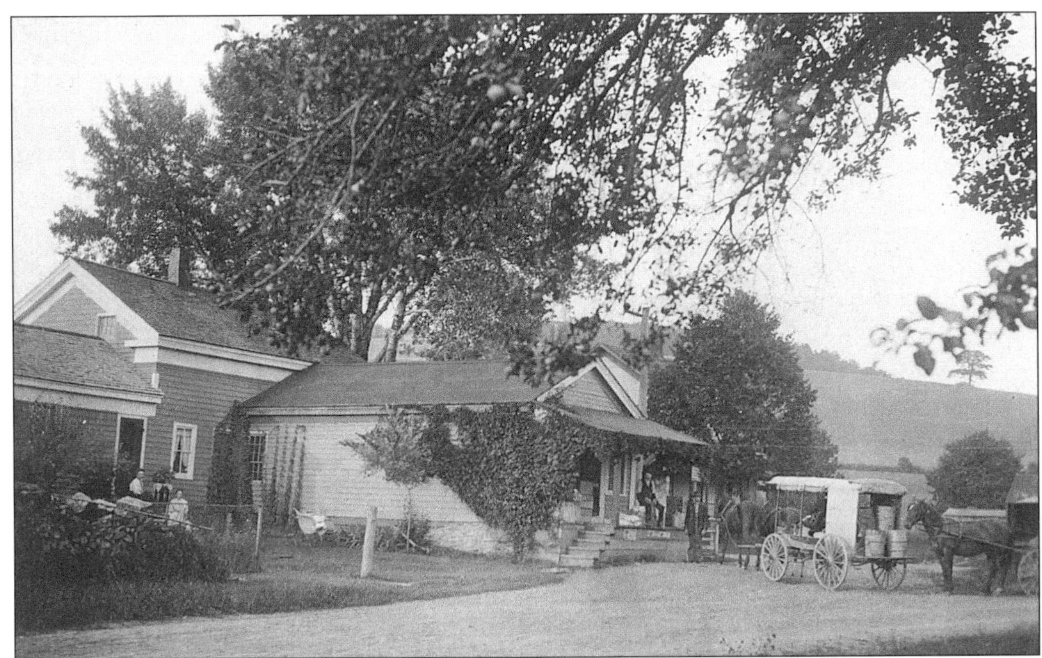

This corner of Jenksville was located in the northwestern part of Newark Valley. It was settled in 1797 and was named for Michael Jenks. The photograph was taken *c.* 1900.

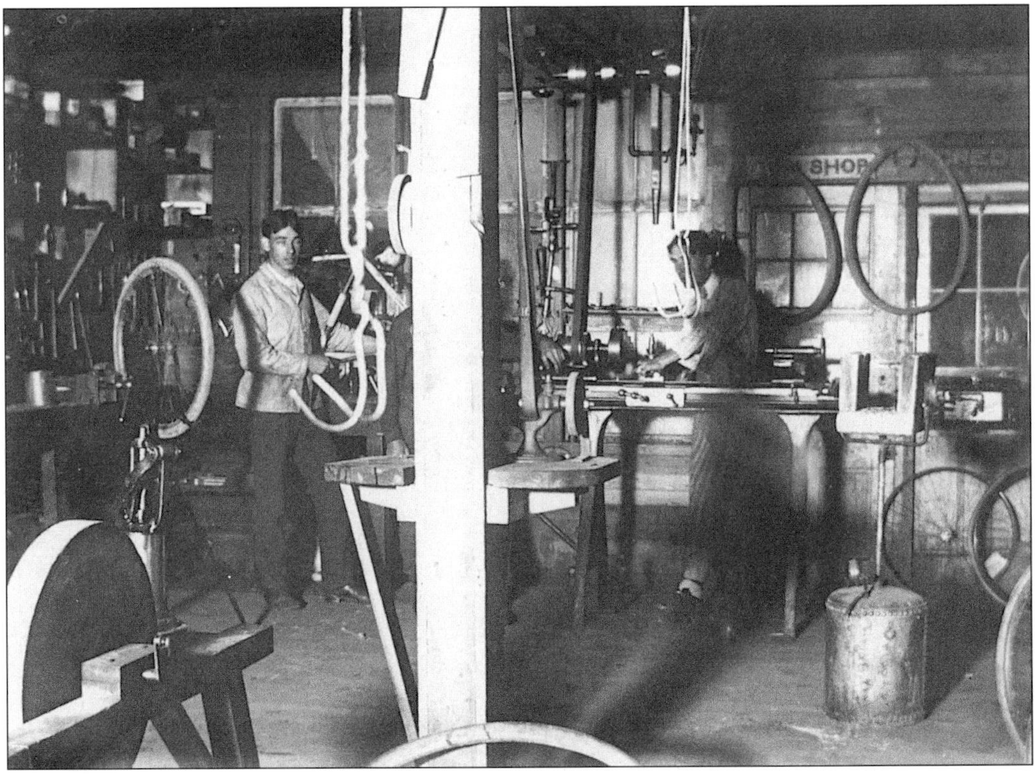

This photograph shows the Strong and Romine Bicycle Repair Shop in Owego *c.* 1900. In 1904, Strong and Romine expanded to sell sporting goods.

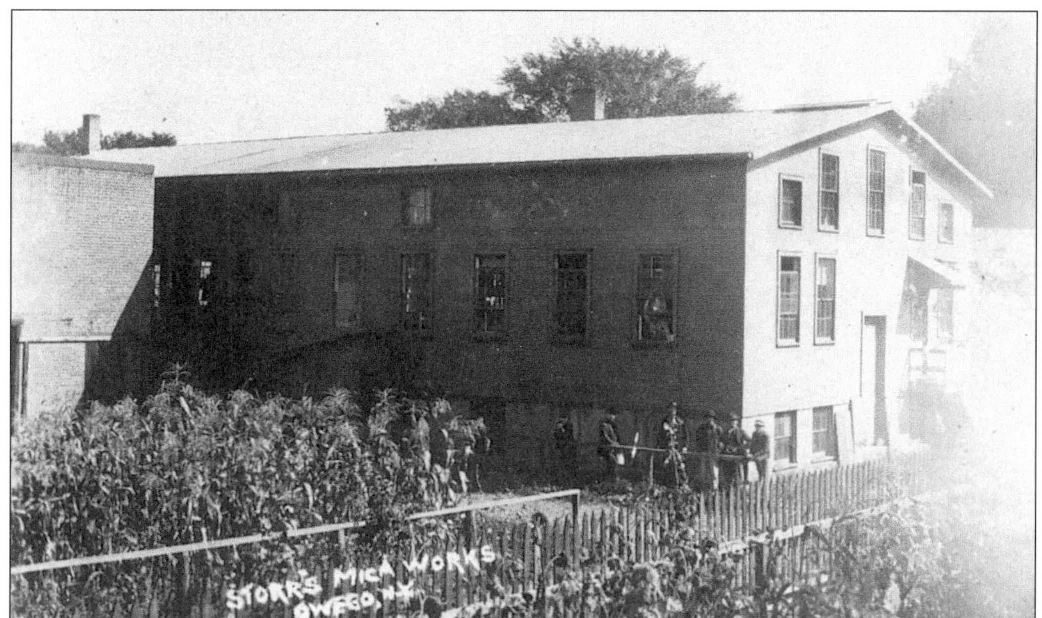

Storrs Mica Works was located on Parkers Lane in Owego. A.P. Storrs built the factory in 1896. He had just patented a mica gas chimney used in the gas lamps of the day. In 1897, Storrs participated in the Gas Exposition in Madison Square Garden in New York City. This photograph was taken *c.* 1910.

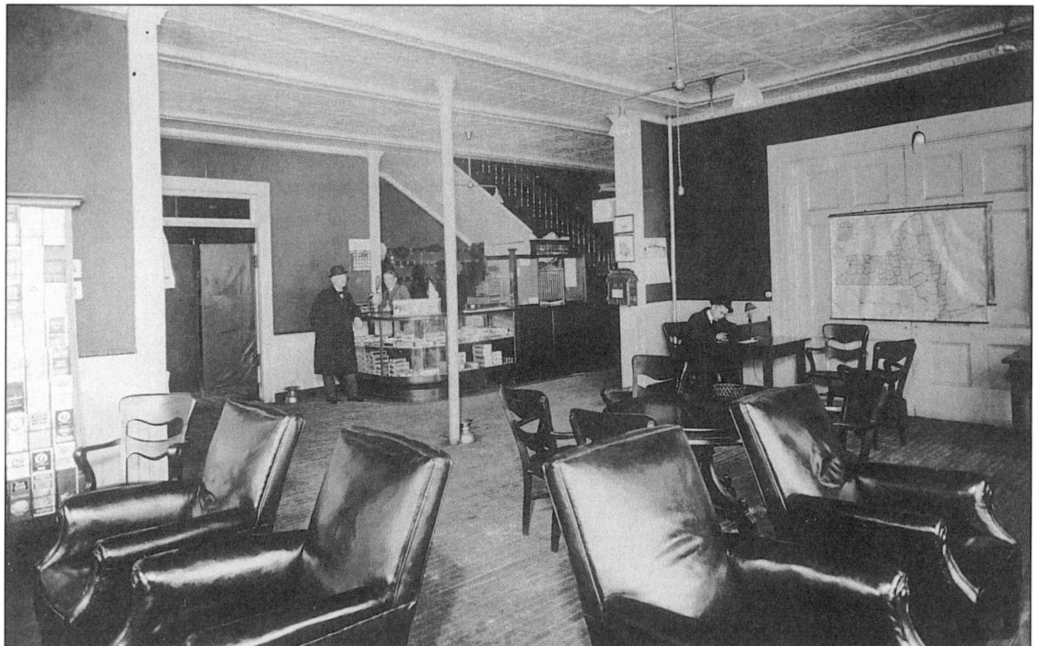

The Ahwaga Hotel was visited by two presidents: Grover Cleveland and Theodore Roosevelt. It was the site of Senator Thomas Collier Platt's famous buckwheat pancake breakfast on November 15, 1904, in honor of the election of Roosevelt. Some 150 Republican dignitaries attended the event. This photograph shows the interior of the hotel *c.* 1910. The Ahwaga was demolished in 1959.

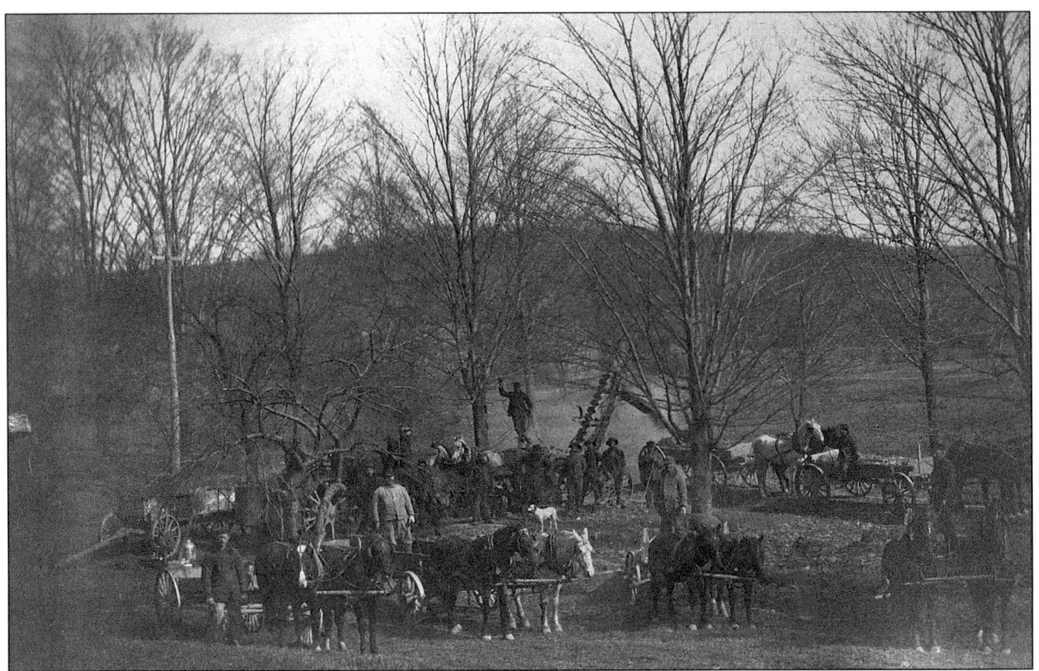

A stone crusher operates in Richford, *c.* 1900. Notice the wagons already filled with crushed stone. The town actually owned the crusher. People who needed crushed stone for their roads or driveways made arrangements to have the crusher hauled to their location and then brought in the fieldstone to be crushed.

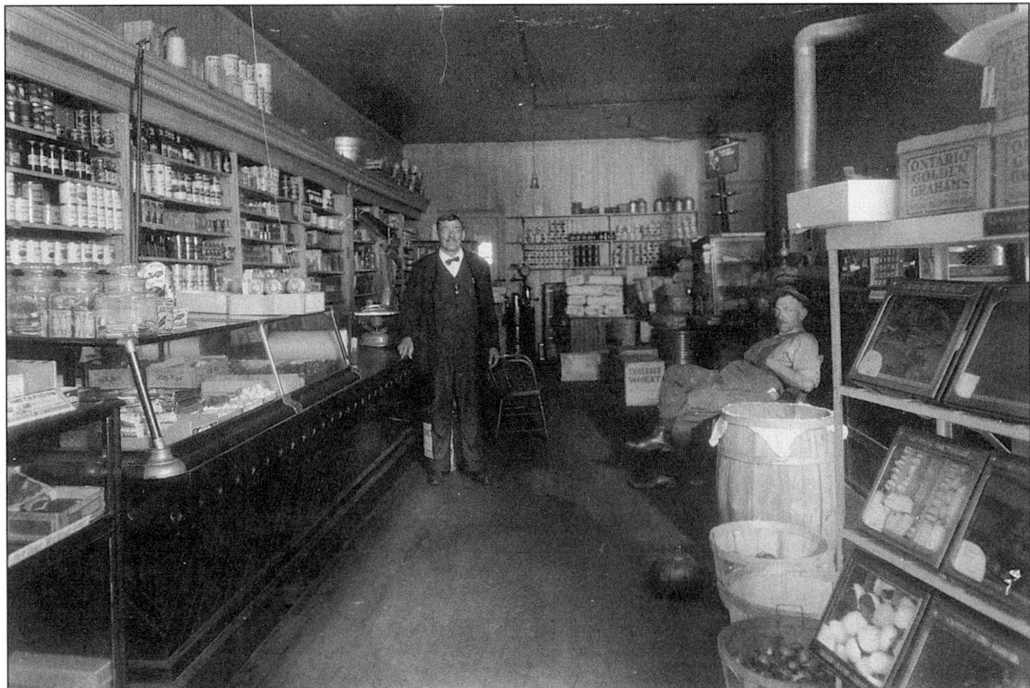

This *c.* 1900 view shows the interior of the Old Richford General Store. DeWitt Finn is the gentleman who is standing.

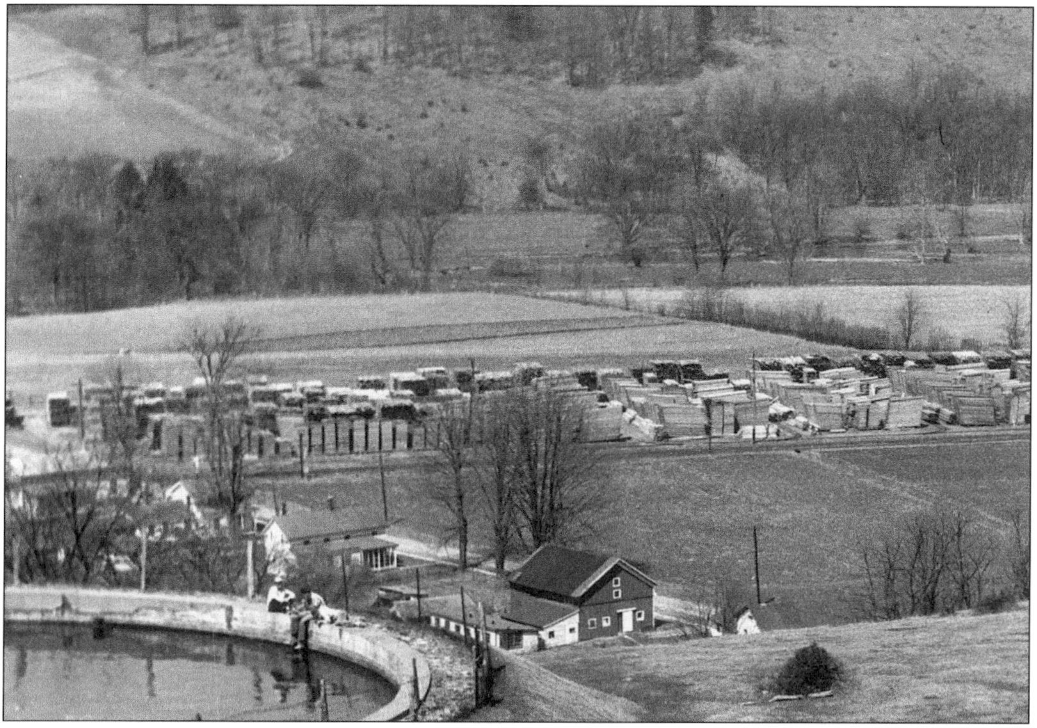

The Chesebro-Whitman Company was founded in 1879 by Denison P. Chesebro and William S. Whitman. The company was incorporated *c.* 1904 under the name Chesebro-Whitman Company Inc. The plant produced wooden steps and extension ladders, pruning poles, and toolsheds. This photograph dates from 1952. Notice the town reservoir on the left.

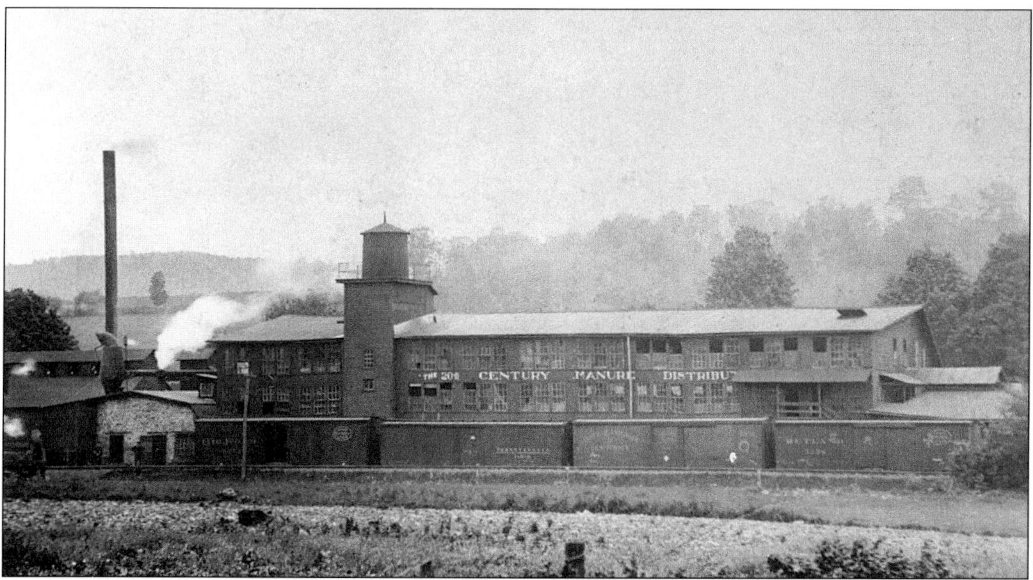

The International Harvester Company in Newark Valley produced manure spreaders to be sold all over the country. The company went from producing 14 machines per day in 1908 to 25 machines a day just two years later. It employed almost 200 hundred men. This photograph was taken *c.* 1910.

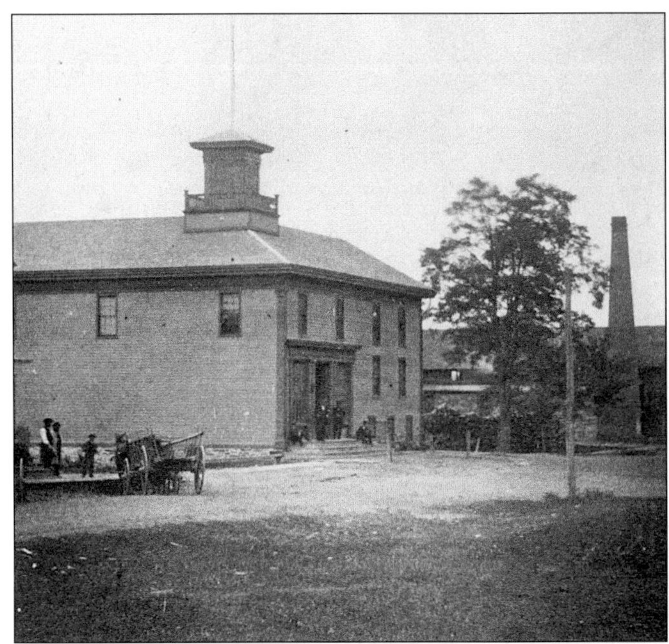

Dean's Tannery was located in Newark Valley. This *c.* 1887 photograph shows the tannery warehouse with the tannery itself in the background. Note the bark cart alongside the warehouse. The typical wage for an 11-hour day in the tannery in the 1880s was $1.10.

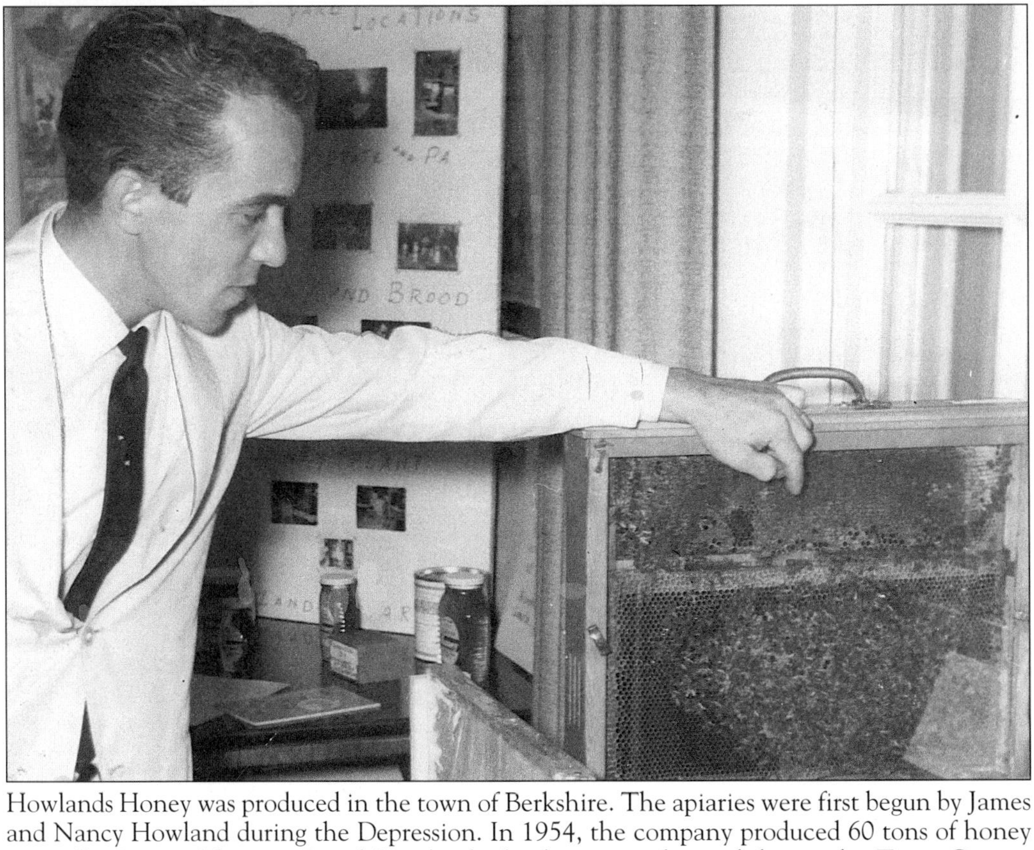

Howlands Honey was produced in the town of Berkshire. The apiaries were first begun by James and Nancy Howland during the Depression. In 1954, the company produced 60 tons of honey annually. Pictured here is David Howland, checking on a bee exhibit at the Tioga County Historical Society in 1964.

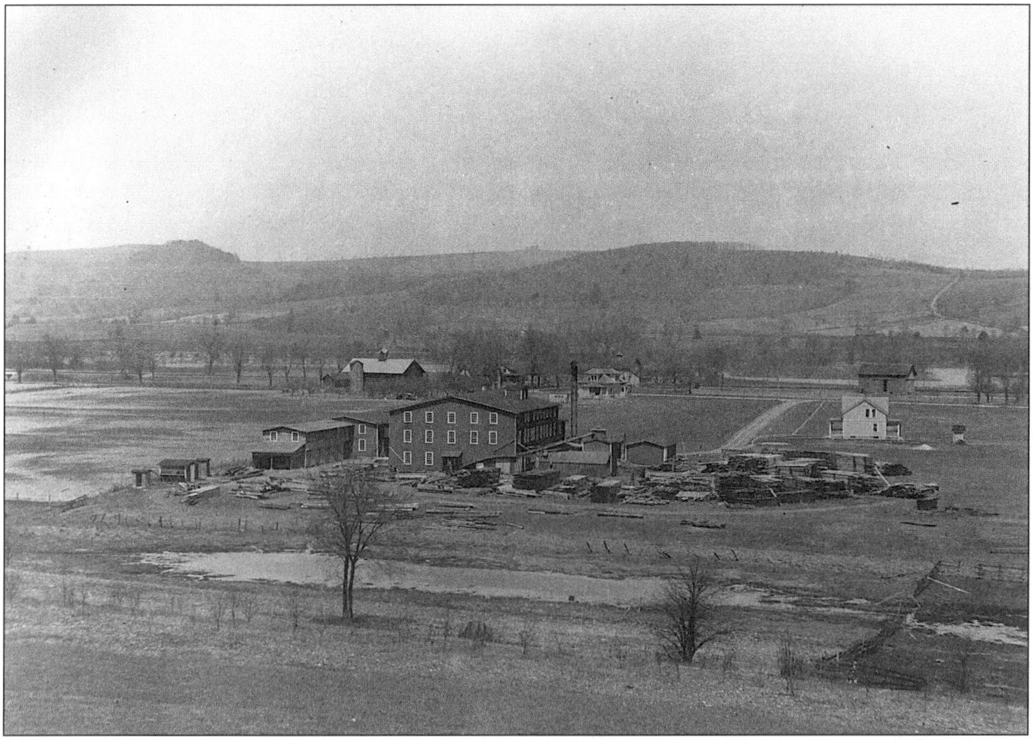

The Johnson Furniture Factory moved to Nichols in 1908. The factory produced a large variety of furniture, including many bedroom pieces. This photograph was taken *c.* 1925. The factory was destroyed by fire in 1947.

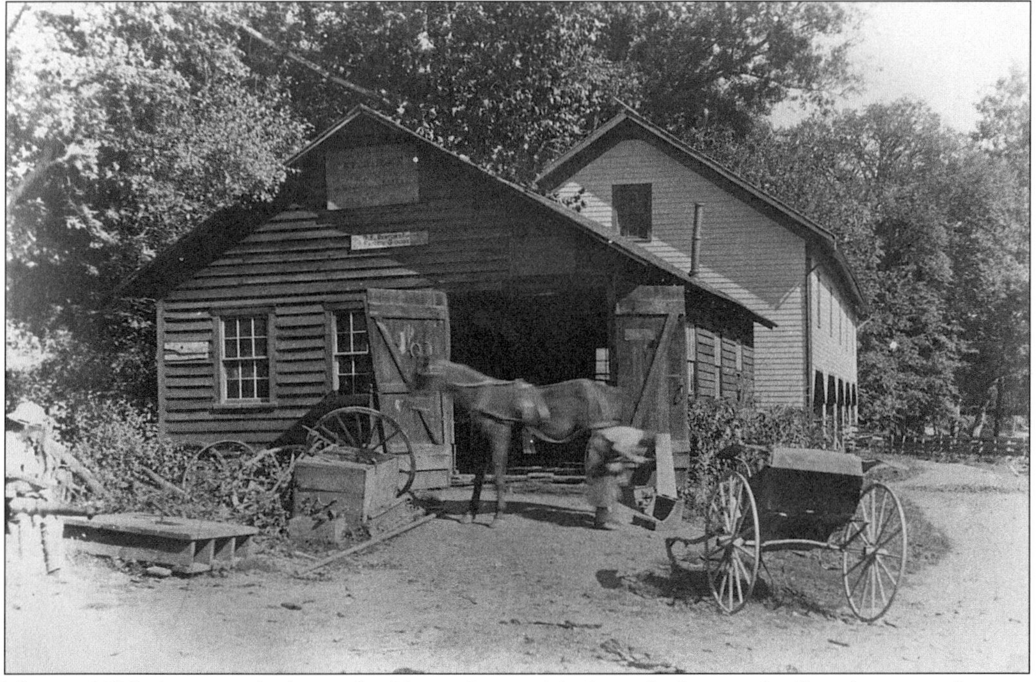

This *c.* 1895 photograph shows the Tioga Center blacksmith shop and roller-skating rink.

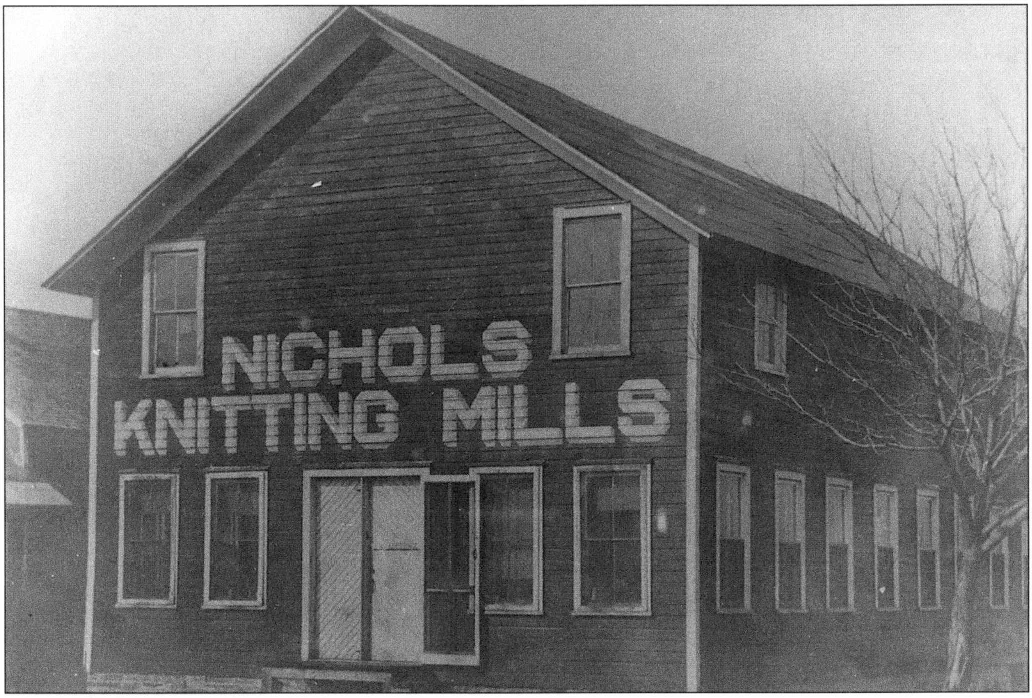

Nichols Knitting Mills was founded *c.* 1900. It produced assorted goods and was in business until 1920. The building is still standing between the former Agway and the Susquehanna River.

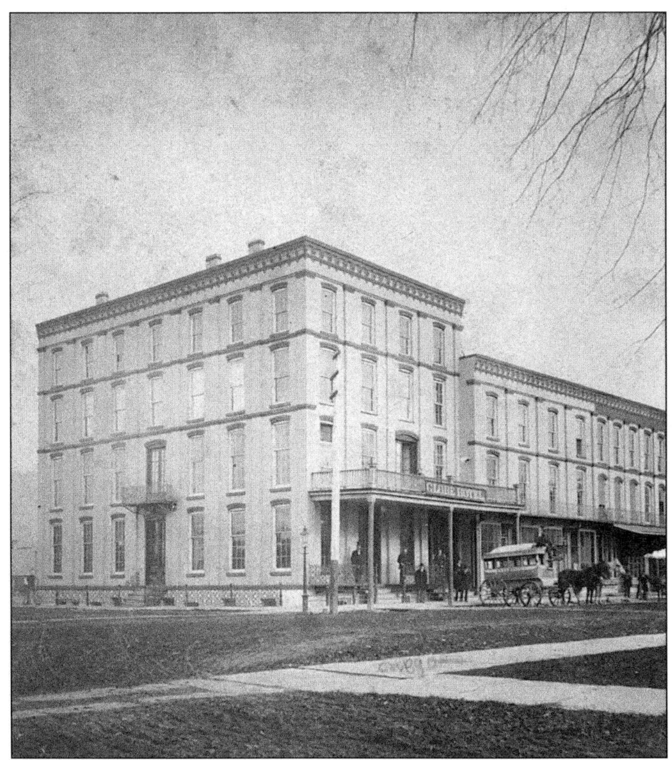

This photograph shows the Globe Hotel in Owego *c.* 1870. The building was originally erected in 1866 by Dr. Wilson, who opened it as the Park Hotel. It was later used as an automobile dealership. Today, the building is the home of United Auto Supply. Located on the corner of Central Avenue and Main Street, it is now only two stories in height.

Melville L. Comfort conducted a jewelry business on Lake Street in Owego for 25 years. He and his wife took great pleasure in entertaining local organizations at the beginning of the 20th century with the latest technology—the phonograph.

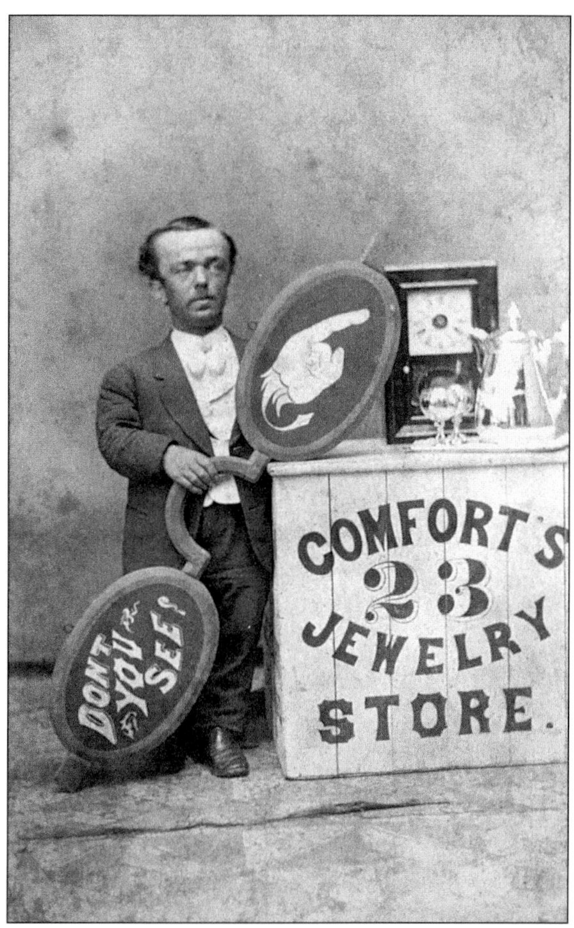

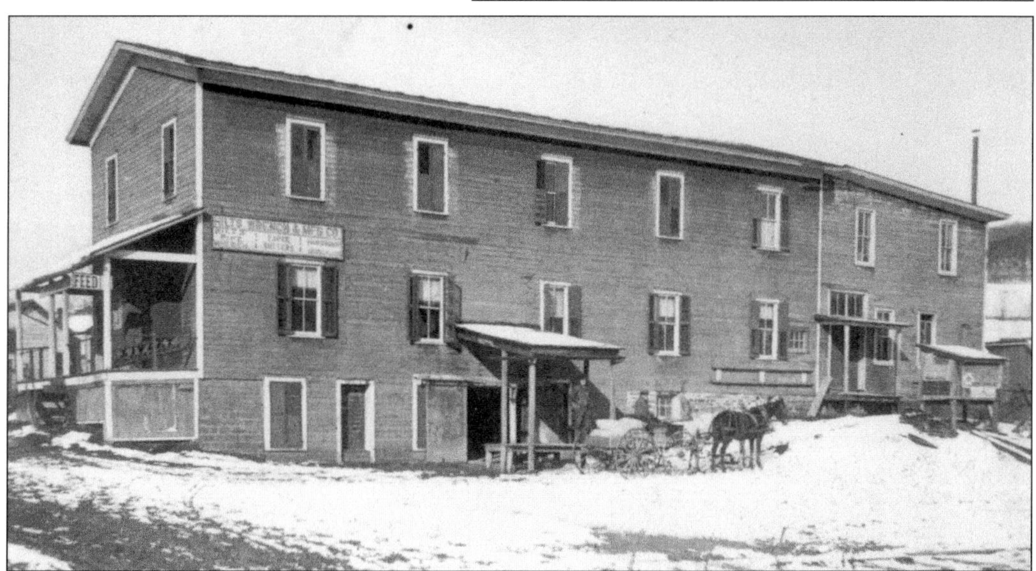

Bovee Hall in Richford was home to the Hilts wrench factory downstairs and the opera house on the top floor. This photograph was taken *c.* 1910.

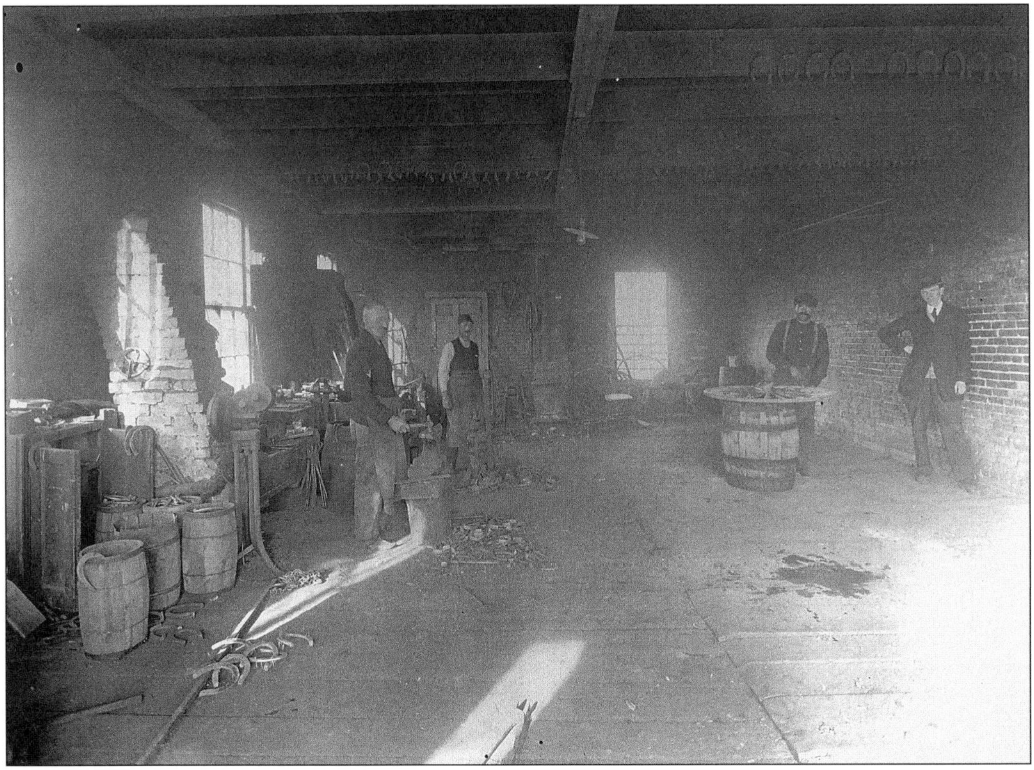

Here is Charles Laing in his blacksmith shop in Spencer. In 1978, this brick building was used as the paint shop of Van Atta Chevrolet.

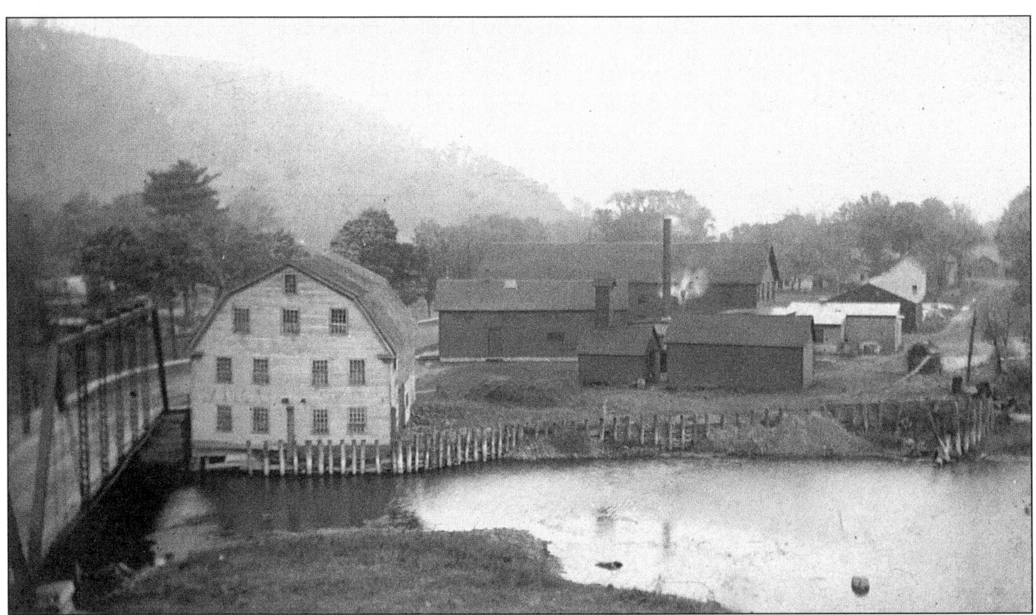

The Candor Blanket Factory was owned by Charles Barager. Barager was a captain in the infantry during the Civil War and was wounded at Gettysburg. He was elected to the New York State Assembly and gave an oration at President Grant's funeral in 1885.

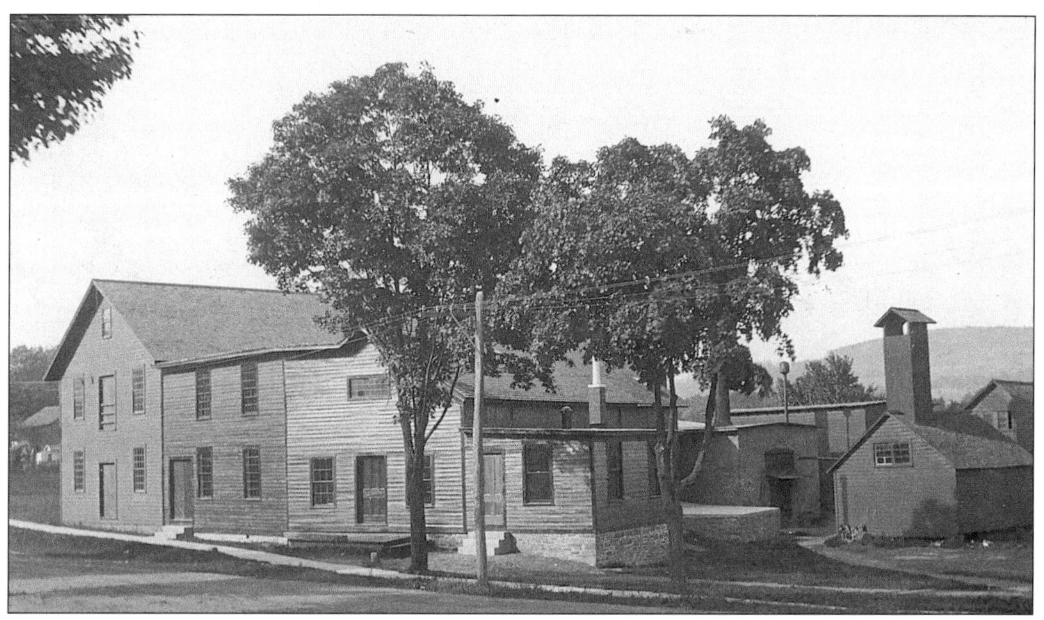

At its height, the Candor Blanket Factory produced 50,000 blankets a year.

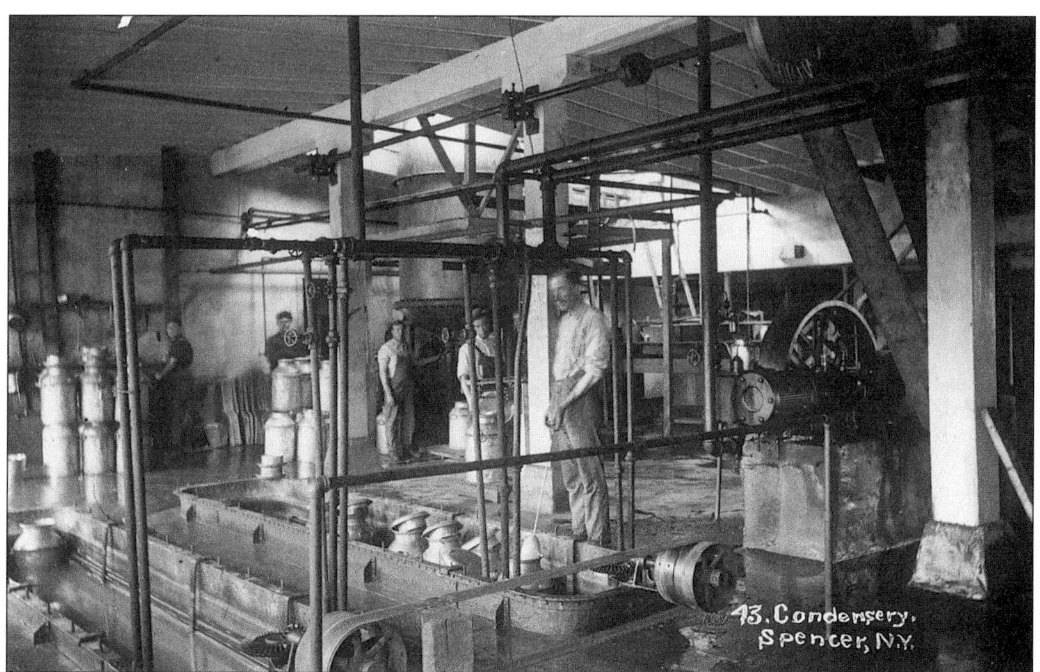

The Spencer Condensery was established in 1911 by C.E. Brigham. Brigham later sold out to the Empire Creamery Company of Pennsylvania. In 1917, the Nestle Company purchased the plant and equipment.

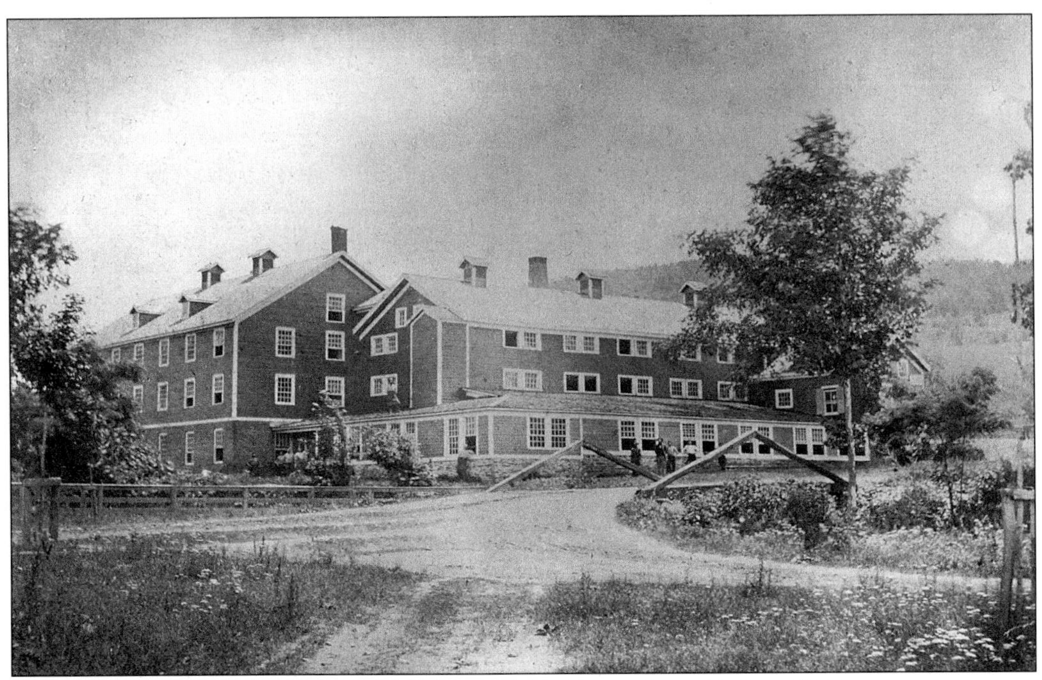

Dean's Tannery operated on Huntington Creek in Owego from 1862 to 1912.

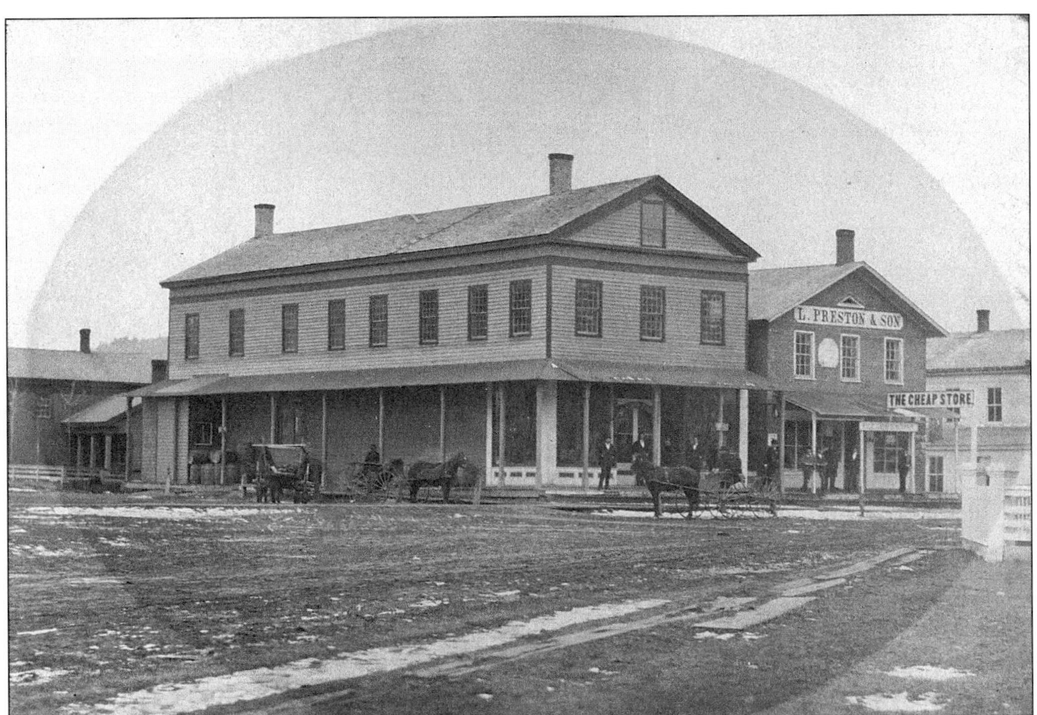

McCarty and Thompson was a general store in Candor. This is how it appeared *c.* 1870. The store burned in 1874 and was replaced with a brick structure. By 1909, ownership had changed to McCarty and Payne.

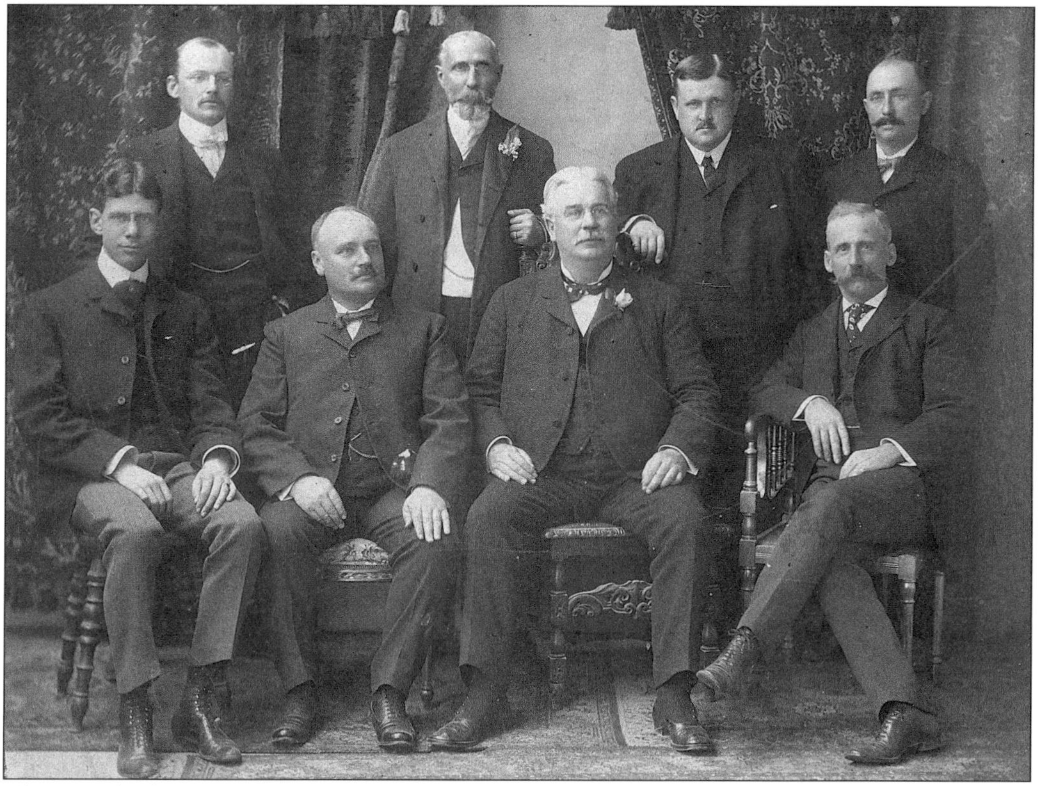

The Standard Butter Company was located on Front Street in Owego. Begun in 1888, the company, at one point, employed 15 men and 2 women. This photograph shows the company board of directors. From left to right are as follows: (seated) George Thompson, George F. Andrews, A. Chase Thompson, and unidentified; (standing) Francis Govers, unidentified, Lyman Stanbrough, and Charles Johnson.

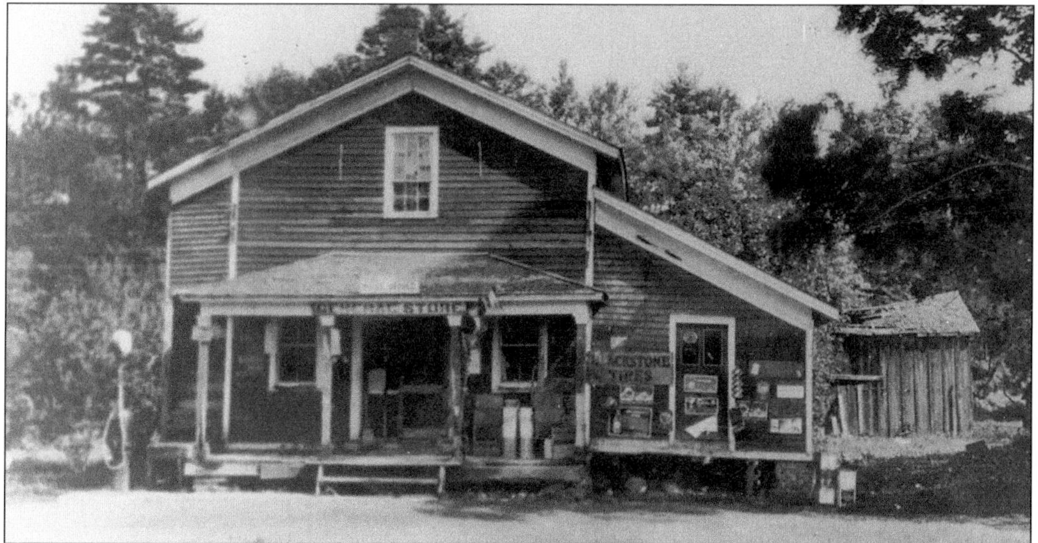

This is how the Straits Corners General Store appeared in the late 19th century. The store was later renovated as a residence.

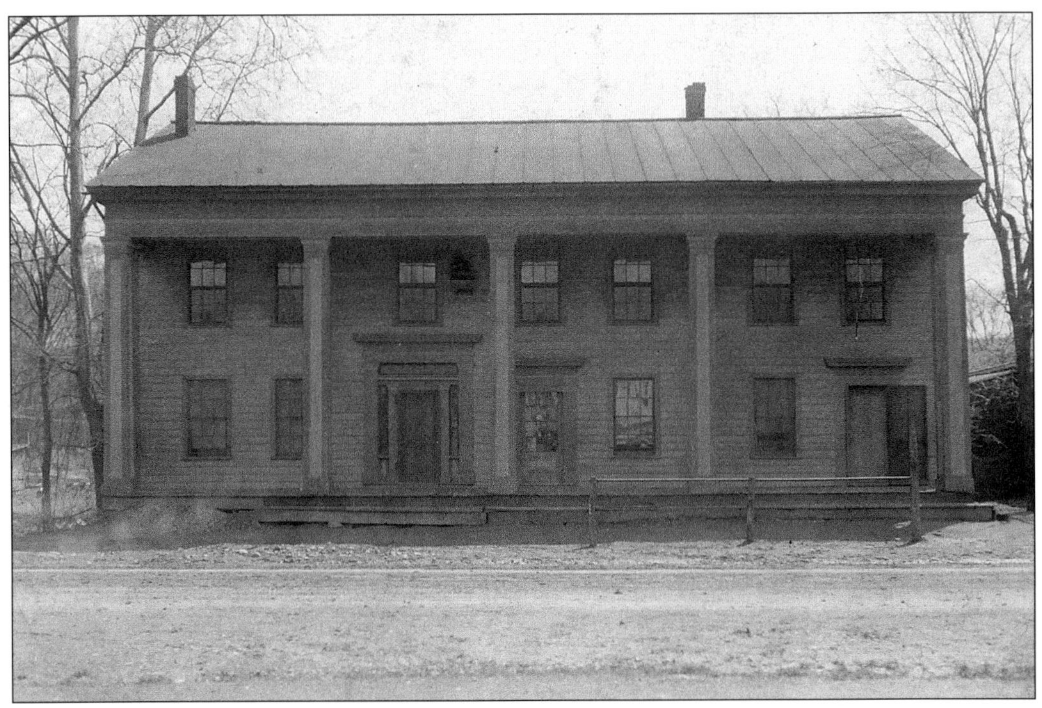

This photograph shows the O'Hart Hotel in Tioga Center.

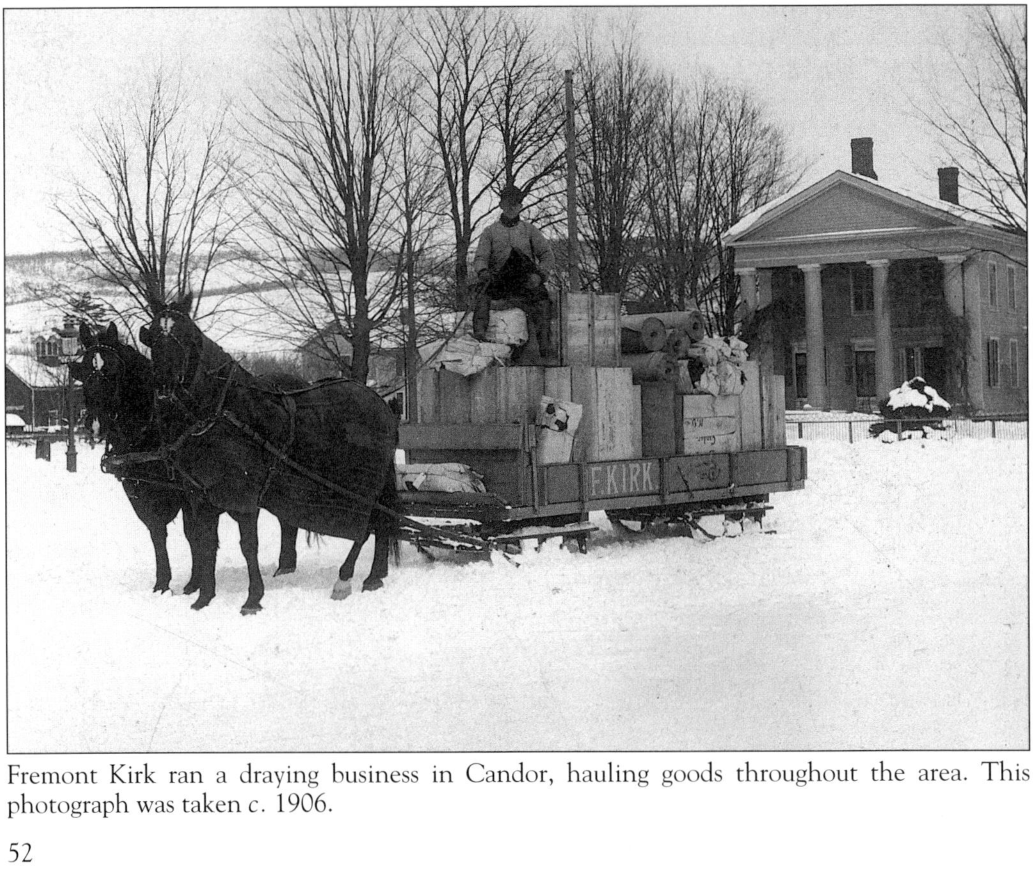

Fremont Kirk ran a draying business in Candor, hauling goods throughout the area. This photograph was taken *c.* 1906.

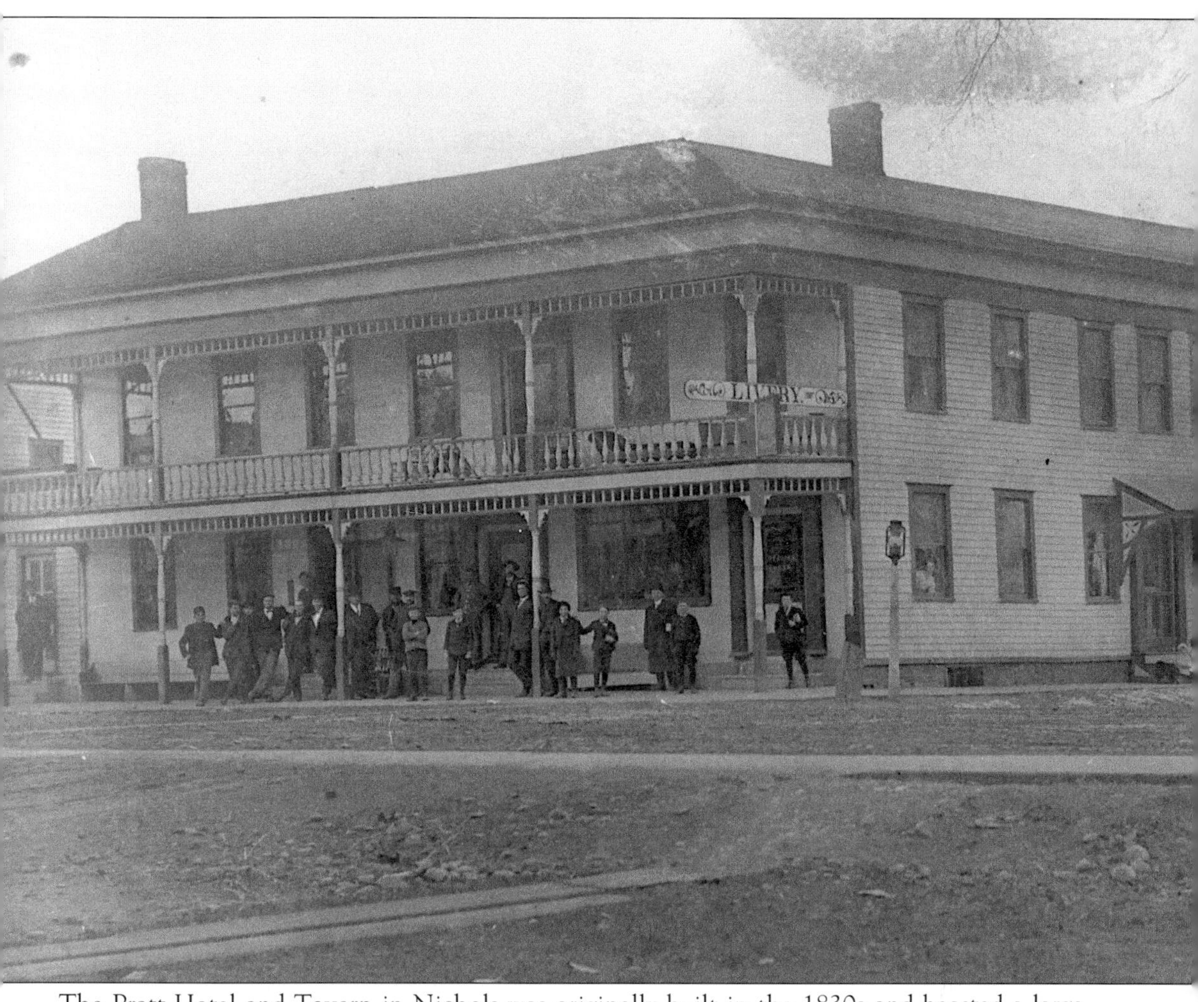

The Pratt Hotel and Tavern in Nichols was originally built in the 1830s and boasted a large ballroom. It is seen here *c.* 1900. To the rear of the building was the livery, located on River Street.

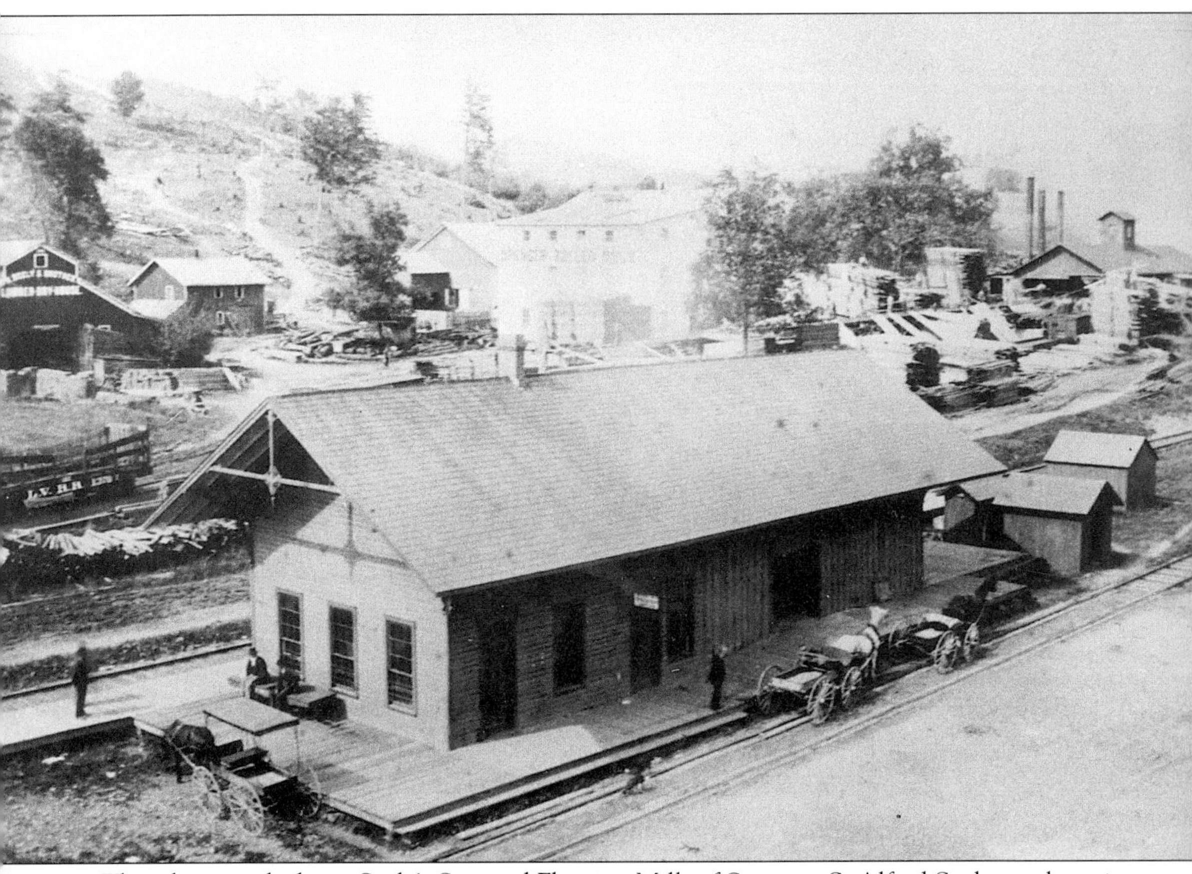

This photograph shows Seely's Saw and Flouring Mills of Spencer. S. Alfred Seely was born in Newfield in 1842. With his brother Seymour Seely, he began a lumber business in Elmira in 1863. In 1874, the Seelys moved their business to Spencer. They expanded further in ensuing years to include the sawmill, creamery, blacksmith shop, carpenter shops, lumber shed, horse and dairy barns, and a glove factory. This portion of Spencer later became known as Seely Town.

Three

Picking Up the Pieces

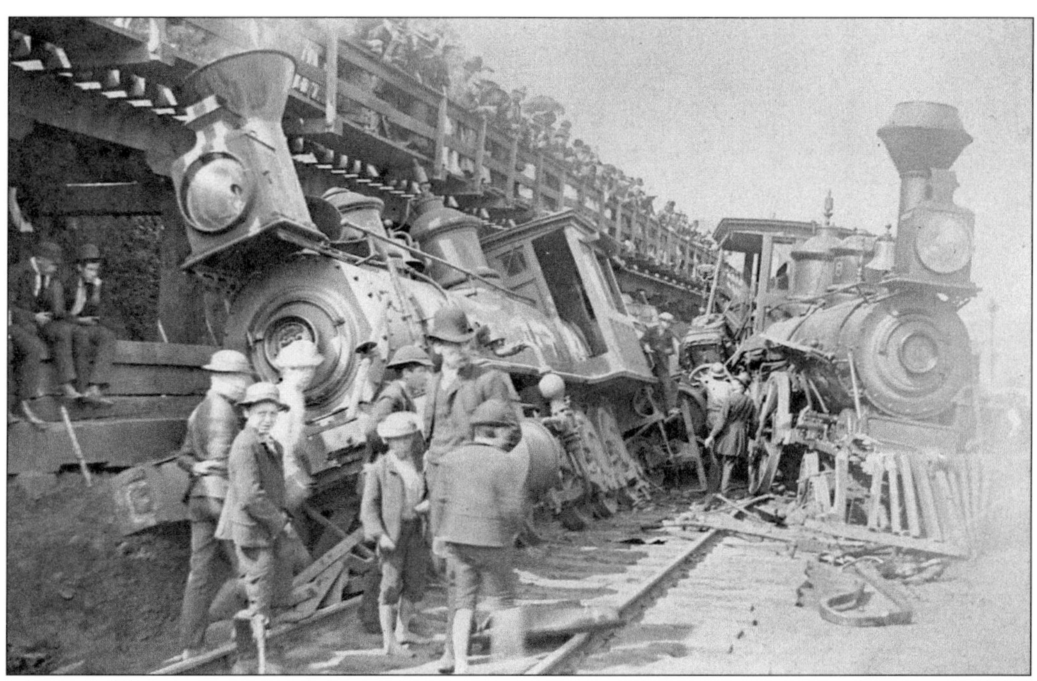

This terrible train wreck of the 1870s appears to have taken place in Waverly near the coal piers. The boy in the foreground has a wooden leg.

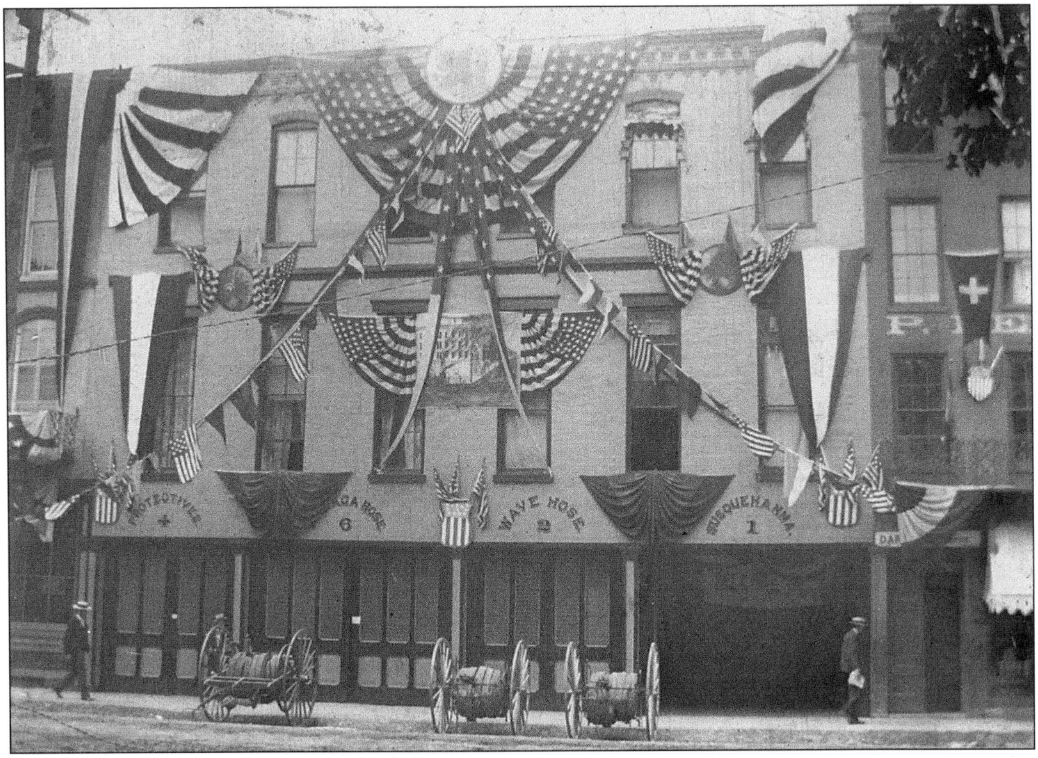

The Owego Fire Department was all decorated for the Firemen's Convention in 1899. The different hose companies are clearly visible.

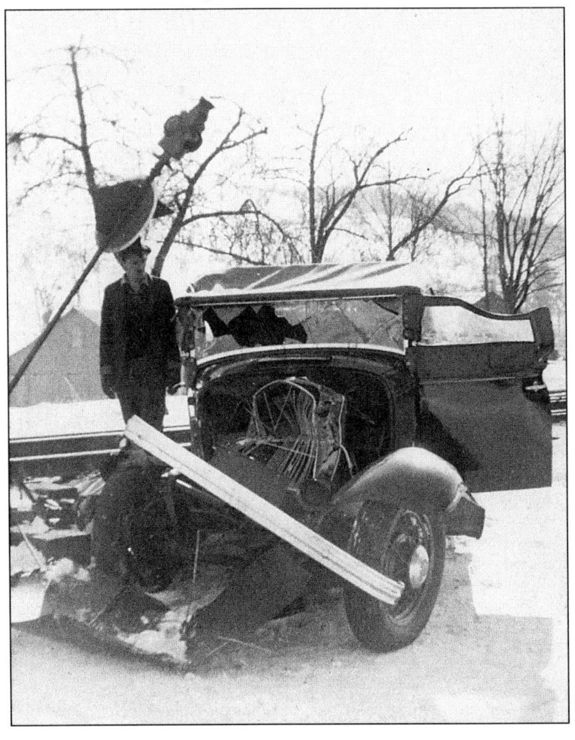

This photograph shows a 1932 Ford after it was hit by a train in Richford.

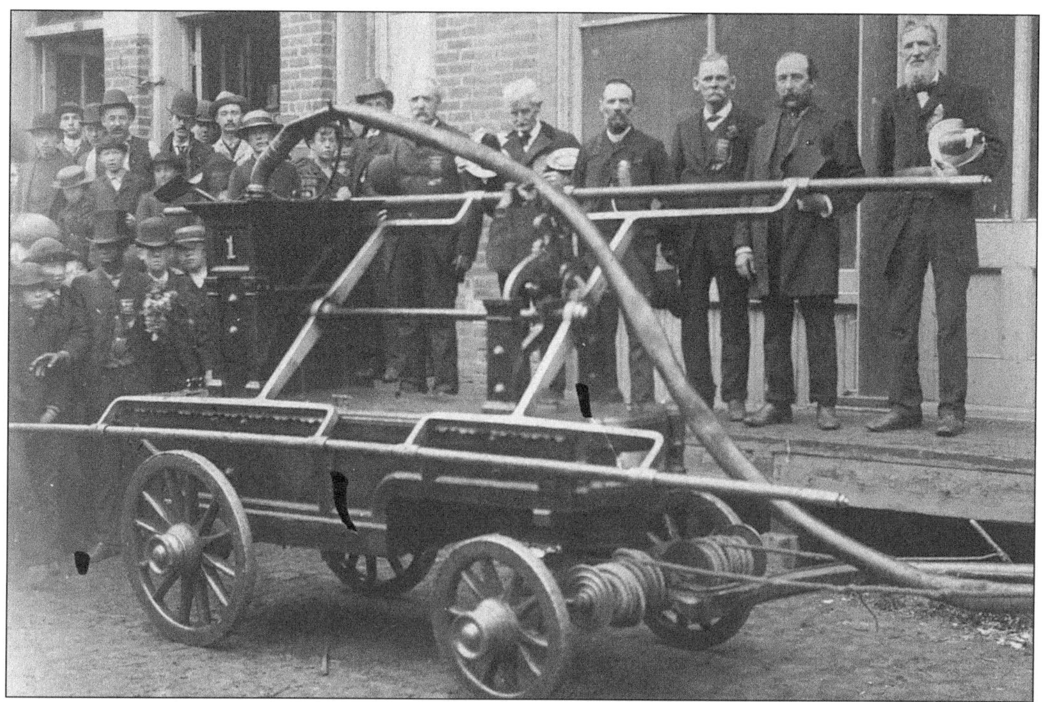

This *c.* 1888 photograph shows an old hand pumper. To provide water pressure in the hose, firemen grabbed the bars on either side and pumped up and down.

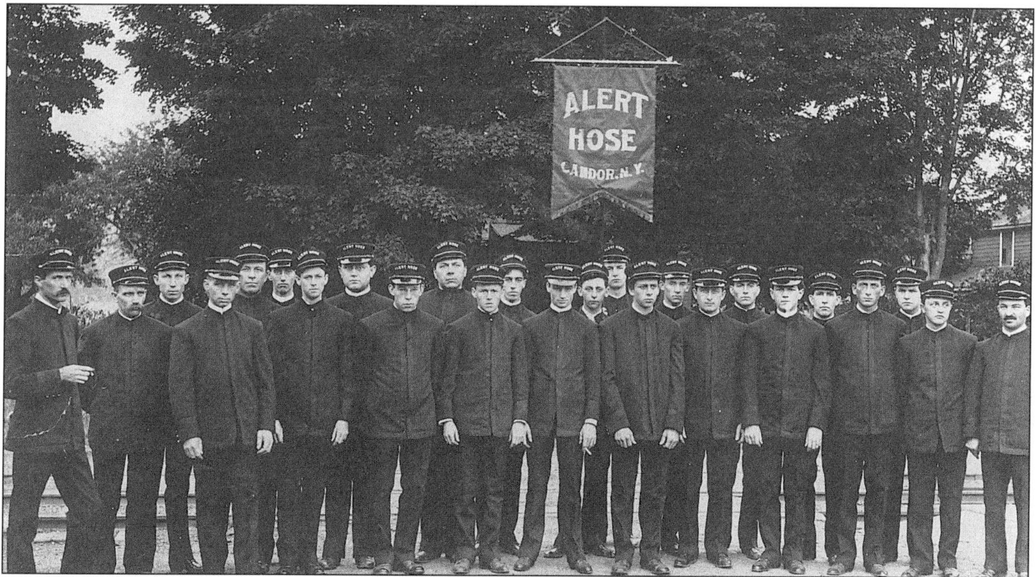

The Alert Hose Company in Candor was organized on August 26, 1911. Members are shown here in 1912 on their way to the State Firemen's Convention. They are, from left to right, as follows: Will Beebe, Will Hulslander, Floyd Monroe, D.G. LaGrange, Merritt Douglass, Lee Haynes, John Brown, Mont Barton, Clarence Booth, Dr. D.G. VanOstrand, Roy Barr, Edwin Harley, William Howard, Roy Bostwick, Homer Brown, Louis Griffin, Mead Wilsey, Archie Allen, Harley Milks, Max Harris, Dr. Moses Roe, Homer Dewey, Floyd Brown, LeRoy Coursen, and Justice Diamon.

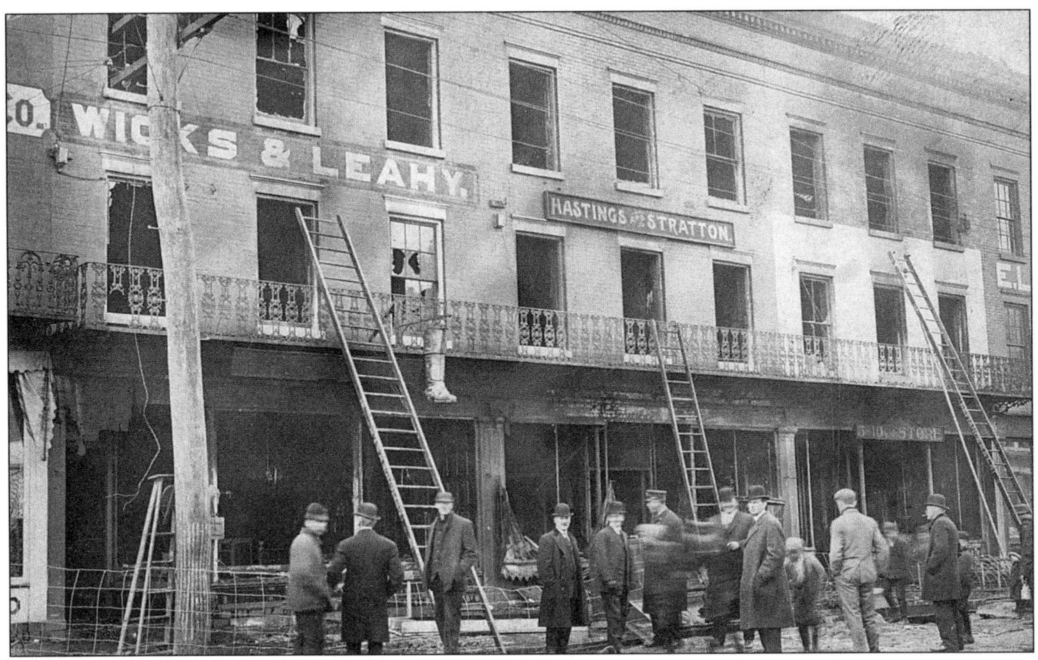

This photograph shows a fire that occurred on Front Street in Owego in 1915.

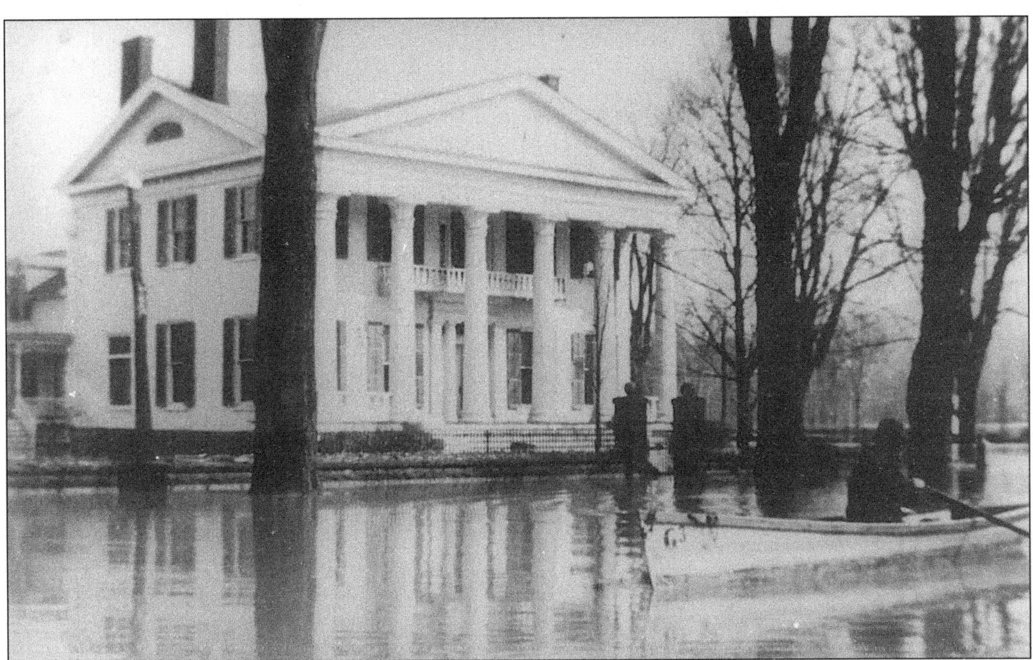
On March 18, 1936, the Susquehanna River flooded, causing severe damage throughout Tioga County. Here, the Cady Mansion in Nichols stands as an island, and someone rows a boat up the road.

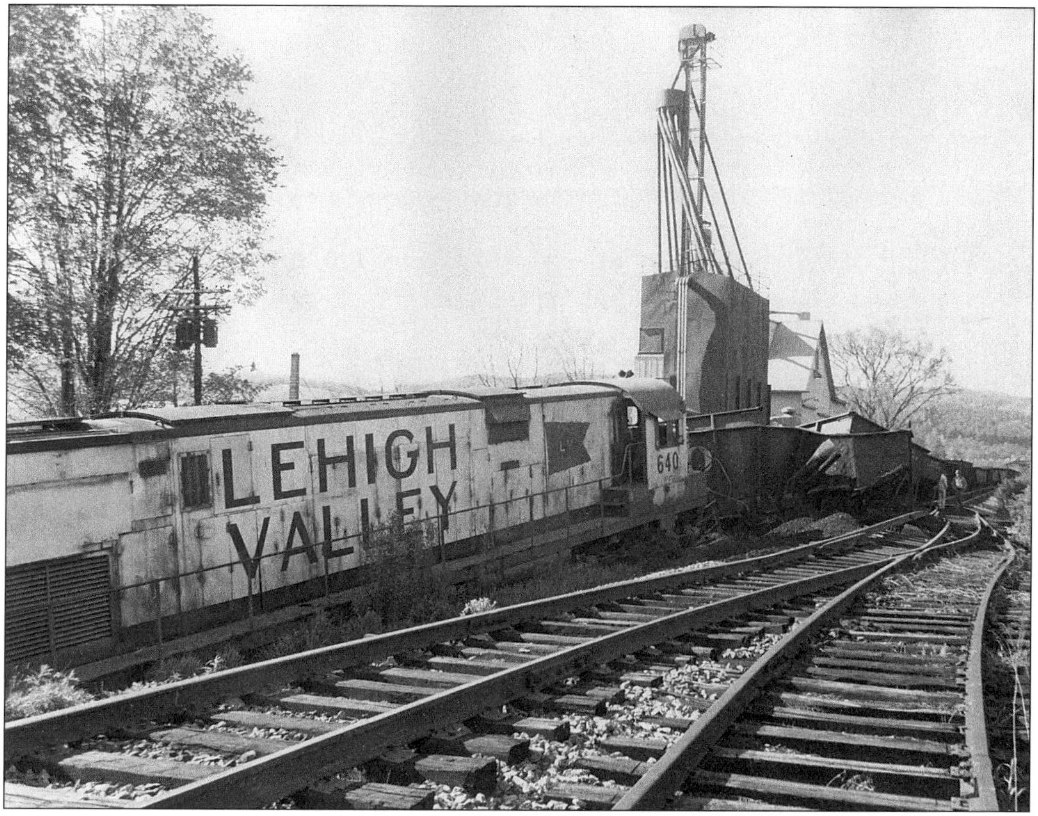

This train wreck occurred in Spencer in 1952. Some children threw the switch, derailing the train. These two photographs were commissioned by the FBI as they conducted the investigation.

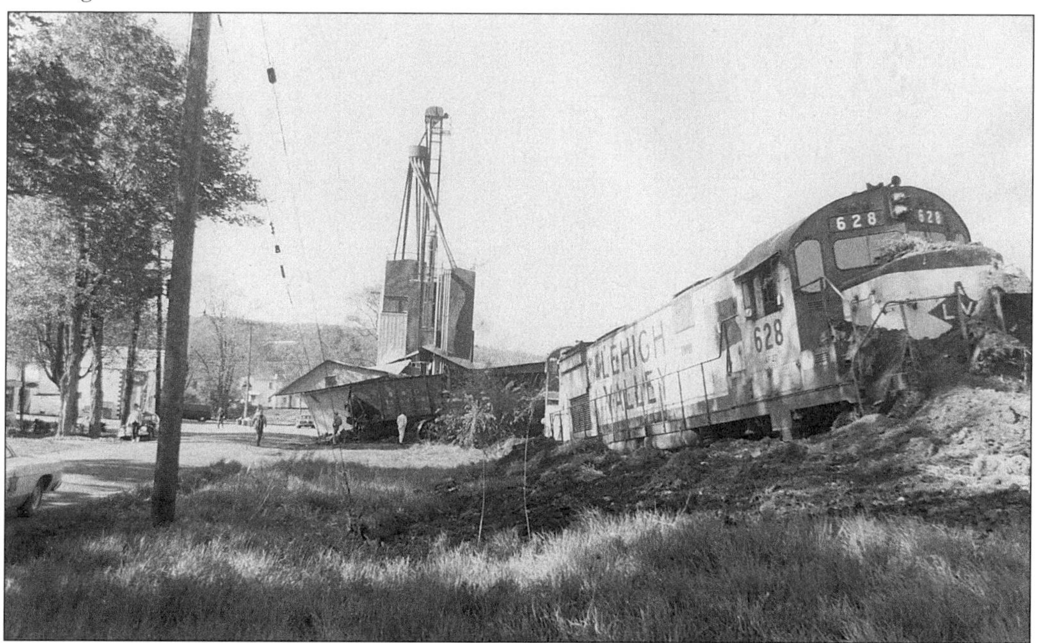

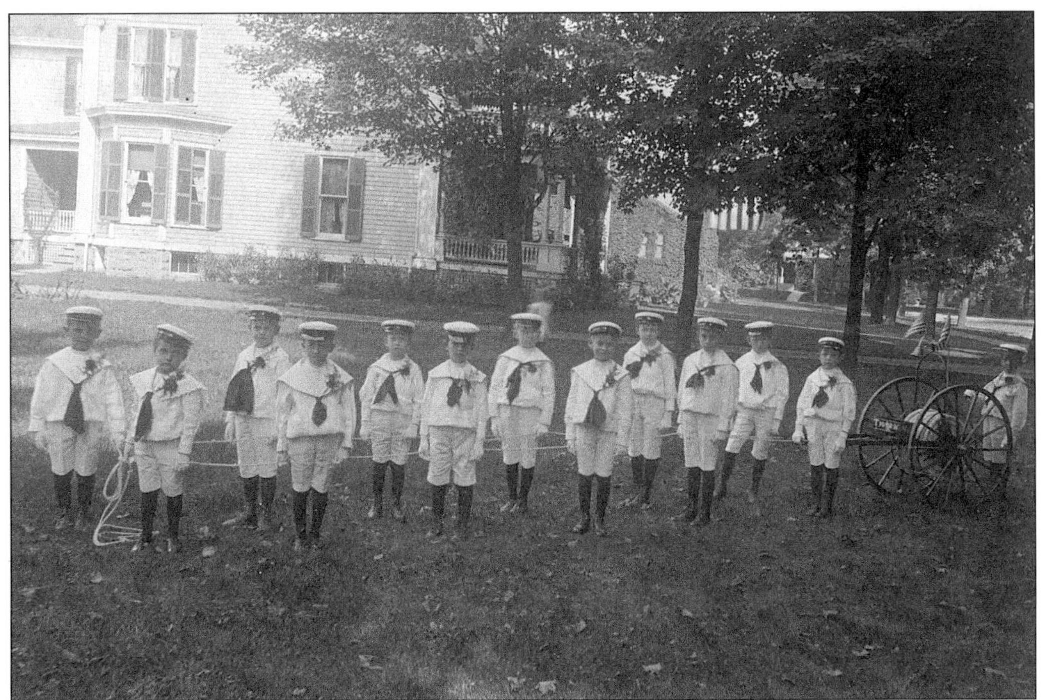

The Tioga Jr. Hose Company takes part in the Firemen's Parade Day on September 18, 1902, in Waverly.

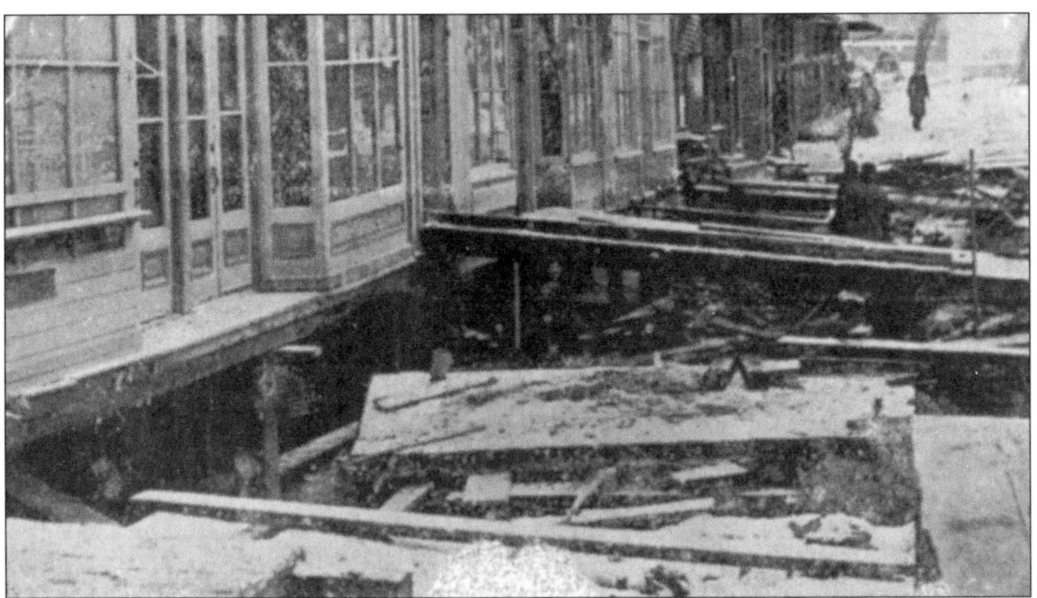

This is how Water Street in Newark Valley appeared after the flood of December 14, 1901.

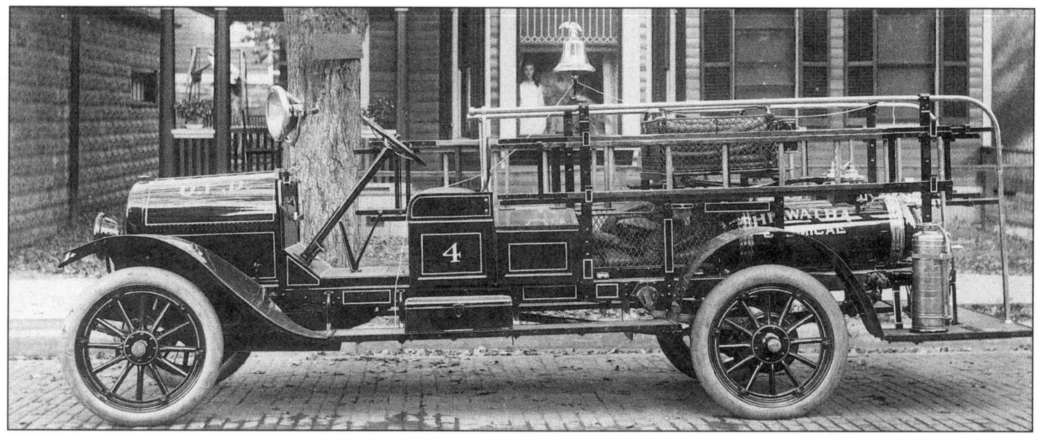

The Owego Fire Department proudly displays its new Hiawatha chemical fire truck *c.* 1920.

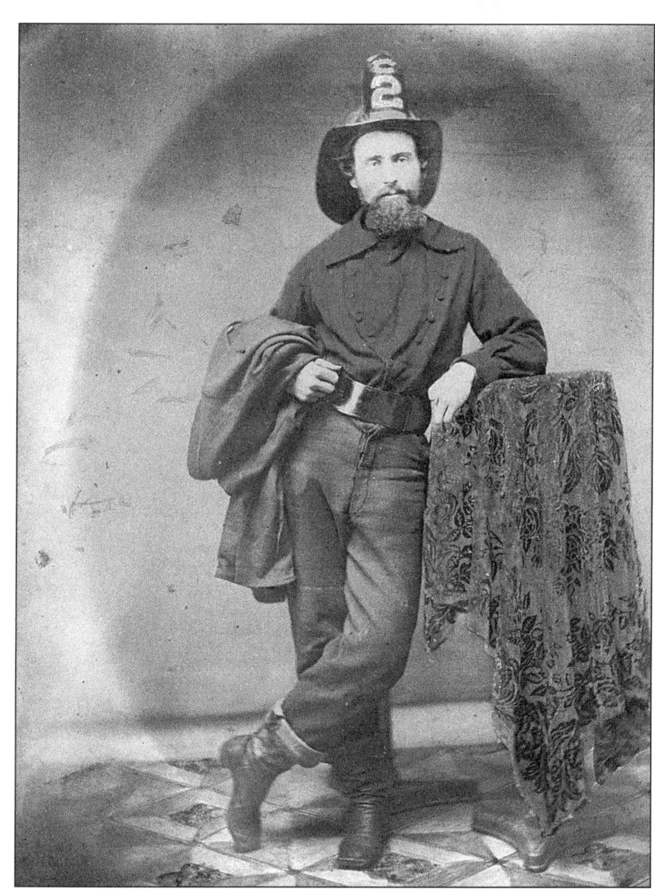

Fireman Marshall D. Pratt poses for this 1863 photograph. The first fire company was formed in Owego in 1828.

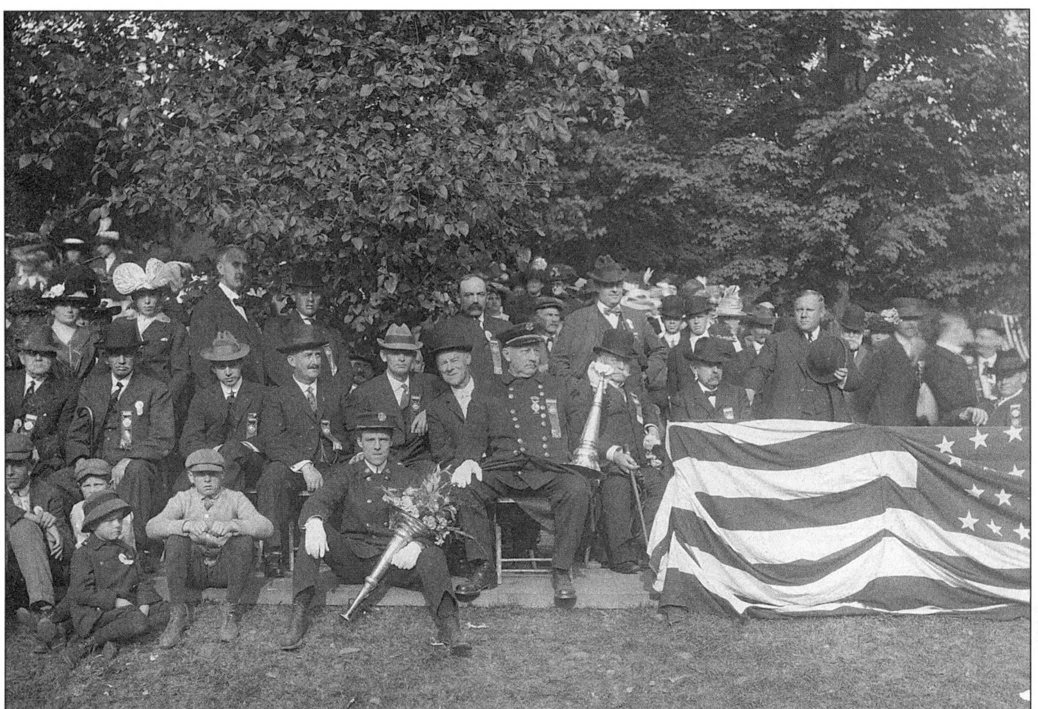

The new fire station in Owego was dedicated on October 3, 1912. The gentleman seated at the left edge of the flag with the mustache and cane is General Isaac Catlin.

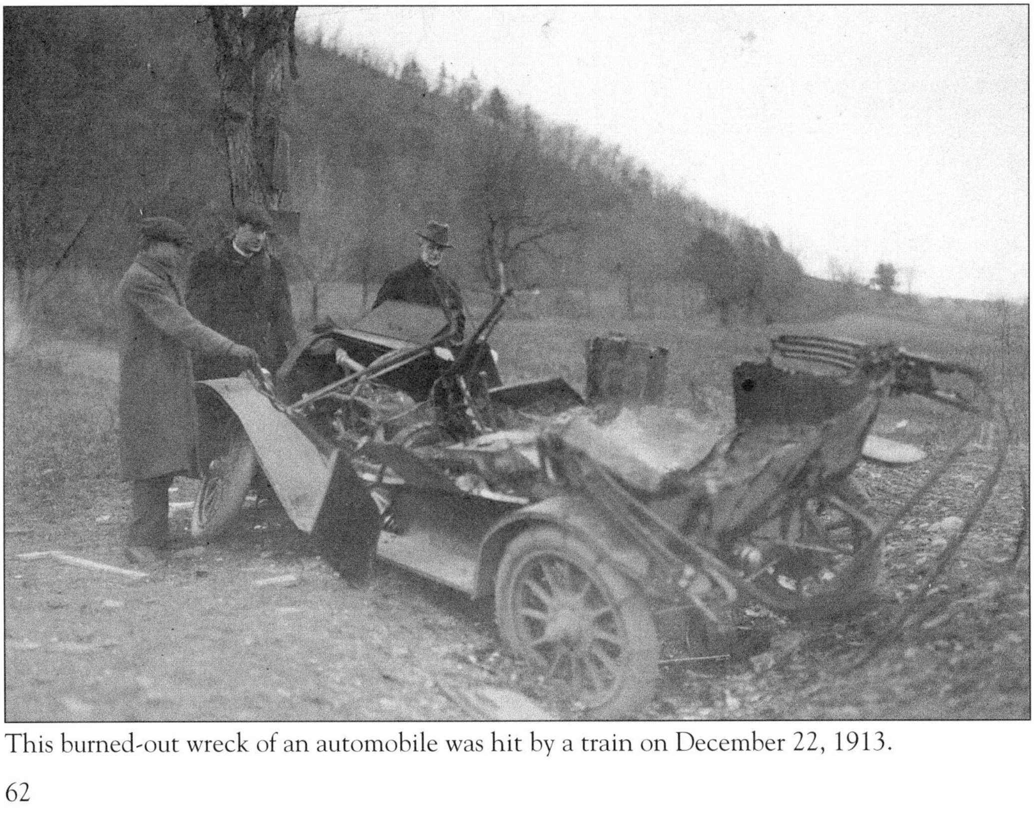

This burned-out wreck of an automobile was hit by a train on December 22, 1913.

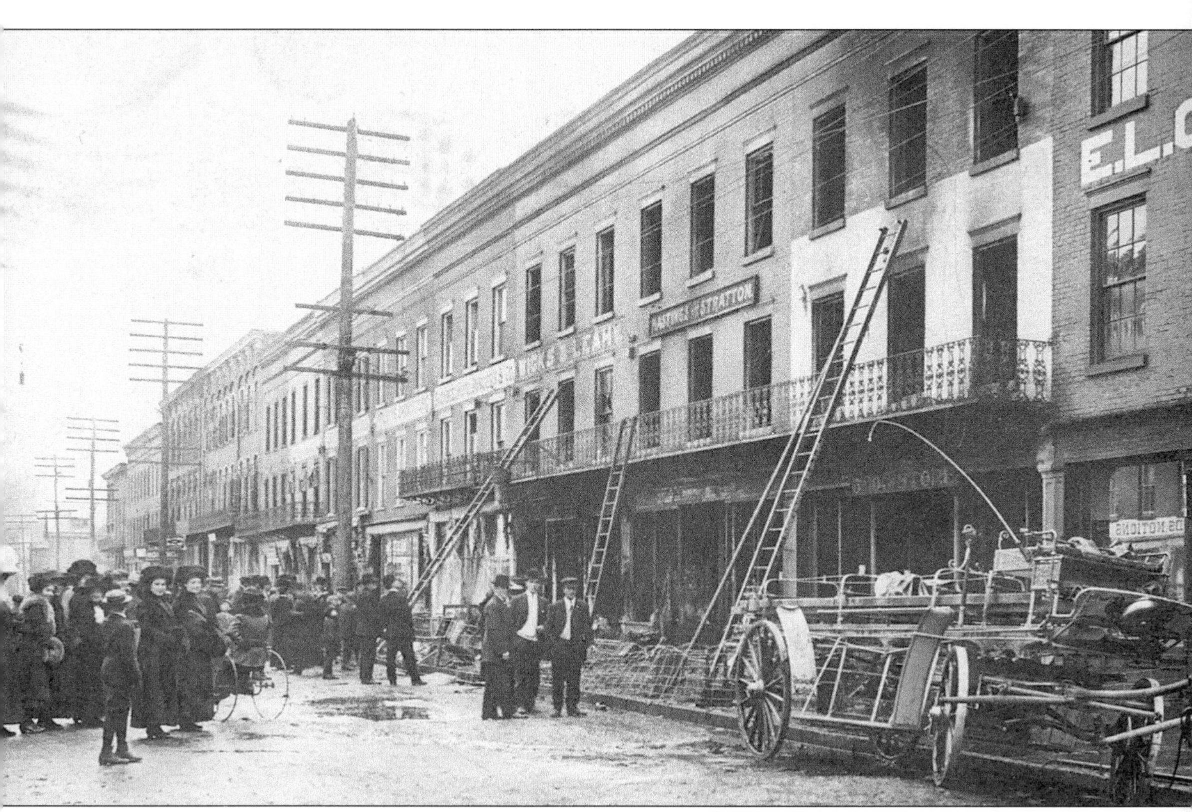

This view shows the damage done by fire on Front Street in Owego in 1915. A horse-drawn fire carriage is on the right.

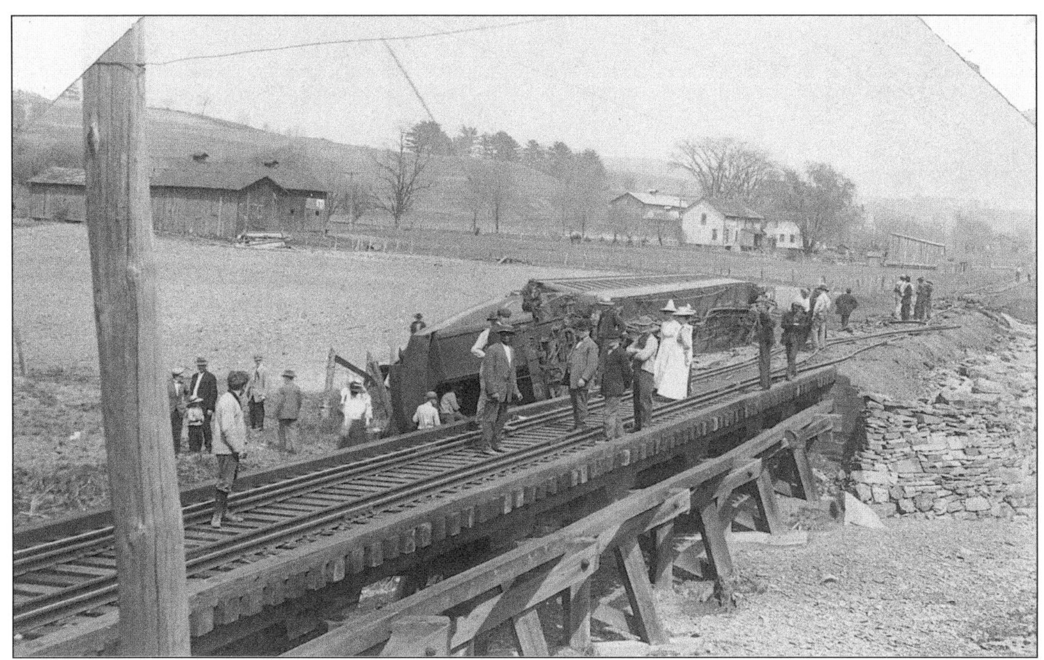

This train wreck occurred in West Candor *c.* 1905.

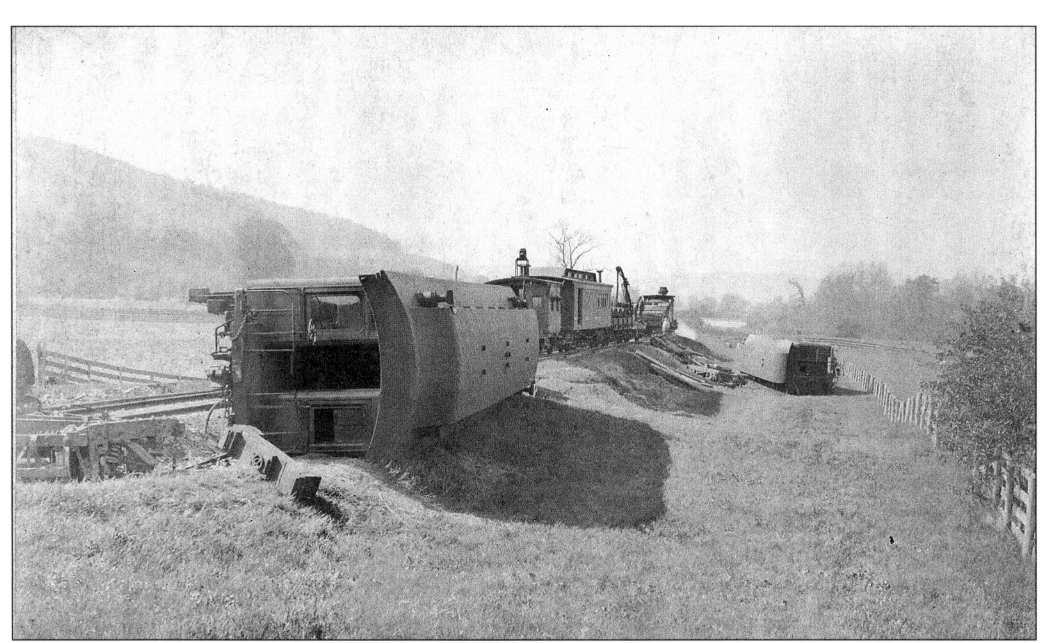

This train derailed on May 14, 1894, near the Tioga County poor farm. Several passengers were badly injured, and a 4-year-old Newark Valley boy was killed.

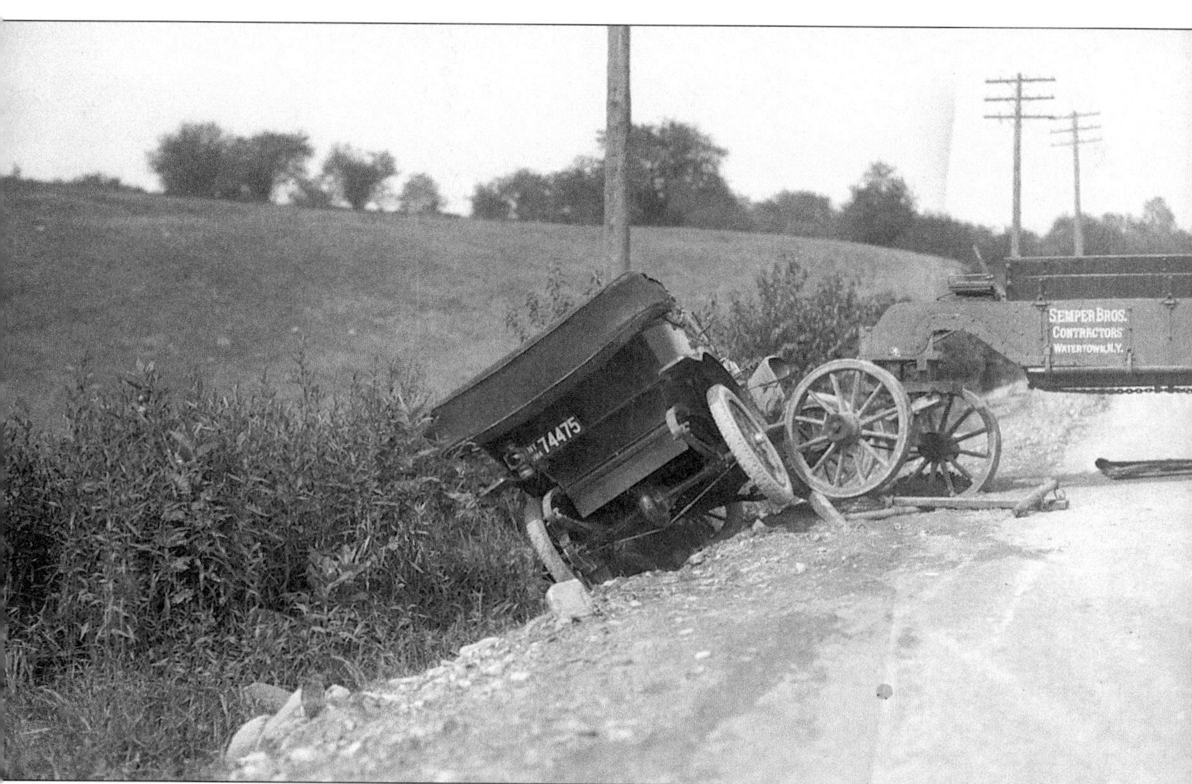

This photograph shows an August 9, 1914 accident scene on the south side of Owego. A car collided with a wagon.

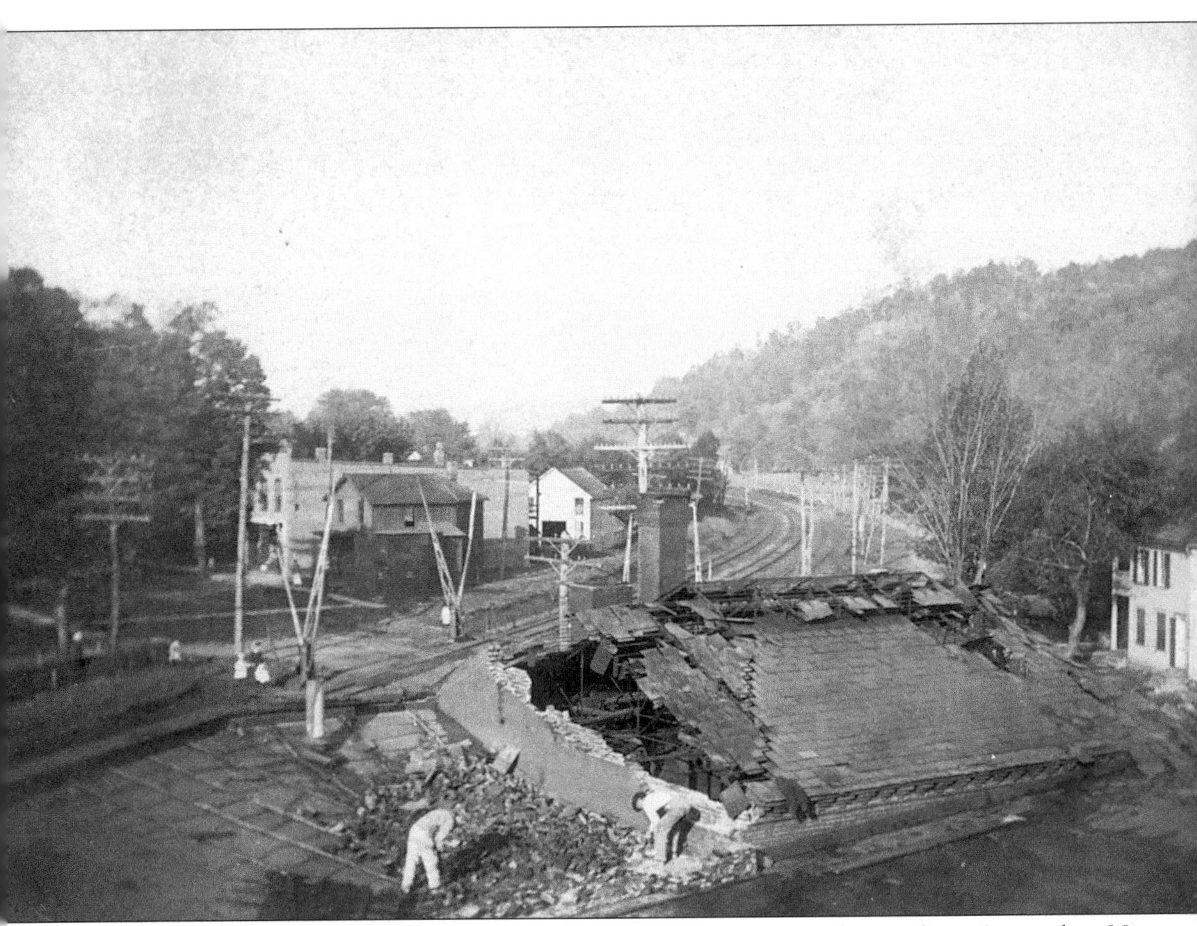

Here is the gashouse on east Main Street in Owego after a tornado struck on September 28, 1908. The tremendous twister caused the walls of the gashouse to collapse.

Four

Over the River and Through the Woods

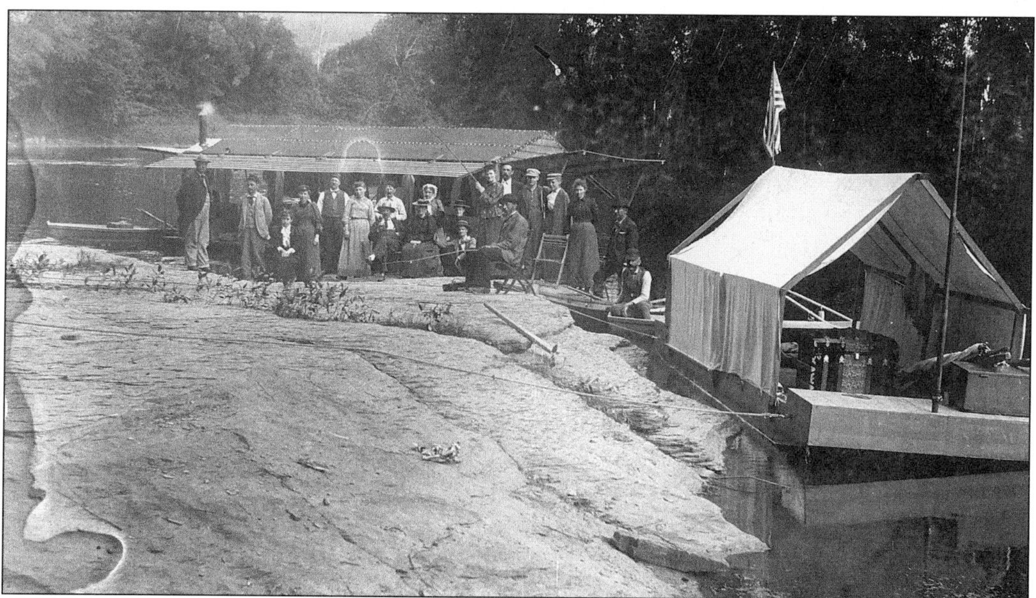

Rafting and boating on the Susquehanna River was an early form of transportation. Here, two groups enjoy an afternoon near Hiawatha Island *c.* 1875.

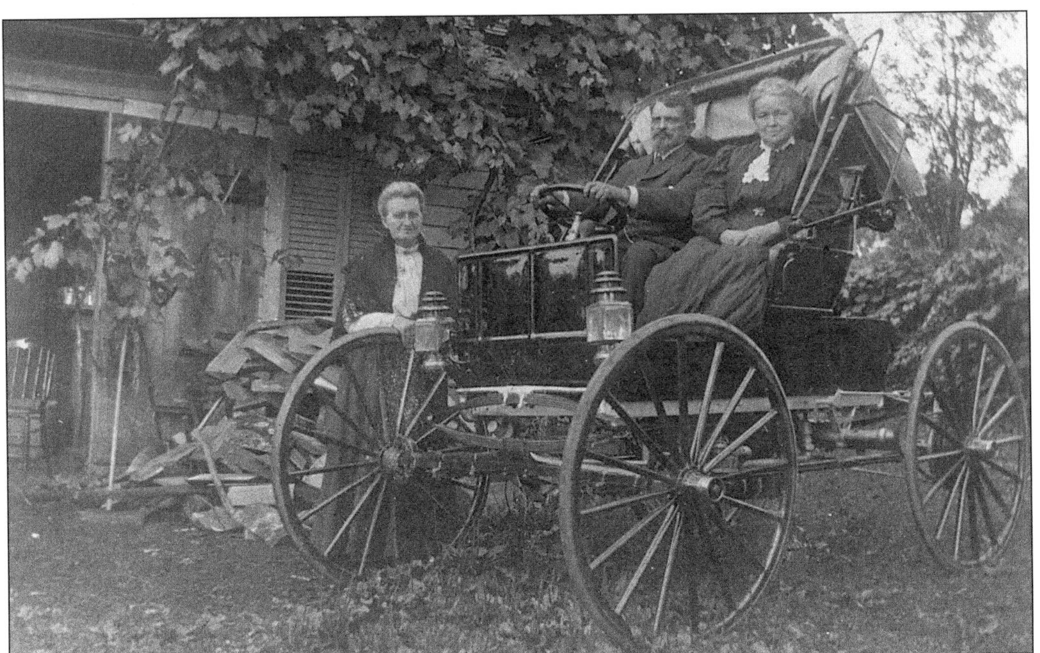

This photograph shows the first automobile in Tioga Center *c.* 1905. The automobile was owned by Dr. Albert Post and his wife, who is standing. With them is Post's sister, Lucy.

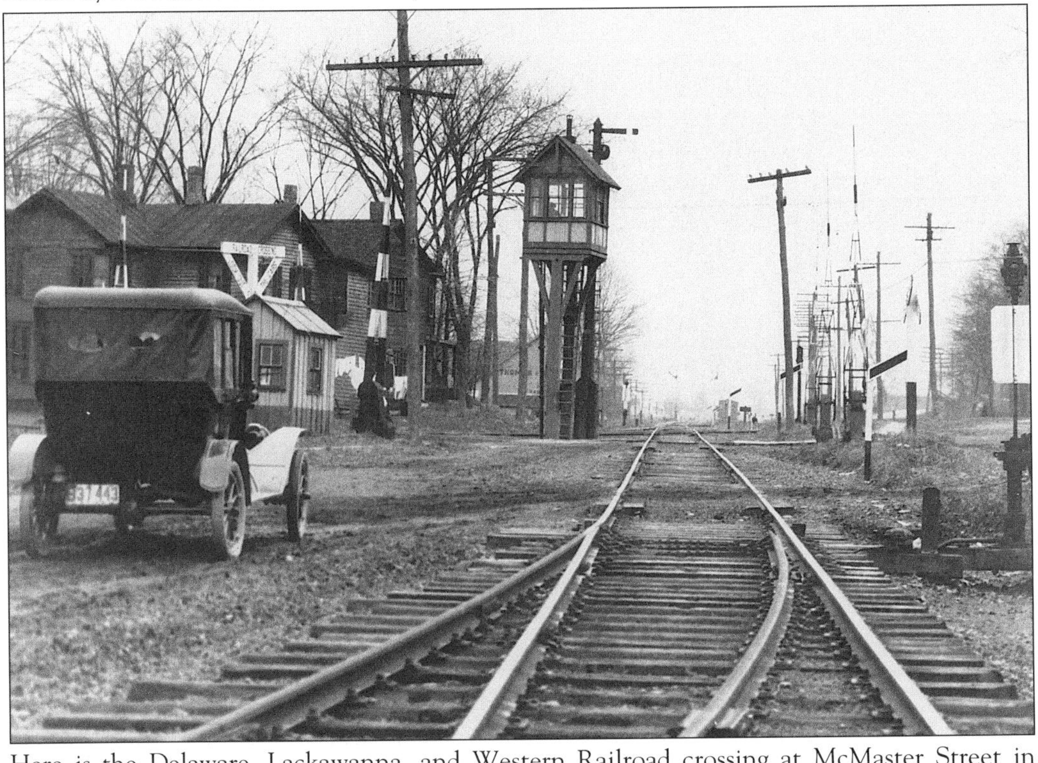

Here is the Delaware, Lackawanna, and Western Railroad crossing at McMaster Street in Owego. This November 1916 photograph was part of a grade-crossing survey being done at that time.

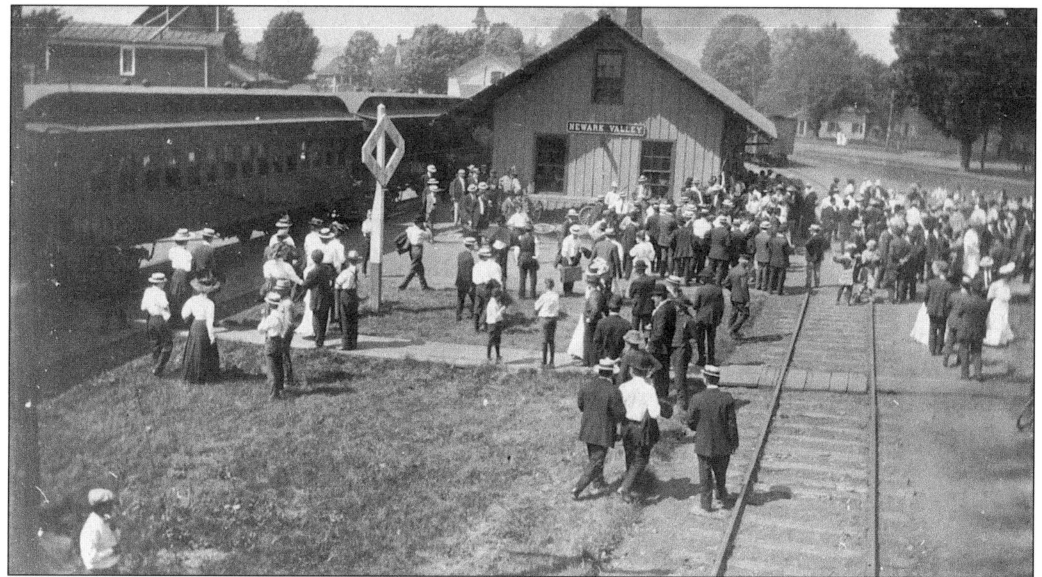

This photograph shows the Newark Valley train depot. After a baseball game between Sayre and Newark Valley, a fight broke out among the spectators at the depot.

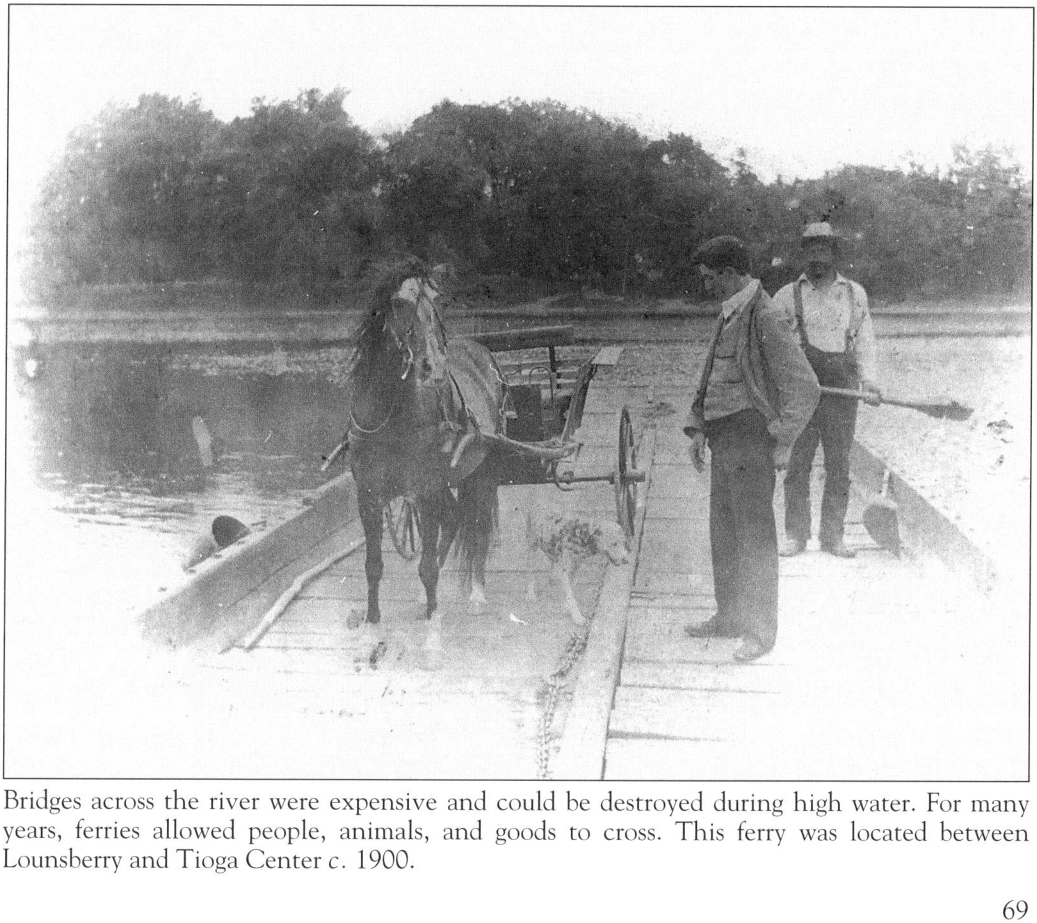

Bridges across the river were expensive and could be destroyed during high water. For many years, ferries allowed people, animals, and goods to cross. This ferry was located between Lounsberry and Tioga Center *c.* 1900.

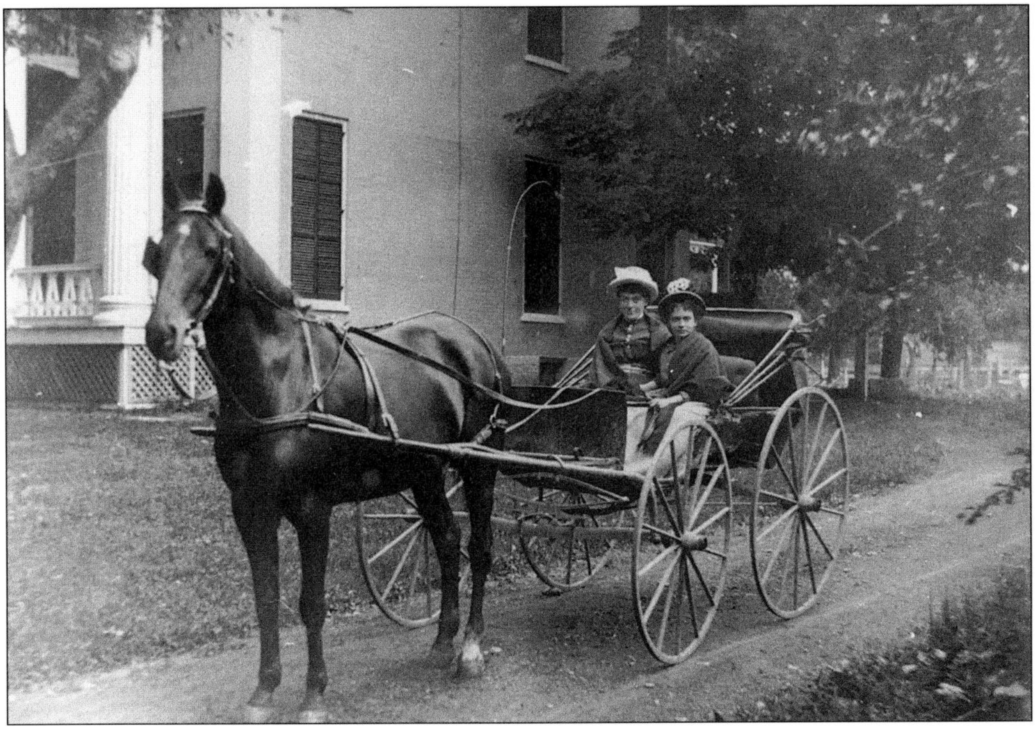

Margaret Cady and Eunice Drisser are ready to take a ride. The photograph was taken in July 1895 on the east side of the Cady Mansion.

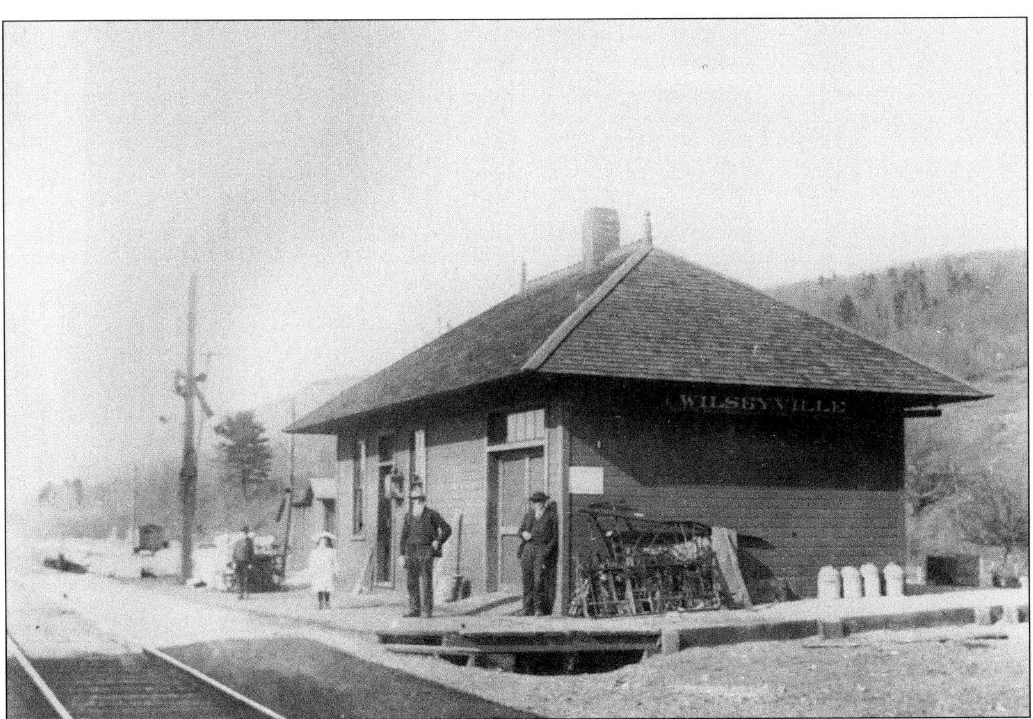

This is a view, *c.* 1910, of the Union Station in Willseyville in the town of Candor.

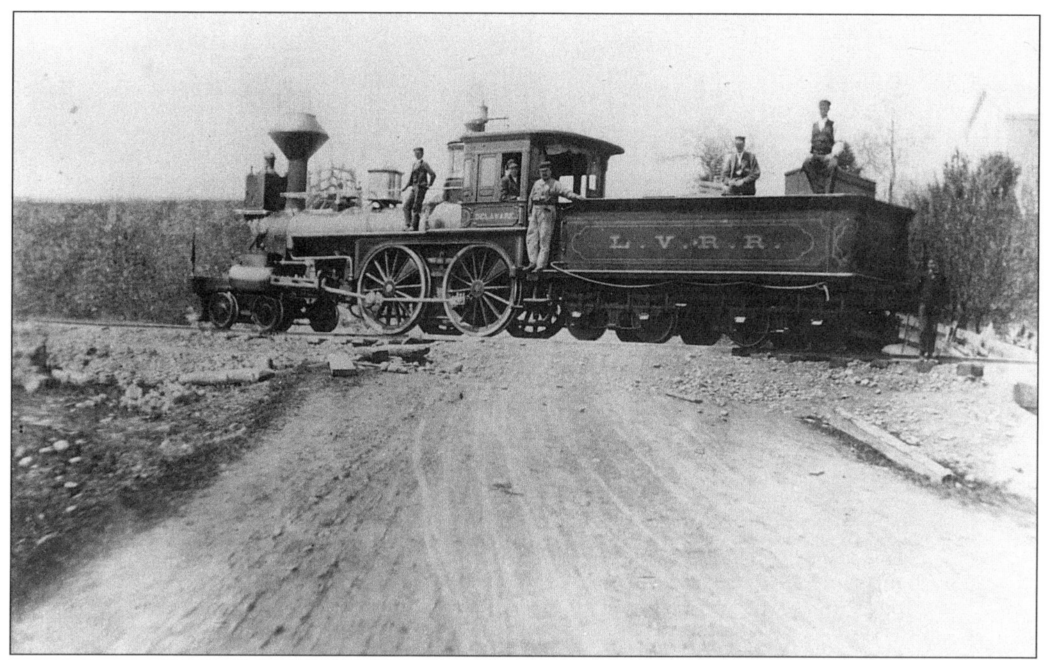

This photograph shows the first locomotive that entered Spencer on the Ithaca and Athens Railroad.

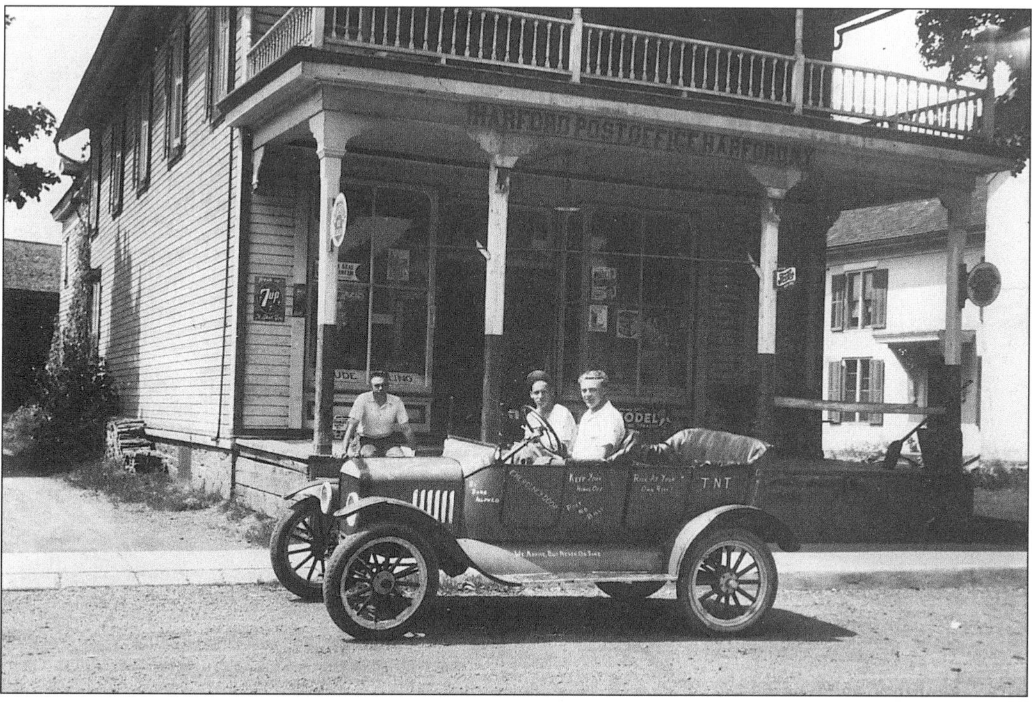

Bud Jewitt parks his Model T Ford in front of Claude Pulling's store in Harford, just outside of Richford, *c.* 1930. In the car with Jewitt is Wilbur Lacey. The hand-painted signs on the car give the impression that these fellows were enjoying themselves.

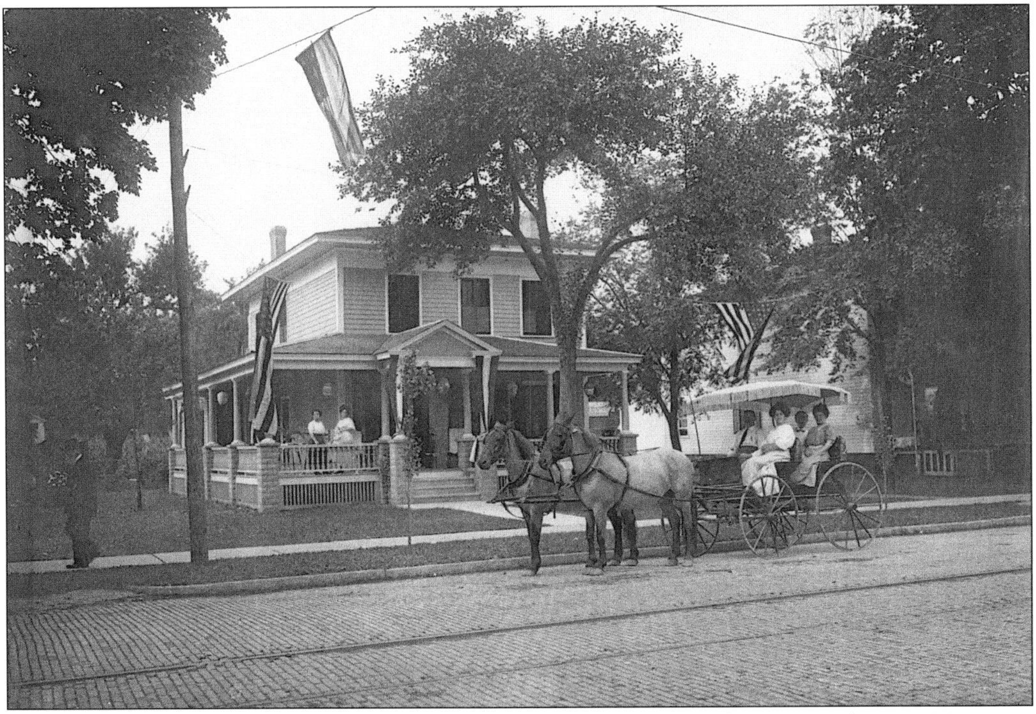

This horse and buggy was photographed alongside the streetcar rails in Waverly *c.* 1900.

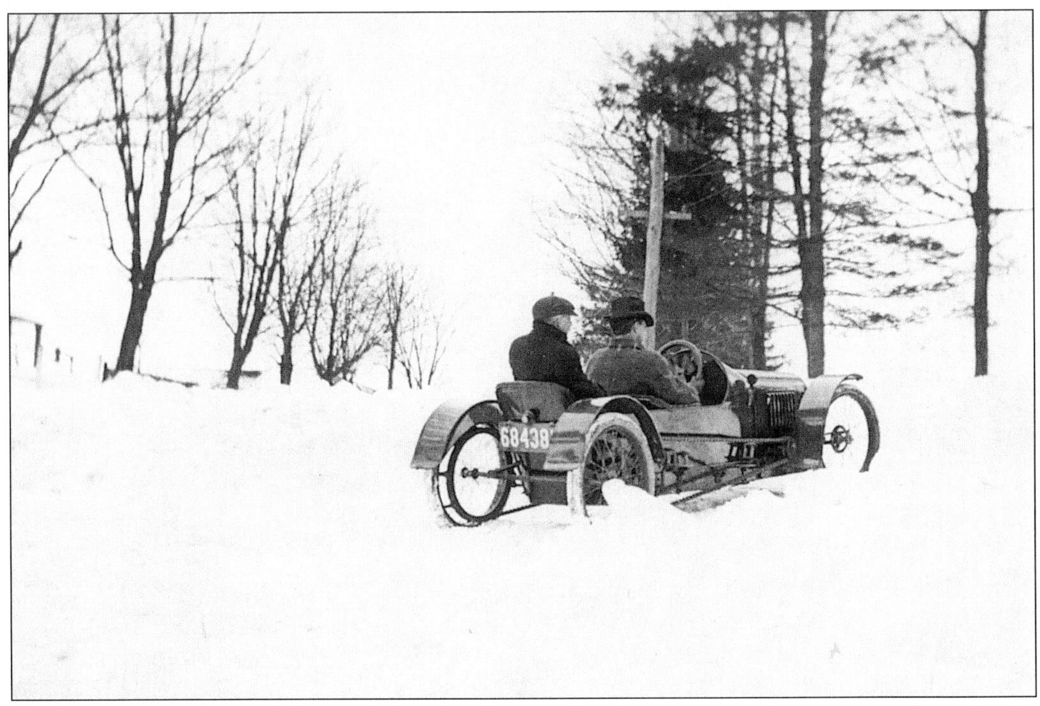

A chain-driven automobile, made by the Owego Car Company, makes its way through the winter roads in 1910.

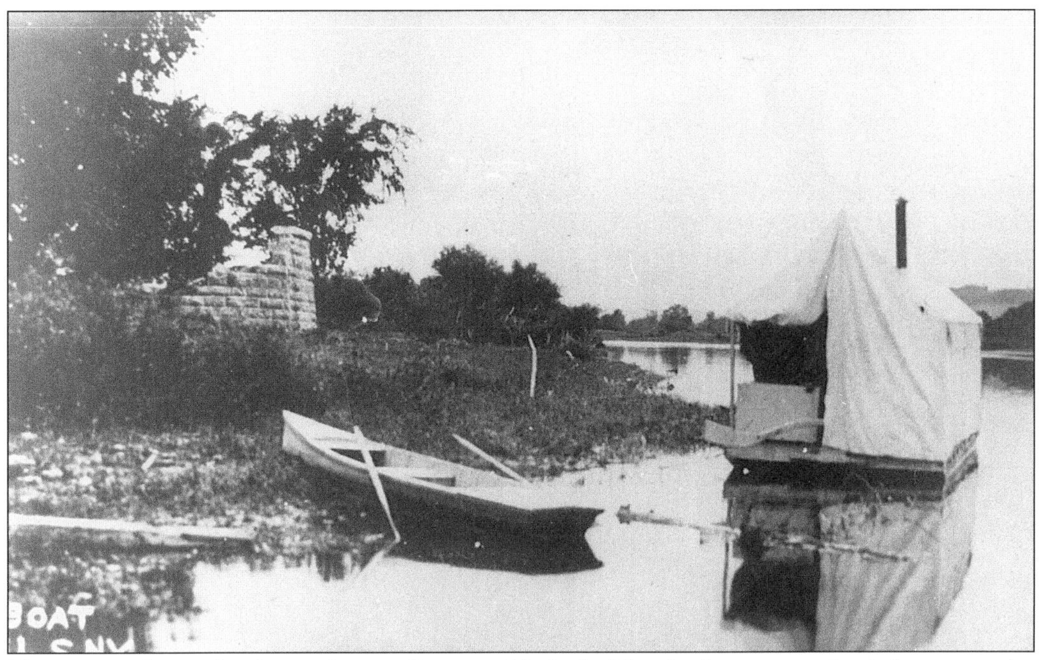

This scene shows the Susquehanna River in Nichols. The bridge pier at the left was on the north side of the river opposite Main Street.

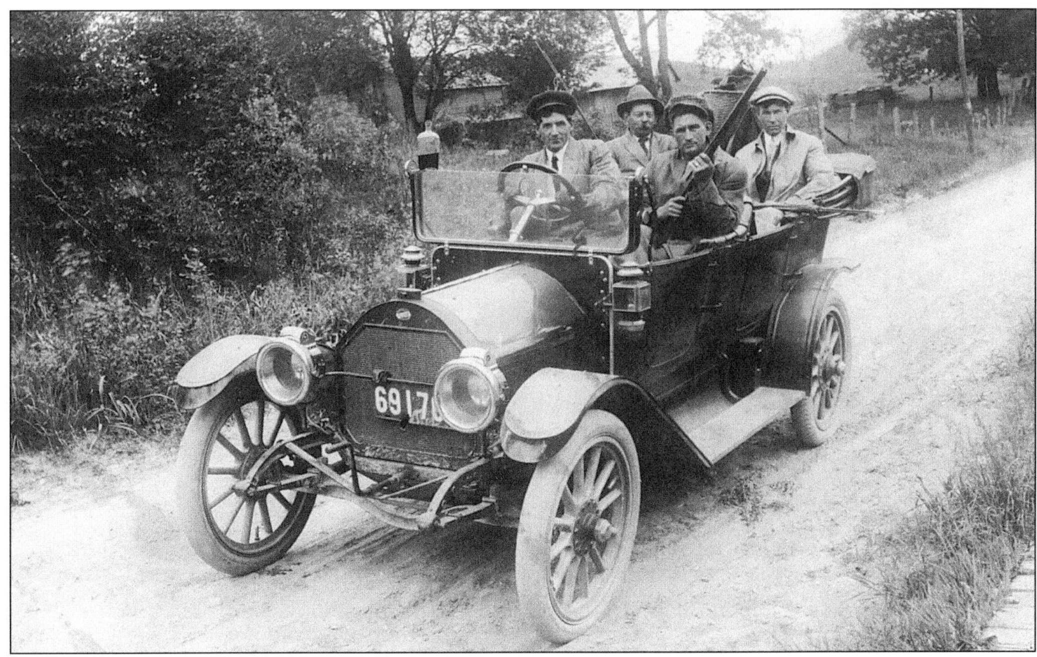

Returning from a hunting trip in the Adirondack Mountains are James Lacey at the wheel, Wallace Hiram behind him, Frank Willard holding shotgun, and Herman Blackman. The photograph was taken *c.* 1909 in Richford.

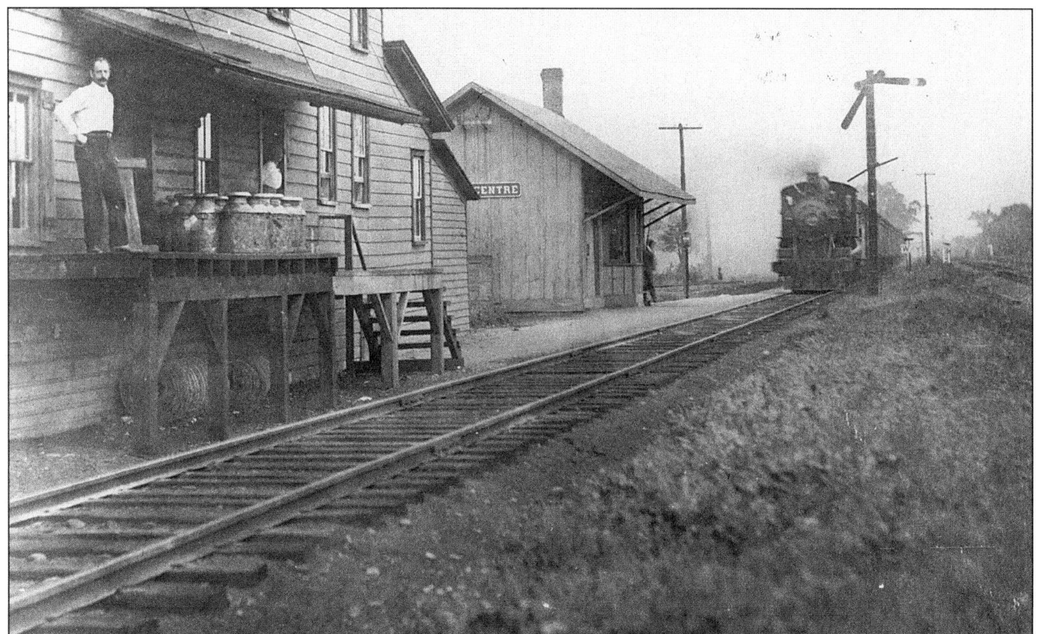

This *c.* 1900 photograph of the Southern Central Railroad on a milk run in Tioga Center was taken looking east.

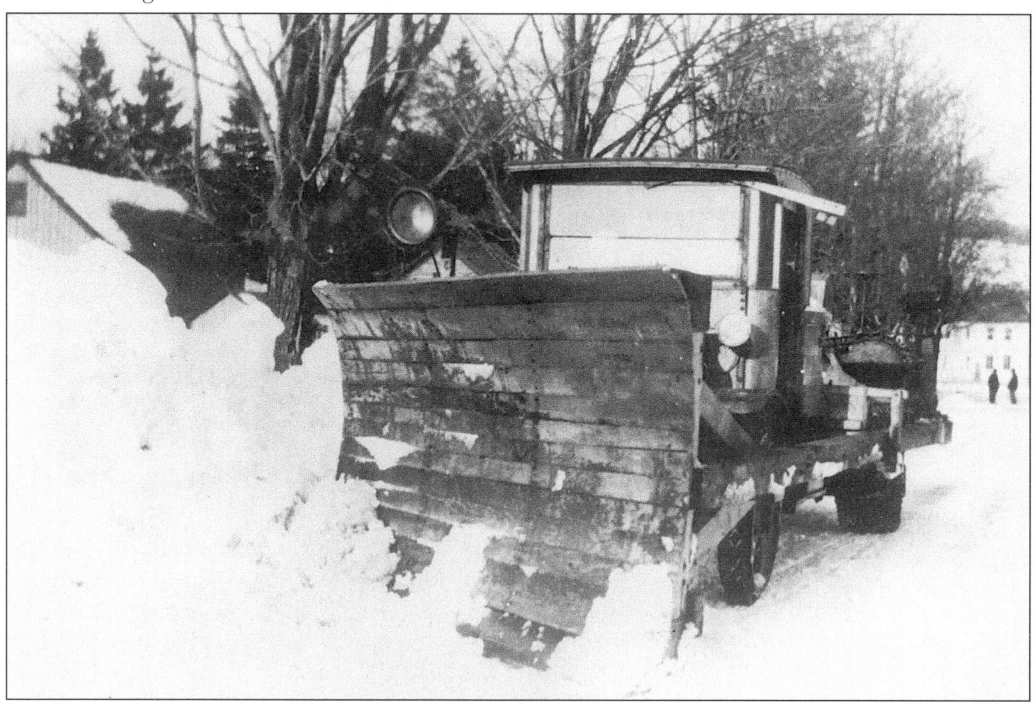

Dave Munson of Richford built this stationary wooden plow blade and then mounted it on his truck. The truck had solid rubber tires, and to add stability, a load of stone countered the weight of the blade. The plow could be driven at speeds of up to 7 miles per hour. Munson patented the design in wood. A few years later, someone took the same idea but built the blade out of steel. This photograph was taken in January 1927.

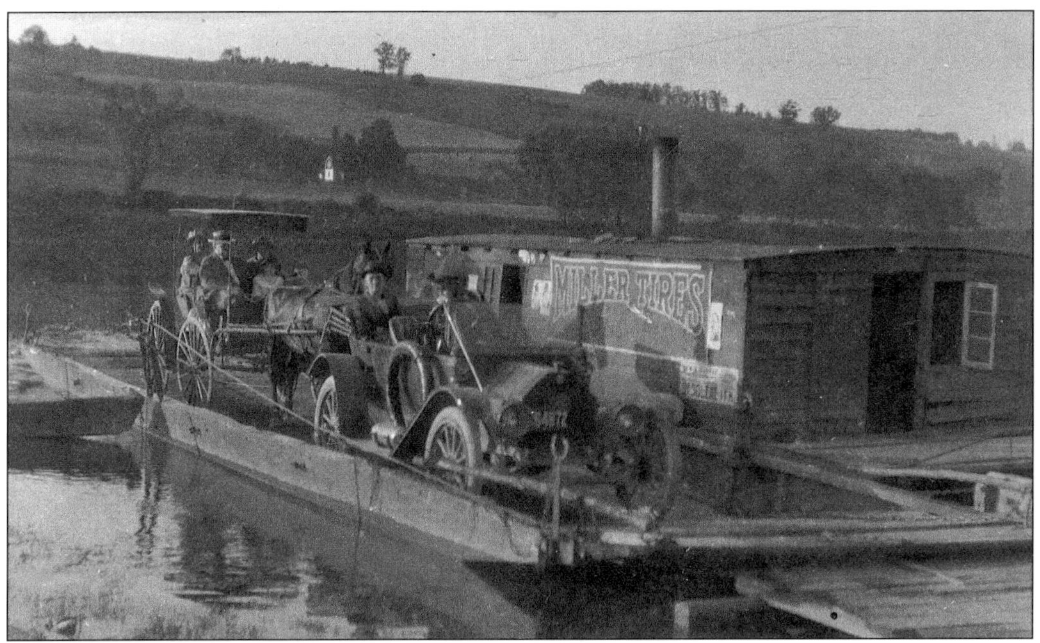

Both times and technology change. Here, the horse and buggy gives way to the automobile, *c.* 1915.

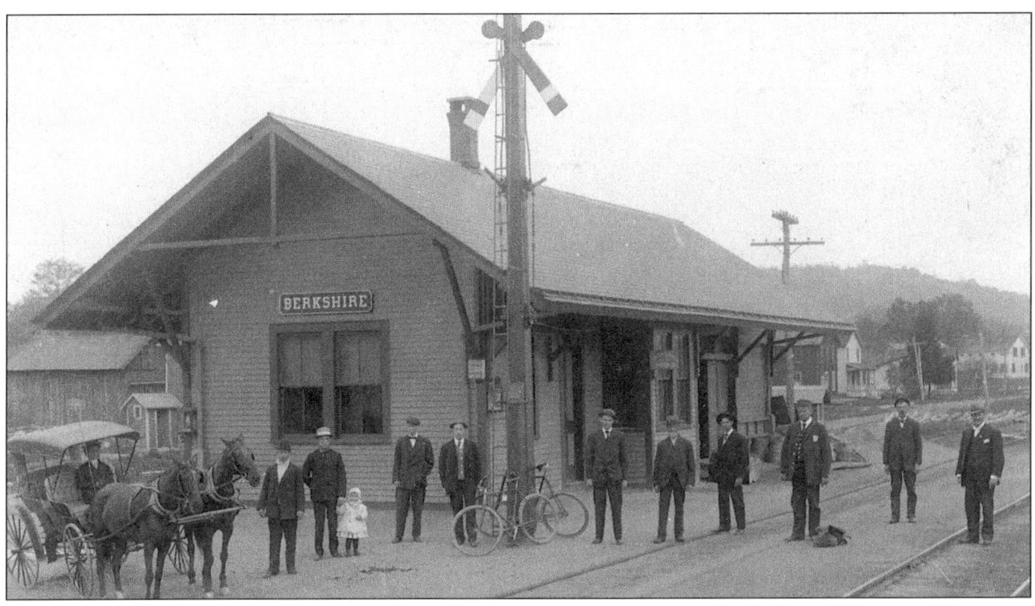

This *c.* 1910 view shows the Lehigh Valley Railroad Station in Berkshire. Western Union, a telegraph service, and the United States Express Company both advertise their services on the side of the building.

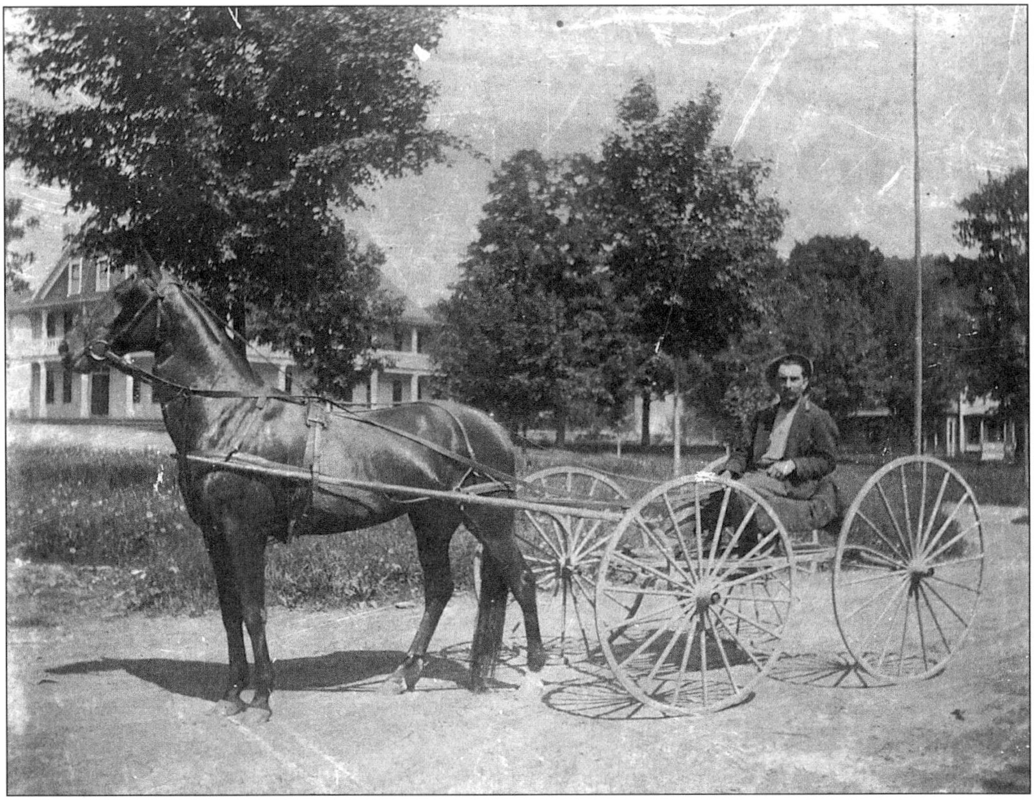

Fred Polley of Richford poses in his gig *c.* 1900.

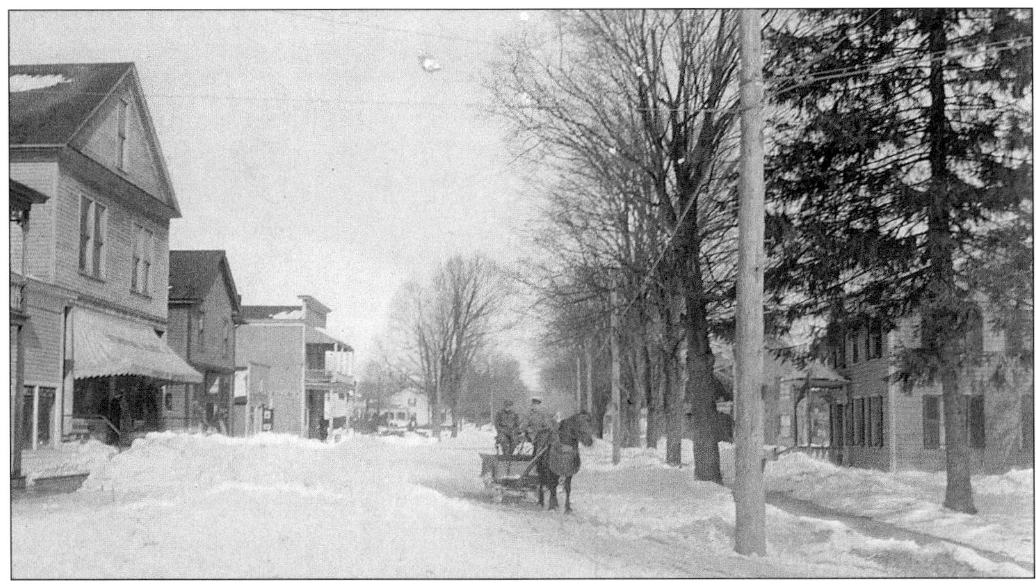

This scene shows people sleighing down Whig Street in Newark Valley *c.* 1910.

This *c.* 1950 view shows the interior of a Delaware, Lackawanna, and Western caboose on the Owego-Ithaca train. The construction was of wood. Bunks, stove, and sinks provided the essentials for long trips.

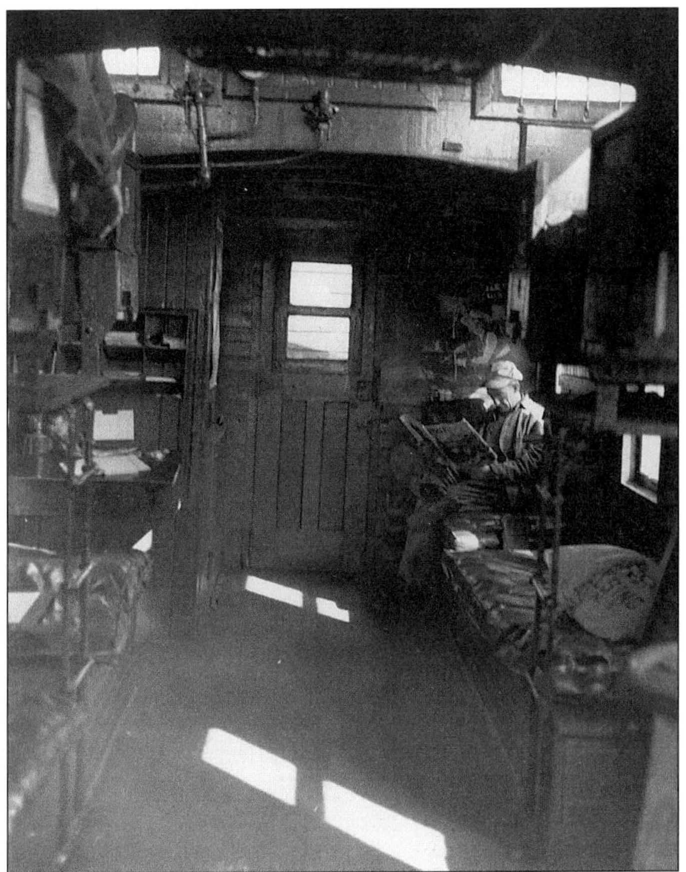

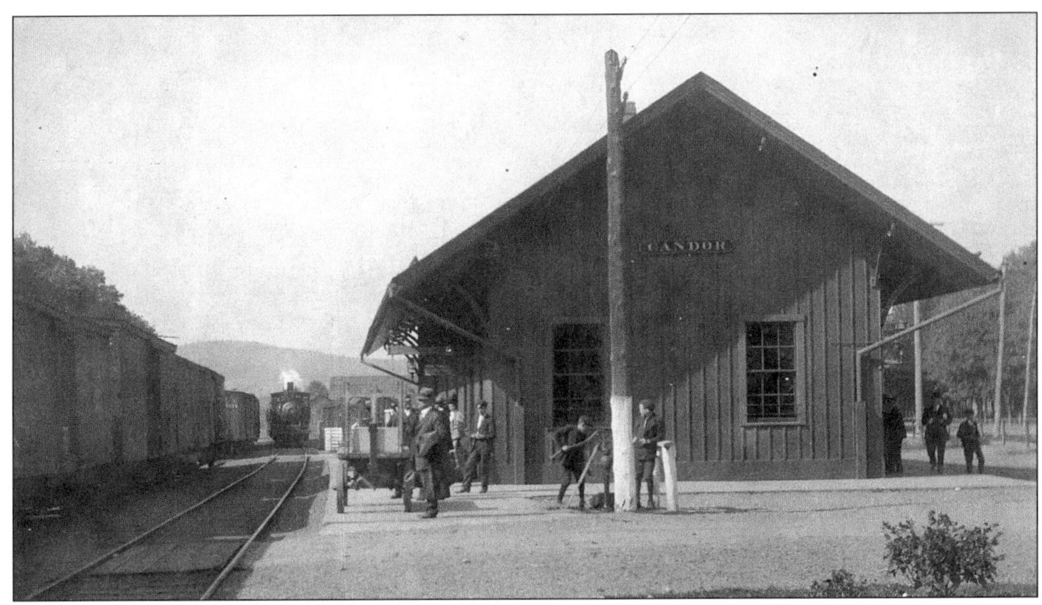

The Lackawanna Station in Candor is shown is this *c.* 1930 photograph.

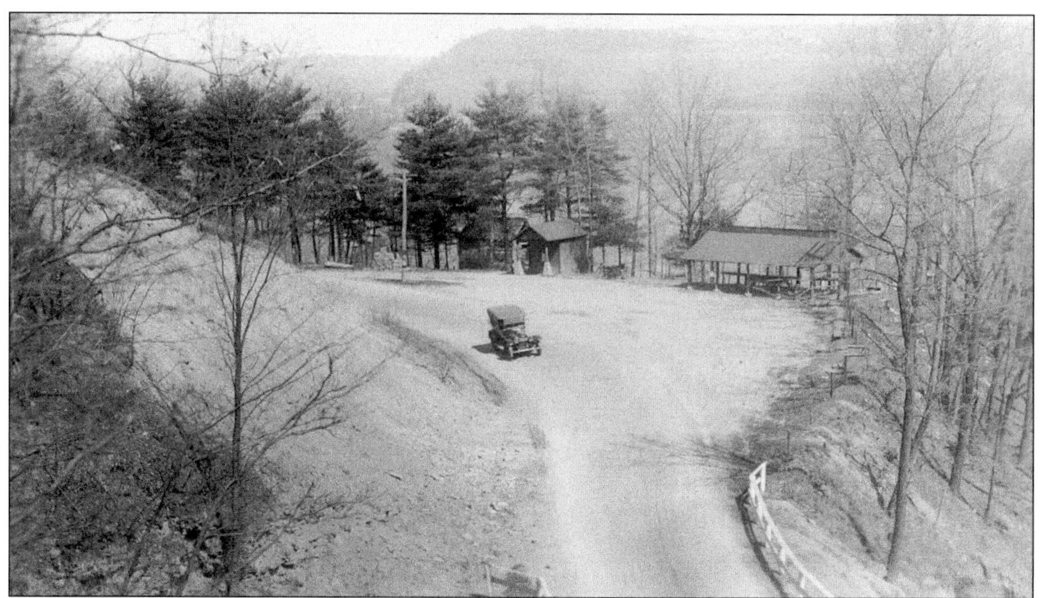

Devil's Elbow is advertised as an "Auto Rest Park" on this postcard mailed from Owego in 1920.

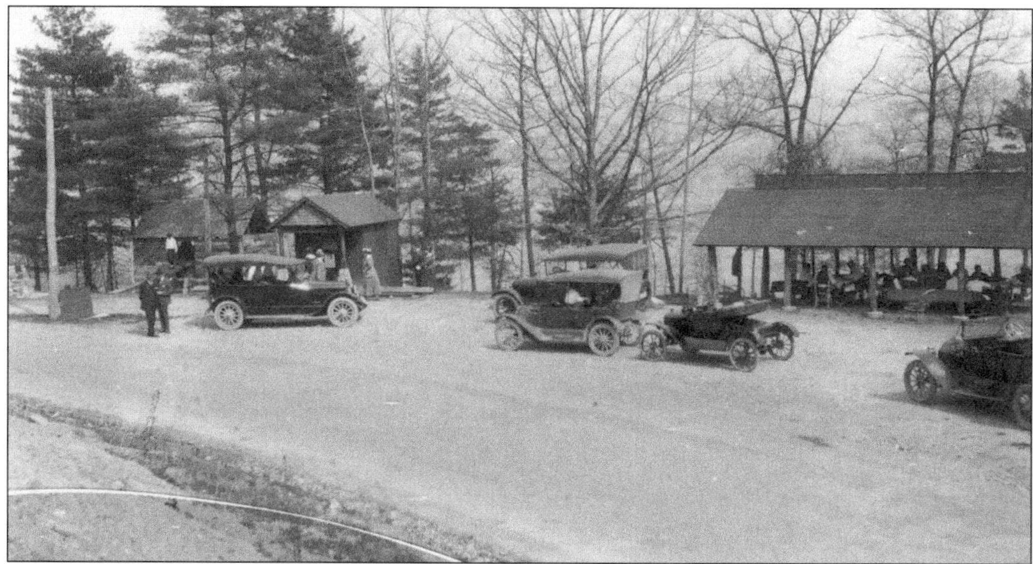

This 1915 photograph shows the first picnic shelter at Devil's Elbow. Located between Owego and Tioga Center, this may have been the first such rest stop in the United States. In actuality, it was built so that the automobiles could cool down after the long uphill drive, not so that the drivers could rest.

Five

FRIENDS AND NEIGHBORS

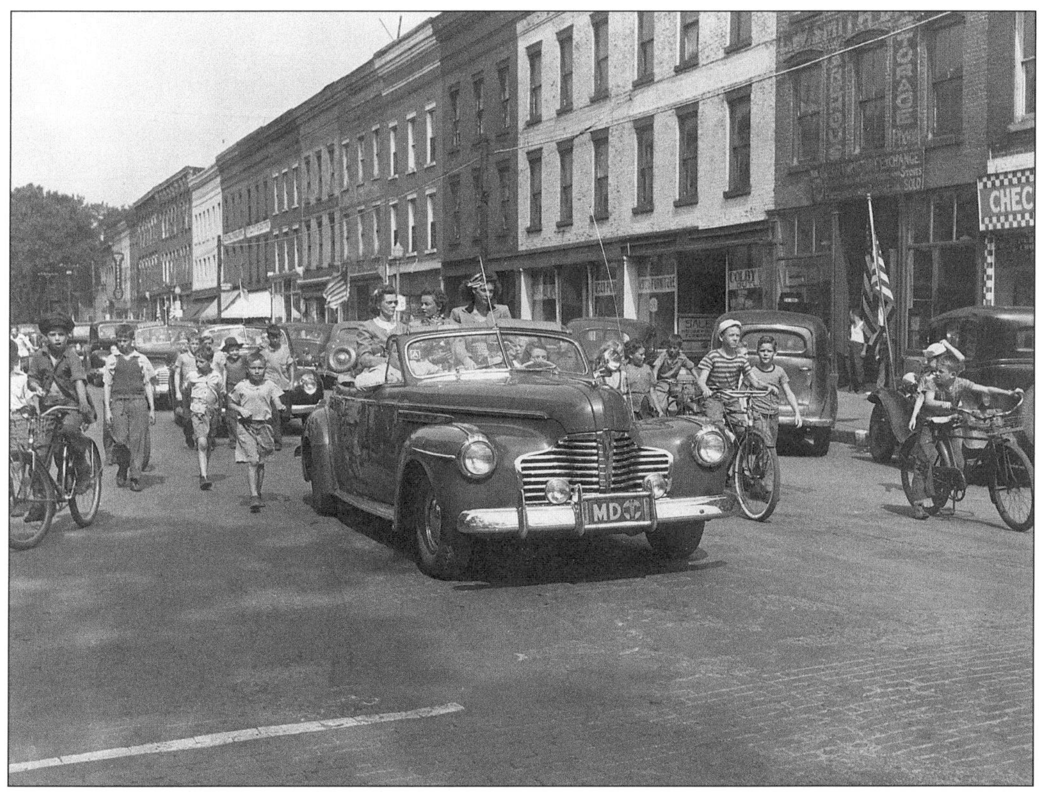

This photograph shows Corporal Margaret Hastings being welcomed back home in Owego in the summer of 1945.

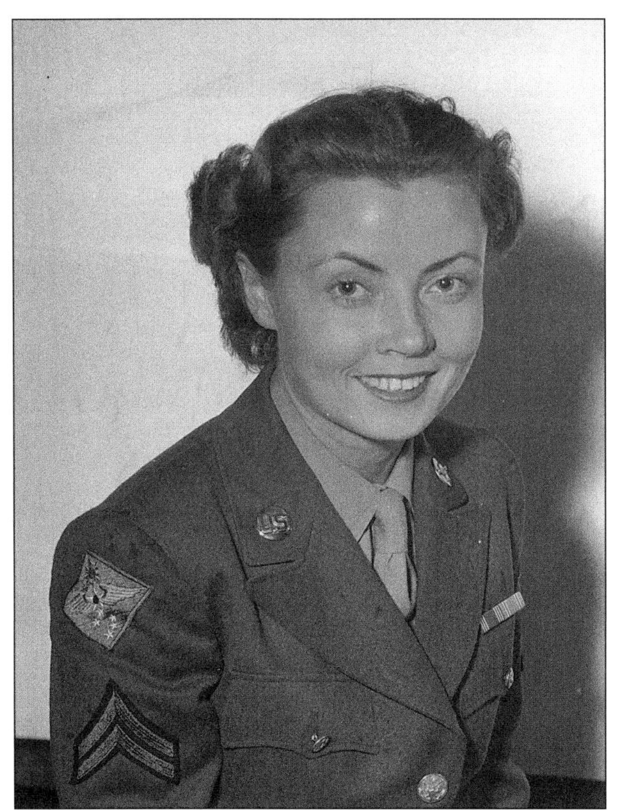

Corporal Margaret Hastings, a WAC during World War II, was stationed in New Guinea. In May 1945, her airplane crashed in the highland jungles of New Guinea. Miraculously, she and two others survived the fiery crash. A tremendous rescue effort ensued, and Hastings and her companions were safely sent home after 47 days in the jungle.

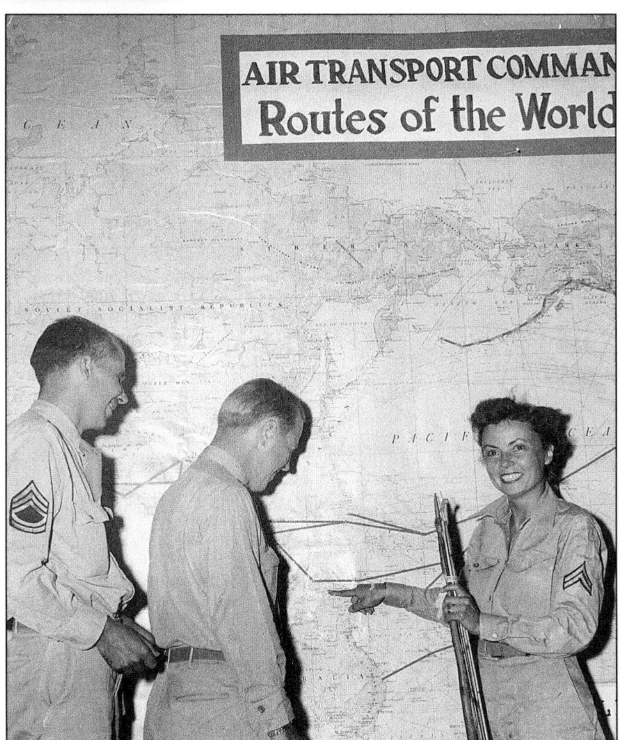

After her 1945 rescue from Shangri-La, Corporal Margaret Hastings shows the location of the crash site.

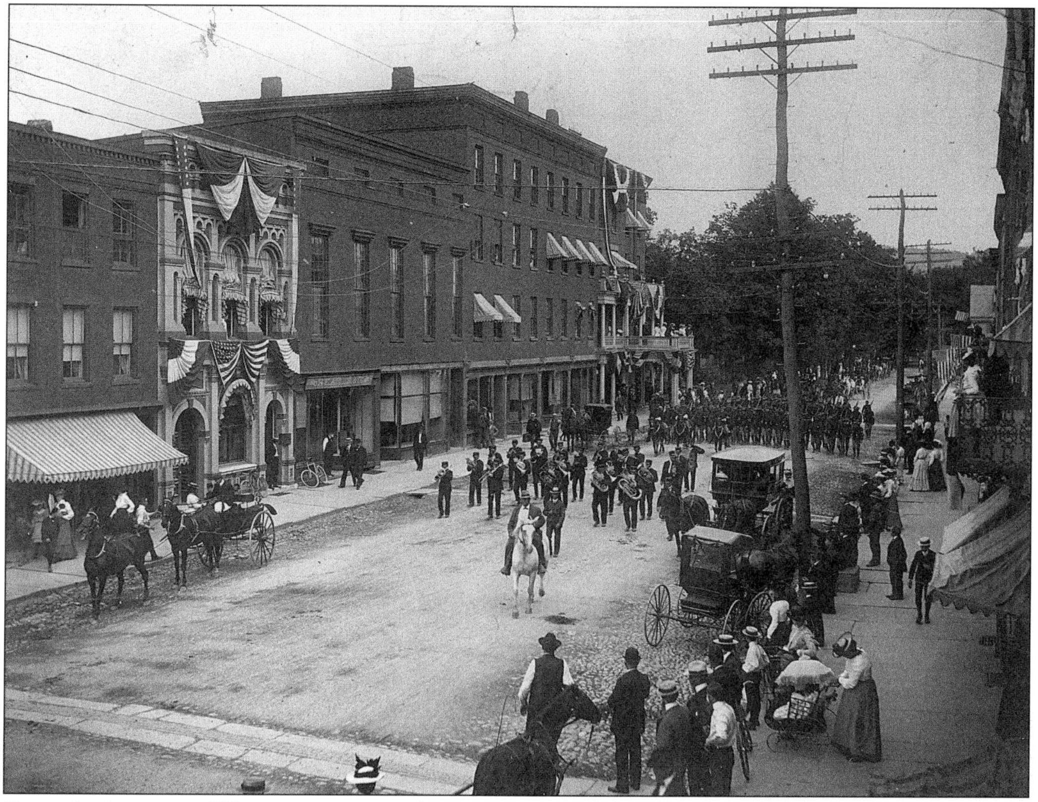

Spanish-American War veterans march in a victory celebration down Front Street in Owego in 1899.

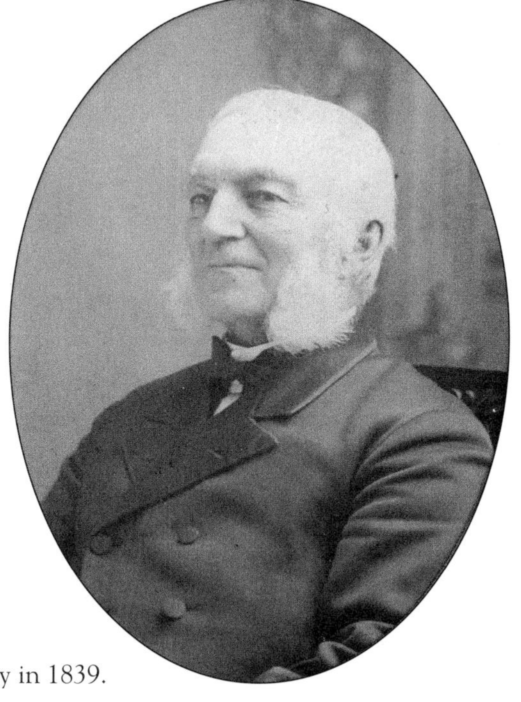

Printice Ransom was the sheriff of Tioga County in 1839.

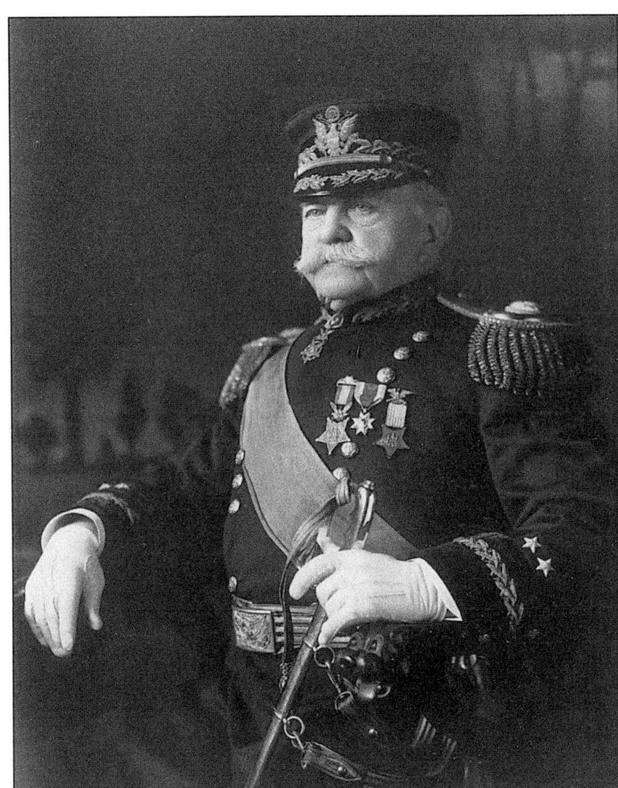

Isaac Catlin was born July 8, 1835, and entered the Union Army at the beginning of the Civil War. In 1862, he was a lieutenant colonel in the 109th New York State Volunteers, along with his brother-in-law, Colonel Benjamin F. Tracy. On July 30, 1864, Catlin led the 109th in Petersburg, Virginia, at the Battle of the Crater. Catlin was struck twice by shell fragments, which severed his right leg just below the knee. He later attained the rank of major general and was awarded the Medal of Honor.

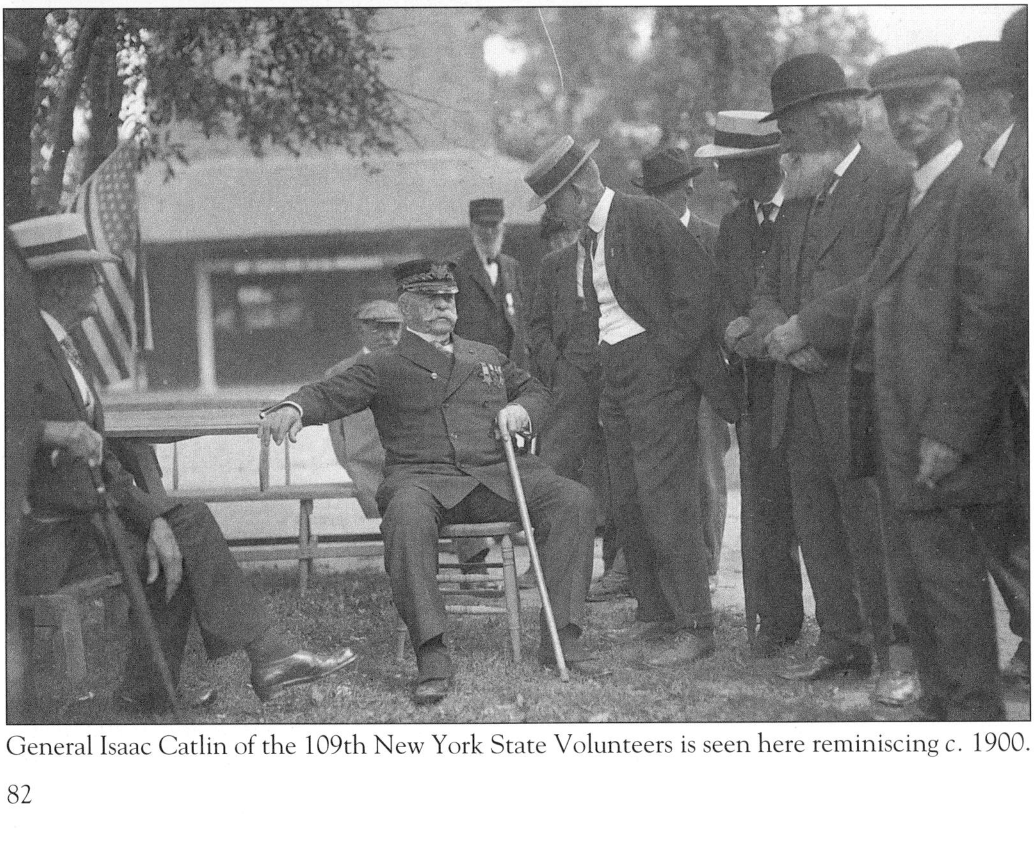

General Isaac Catlin of the 109th New York State Volunteers is seen here reminiscing *c.* 1900.

Captain Horace B. Monroe is shown being decorated with the Oak Leaf Cluster to the Air Medal and with the Purple Heart by Brigadier General J.V. Crabb c. 1942. After World War II, Monroe, who was a pilot, organized area air shows and ran the Owego Flying Service.

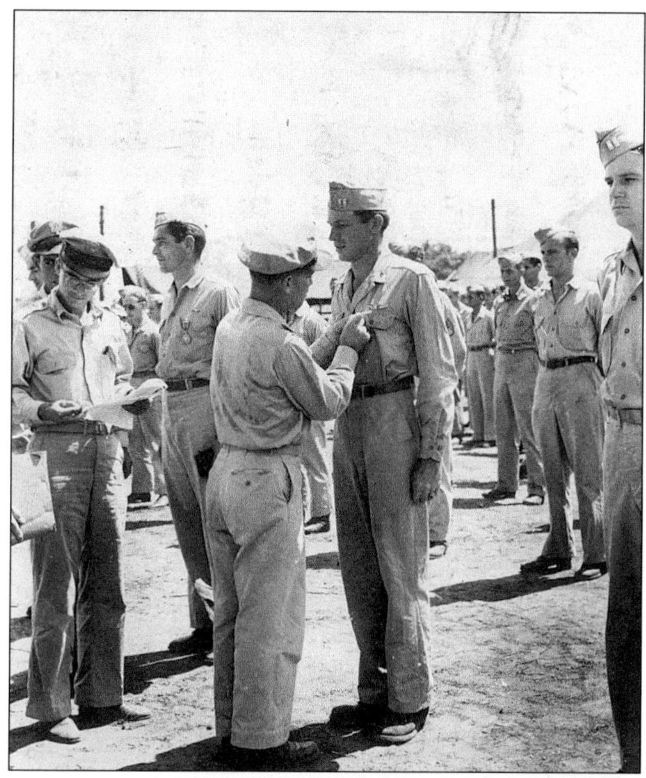

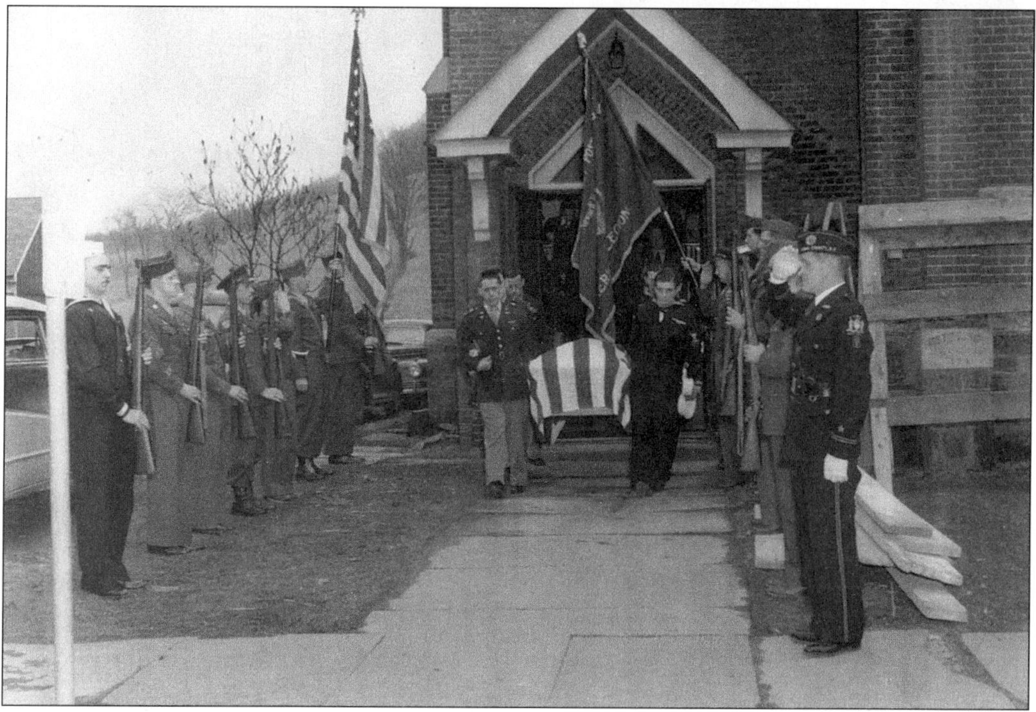

A military funeral was held for Hiram Saddlemire in Newark Valley in early 1945. Saddlemire, a private in the 94th Infantry division, was killed in action.

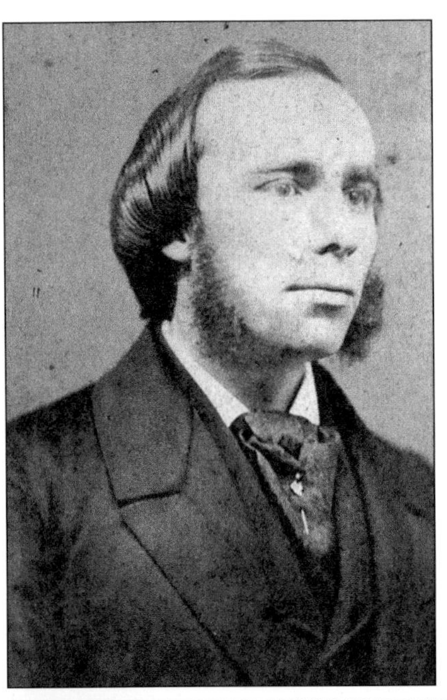

Washington Gladden was a nationally famous Congregationalist minister, editor, author, and educator. He resided in Owego from 1841 to 1860.

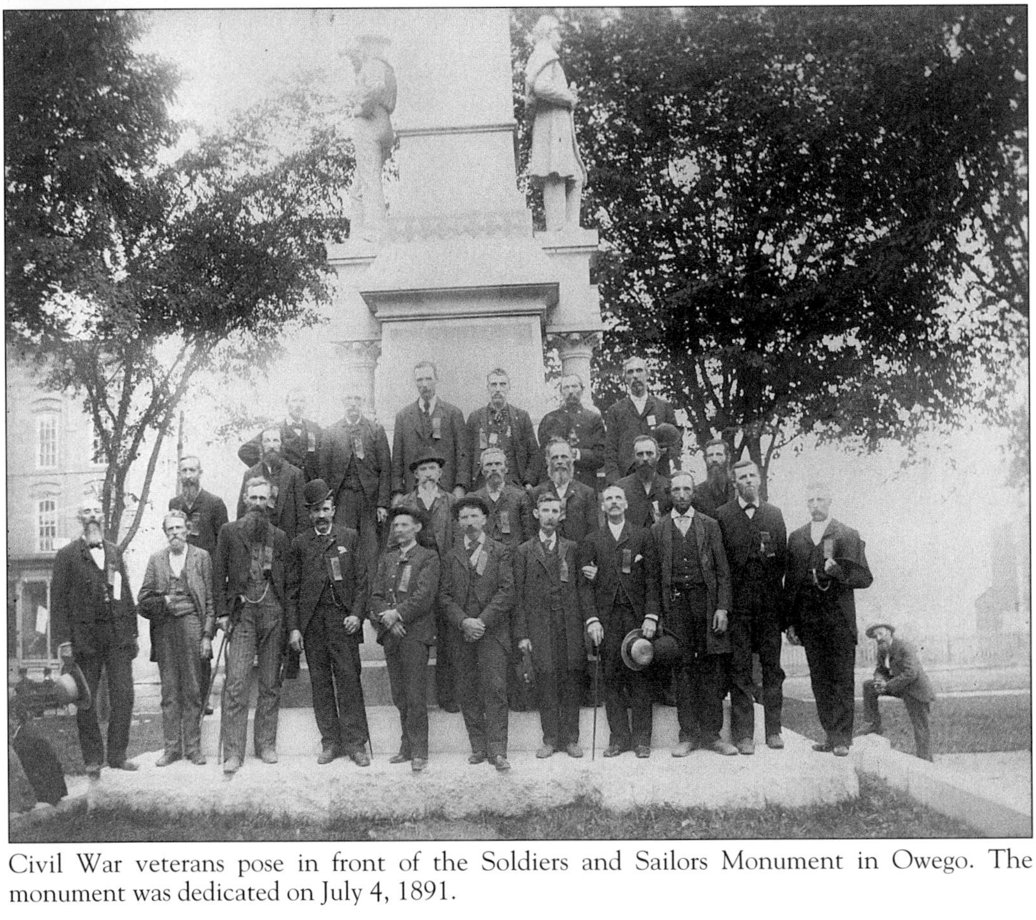

Civil War veterans pose in front of the Soldiers and Sailors Monument in Owego. The monument was dedicated on July 4, 1891.

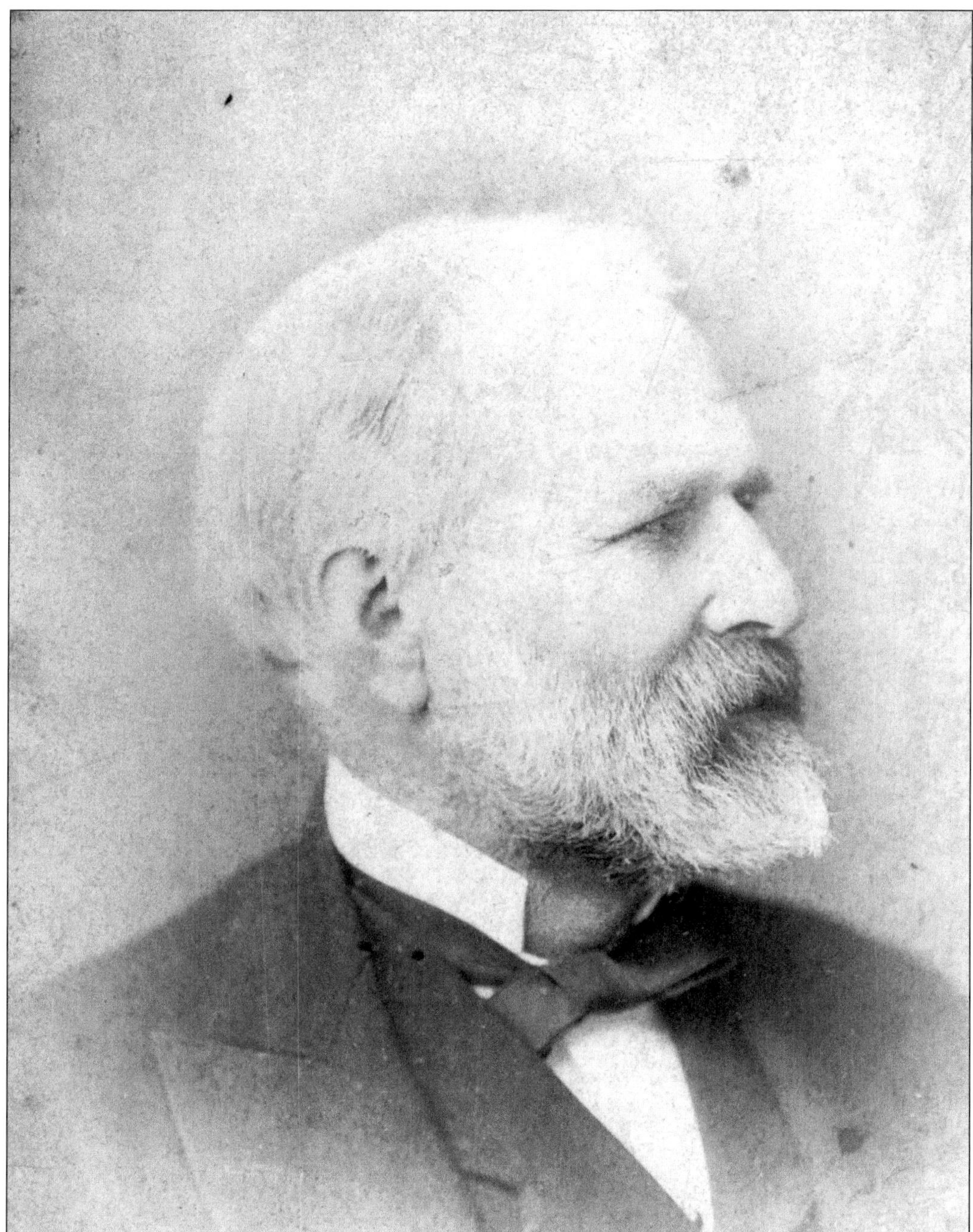

Benjamin Franklin Tracy grew up on the family farm on Marshland Road in Apalachin. Born in April 1830, he was elected district attorney for Tioga County in 1853. By 1860, he was a New York State assemblyman. In 1862, following President Abraham Lincoln's call for 300,000 more troops, Tracy returned to Owego to recruit two regiments of volunteers, the 109th and the 137th. In May 1864, Tracy led his troops in the Battle of the Wilderness, where he won the Medal of Honor for gallantry in battle. Due to health problems, he was reassigned as the commanding officer of the Elmira Prisoner of War Camp. After the war, Tracy was appointed to President Benjamin Harrison's cabinet as secretary of the navy and served from 1889 to 1893.

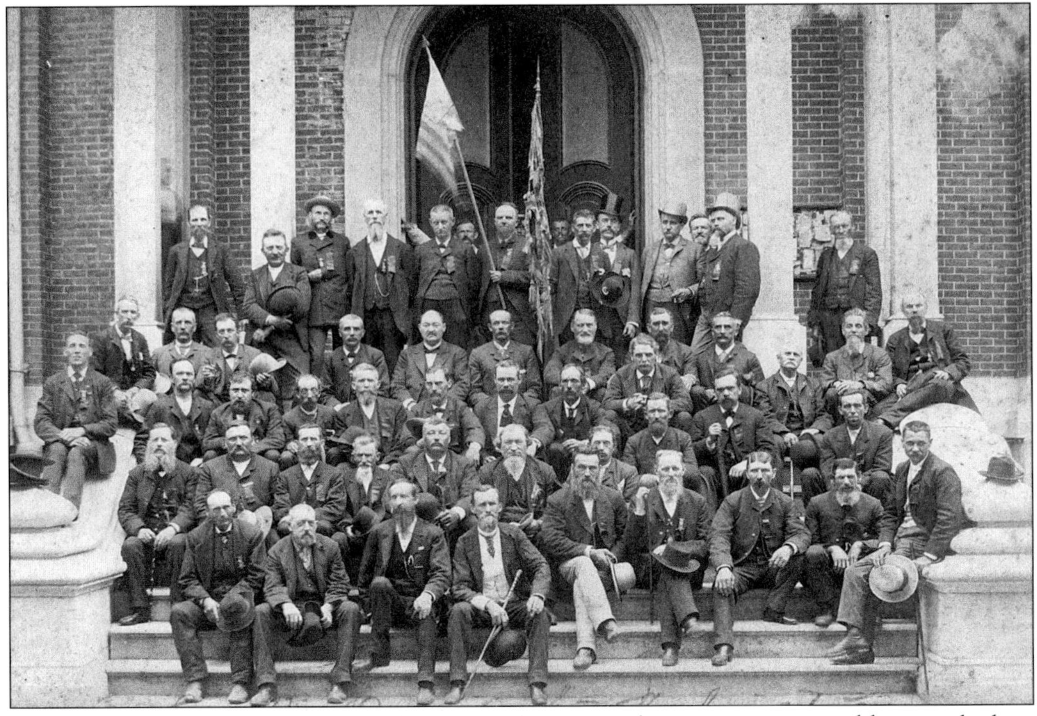

The Civil War veterans of the 137th New York State Volunteers are pictured here with their tattered battle flag *c.* 1895. The regiment was recruited in 1862 by then New York state assemblyman Benjamin F. Tracy of Owego. The regiment consisted of Tioga, Broome, and Tompkins County men. They served with distinction at Gettysburg, and they were present at the surrender of Confederate General Robert E. Lee at Appomattox.

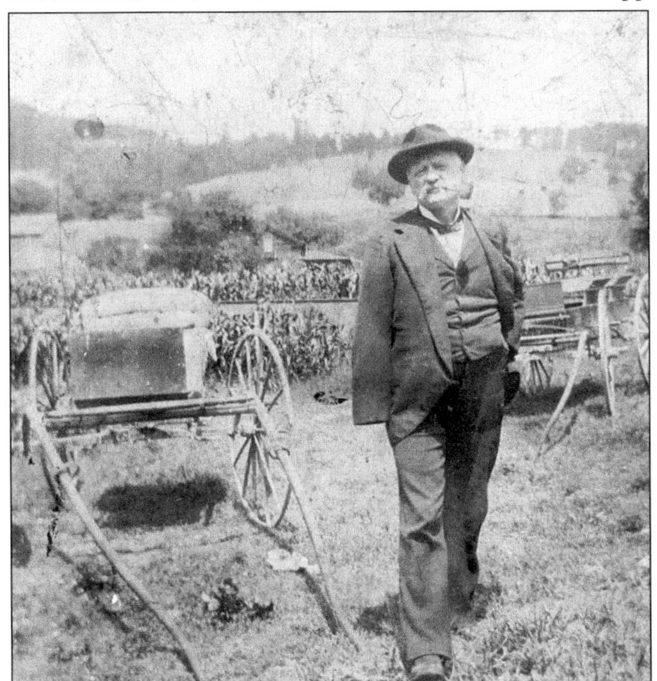

Richard S. Stout enlisted in the navy during the Civil War and served aboard the *Isaac P. Smith*. In the midst of battle, Stout's right arm was shattered, and he lost consciousness from the loss of blood. His arm was later amputated. He received a Bronze Medal for his gallantry. Stout is shown here *c.* 1890.

Dr. Charles L. Stiles was born in Sussex County, New Jersey, in 1837. He graduated from Geneva Medical College in 1865. He came to Owego in May 1868. He was elected president of the Tioga County Medical Society in 1895. He was also vice president of the New York State Medical Society and was the surgeon for the Erie Railroad Company.

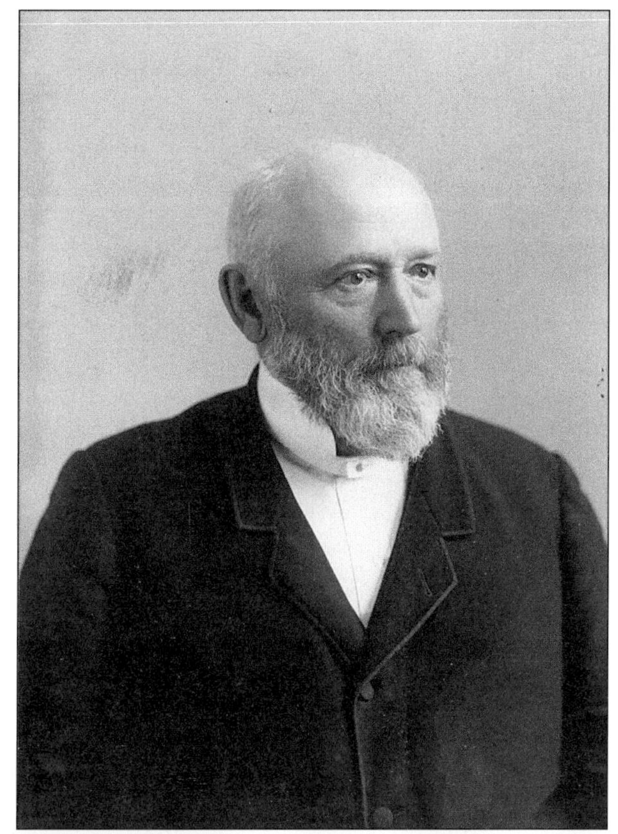

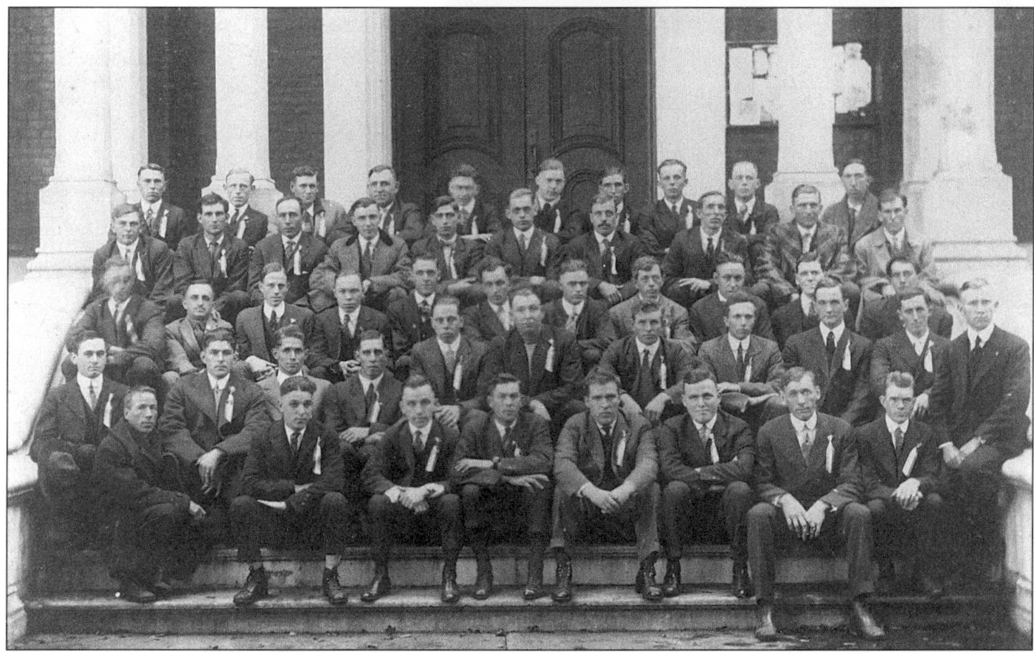

Soon to be veterans, these men pose on the steps of the county courthouse as they prepare to leave for Camp Dix, New Jersey, in 1917.

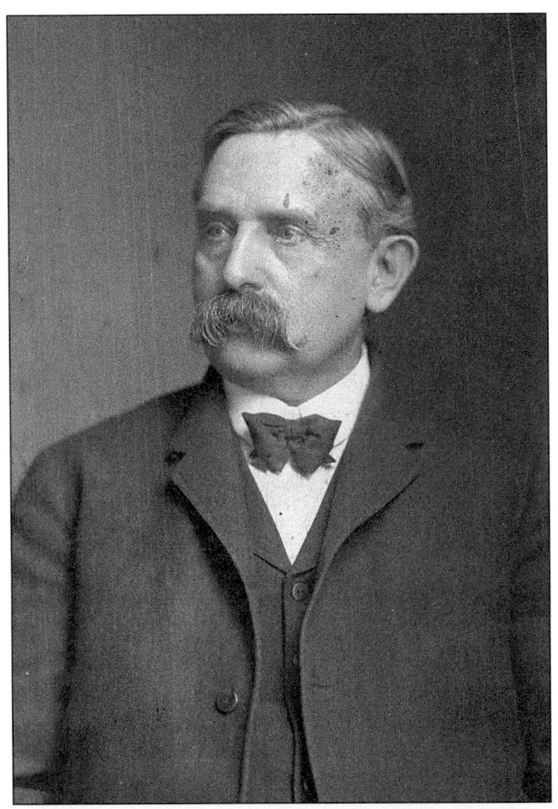

Frank Baker was born in Owego on March 26, 1846, and was a graduate of the Ames Business University in Syracuse. In 1896, he was appointed railroad commissioner by New York Governor Morton. He was involved in the organizing of the New York State Firemen's Association and was the chief engineer of the Owego Fire Department in the late 19th century. Baker donated the fireman's fountain to the town of Owego as a memorial to his son, a fireman who was killed in an automobile accident.

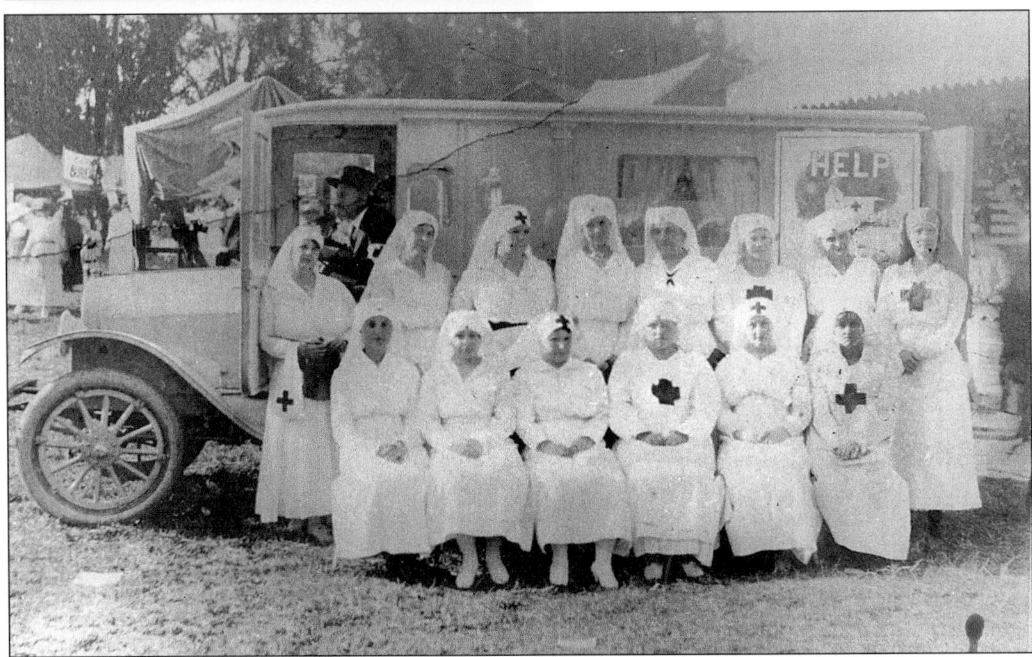

J. Alden Loring, a world-famous naturalist who accompanied President Theodore Roosevelt on his African safari in 1909, was an ambulance driver during World War I. This photograph was taken *c.* 1920 at the Tioga County Fair.

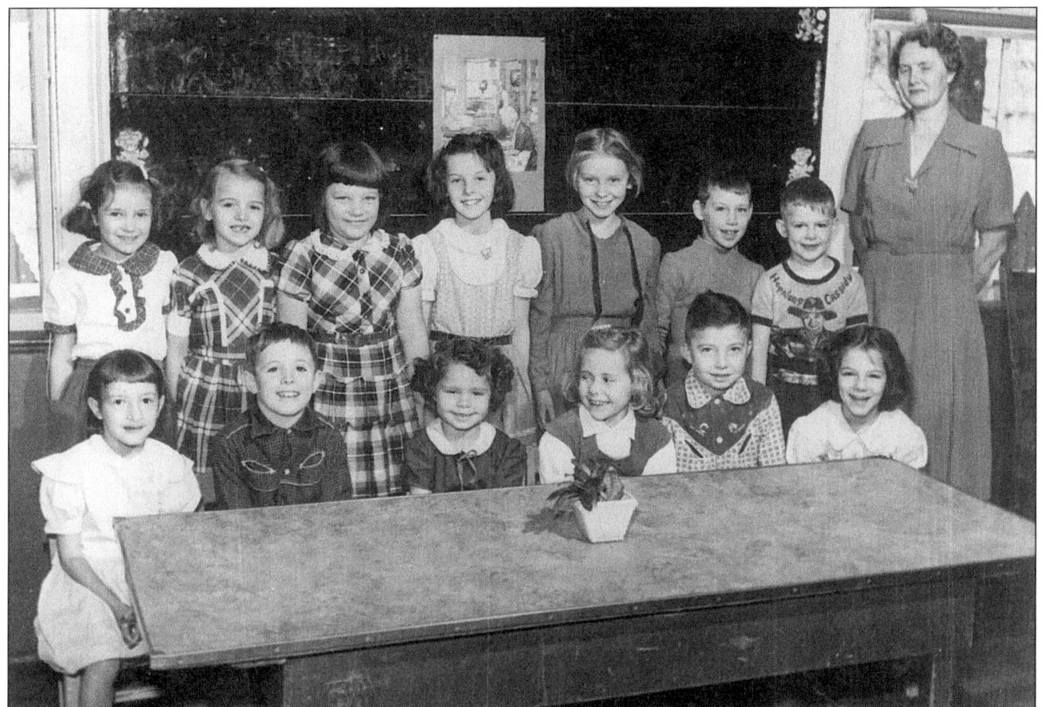

This photograph shows grades one, two, and three of the old Richford School on Route 38. These were the last students to attend class in the school, which closed in June 1955. They are, from left to right, as follows: (front row) Sandy Rundell, Michael Conway, Jane Kobylarz, Susan Lacey, Robert Marshall, and Shirley Canfield; (back row) Bonnie Seymour, Susan Jewett, Mary Weston, Waneta Nixon, Marietta Ellis, Dan Stineford, and Kenneth Canfield. With them is their teacher, Marie Gormel.

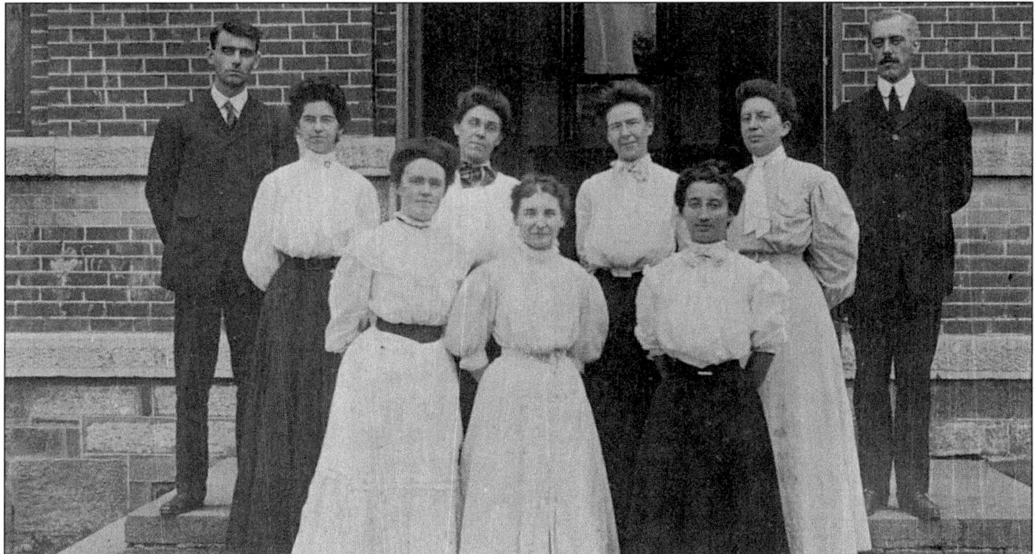

Teachers in Newark Valley in 1908 were, from left to right, as follows: (front row) Charlotte Roberts, Jesmine Elwell, and Bessie Rhines; (back row) Professor Barford, Kate Benham, Bessie Belcher, Jennie Pearsall, Mary Goslin, and Edward Eastman.

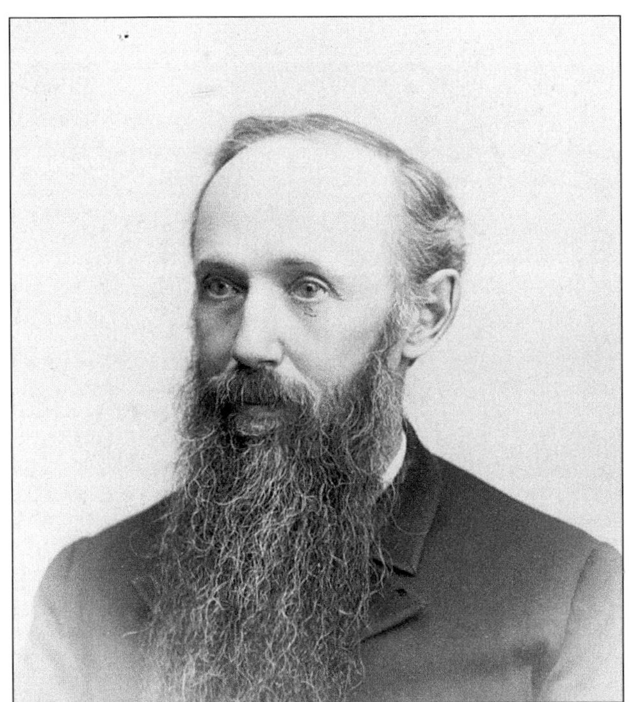

Ezra J. Peck was born December 19, 1830, at Seneca Castle in Ontario County. He served in the Civil War as a first lieutenant in Troop D of the 8th Cavalry. In 1886, Peck became principal of the Owego Academy. Previously, he was a teacher and principal in Auburn and Homer. He retired in 1901 after 35 years in public and private education.

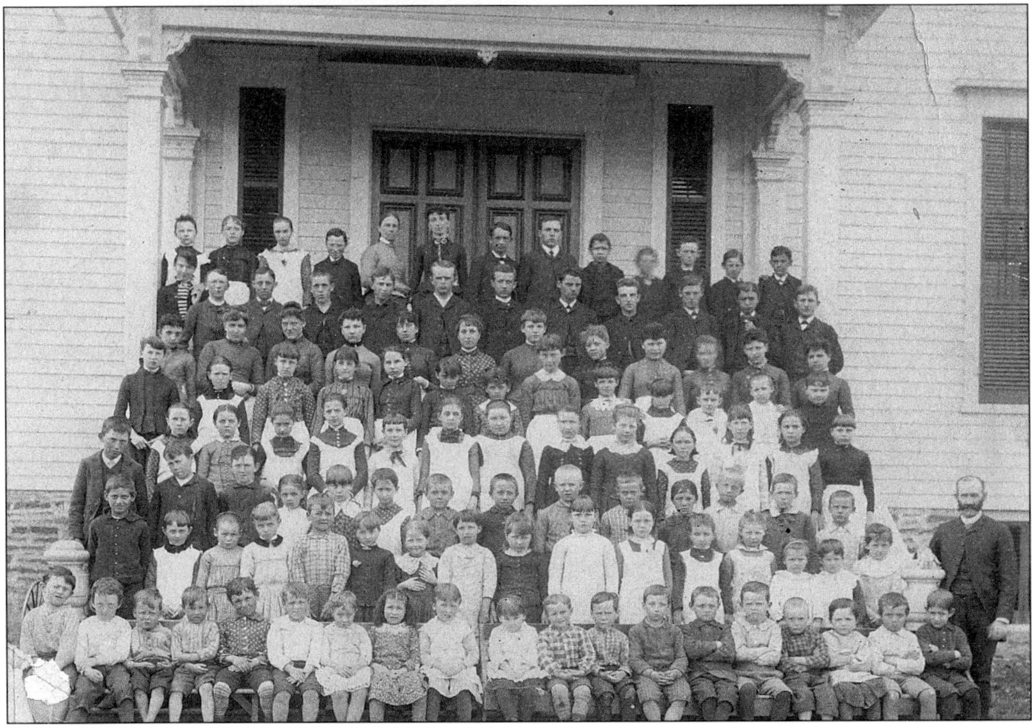

This frame schoolhouse was opened in September 1884 due to overcrowding in the District 14 School. Newark Valley students paraded from this school to the new brick schoolhouse. This building was then used as a cigar factory. Mrs. Minturn, who also appears in the Teacher Training Institute photograph, is pictured here in the top row, fifth from the left.

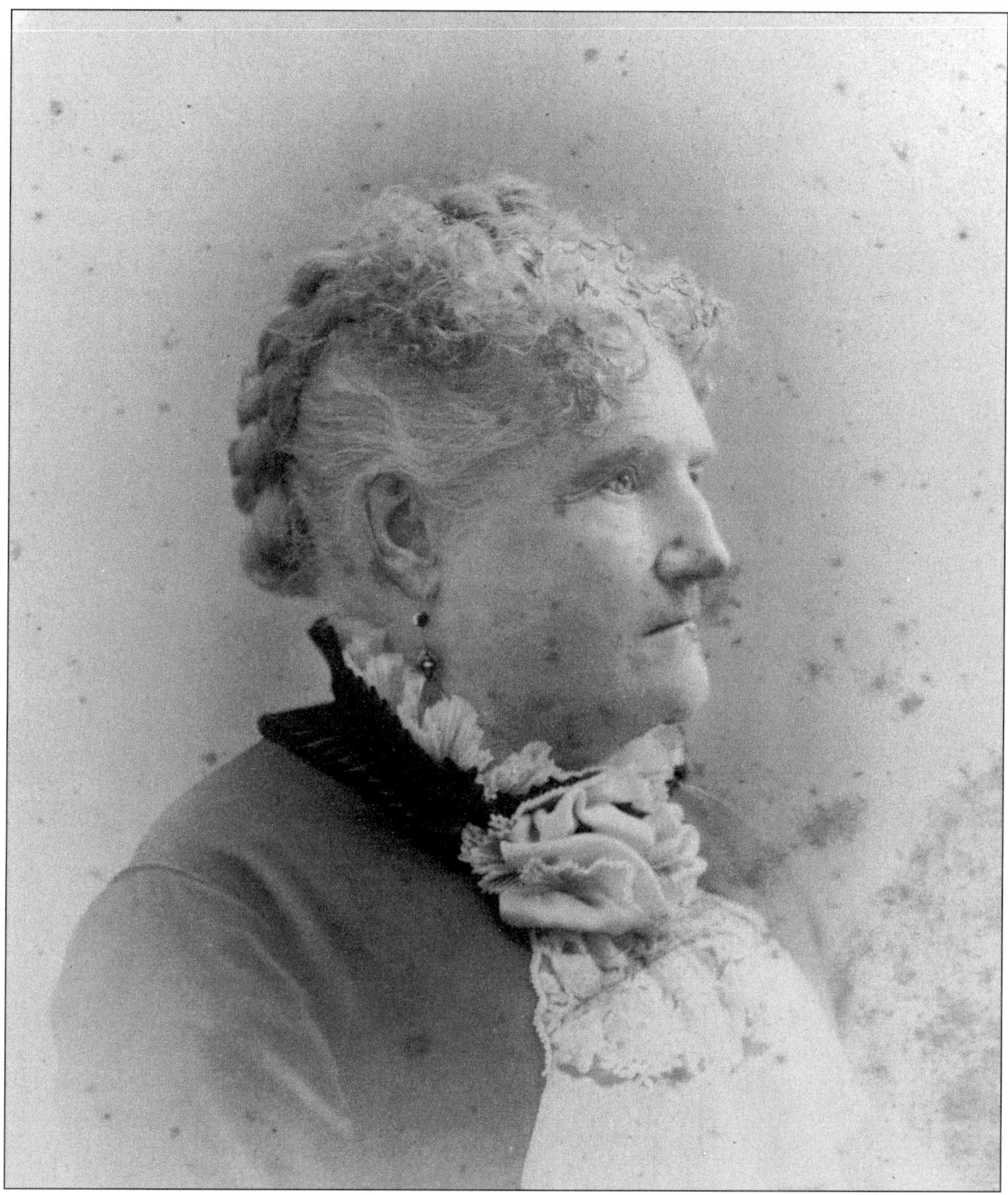

Esther H. McQuigg Morris was born in Spencer in 1812. As a young girl, she moved with her family to Owego. Later she moved westward to the Wyoming Territory. There, in 1869, she was appointed justice of the peace, the first woman to hold that position in the United States.

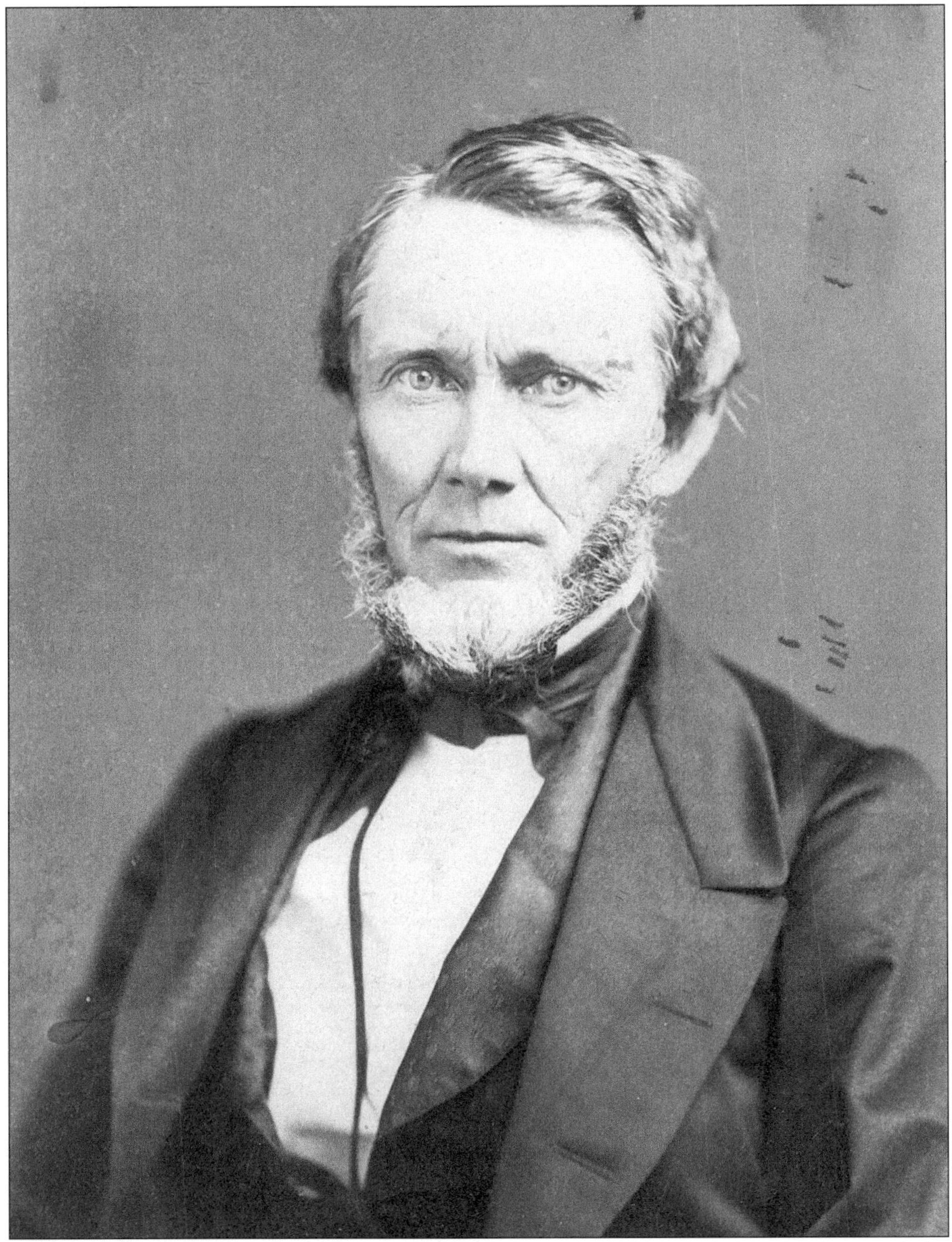

John J. Taylor moved to Owego in December of 1834. He was a leading Democrat and the Court of Common Pleas district attorney for five years beginning in 1838. He was elected to Congress in 1852 and served on the foreign affairs committee. In 1858, he was the Democratic candidate for lieutenant governor but was defeated.

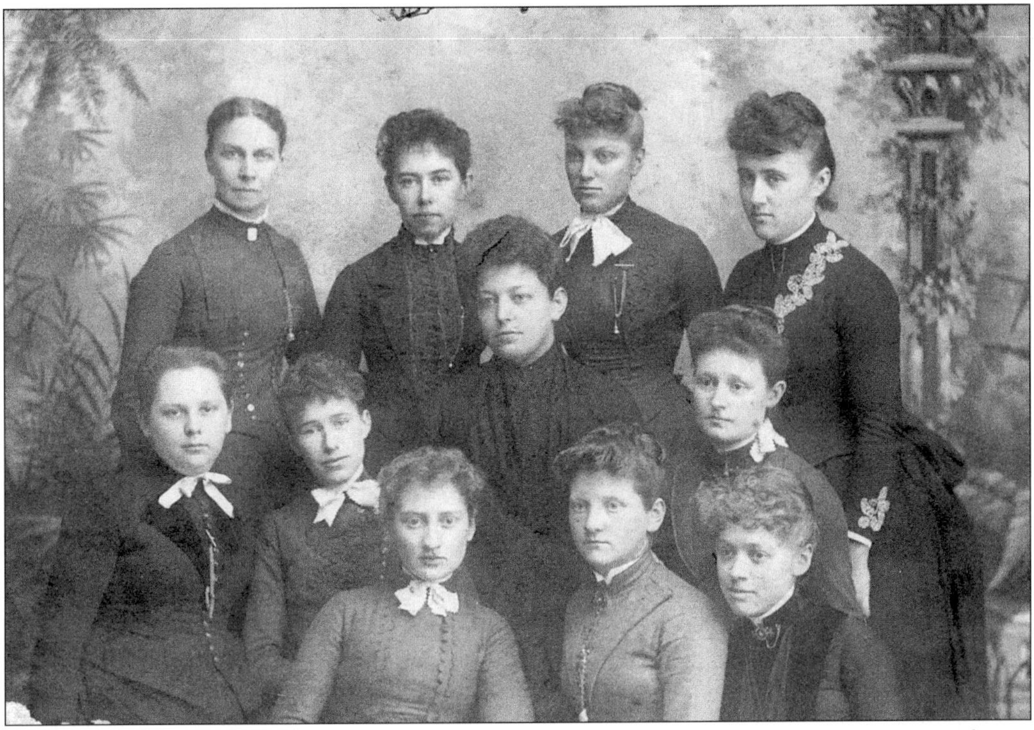

Posing for their photograph on March 26, 1889, are the Teachers Training Institute graduates from Newark Valley. They are, from left to right, as follows: (first row) Eva Zimmer, Fran Sherwood, and Mame Smith; (second row) Levantia Westfall, Helen Butler, and Mabel Holden; (third row) Rosa Thomas; (fourth row) Mrs. A.P. Minturn, Anna Jayne, Susie Patterson, and Iva Culver.

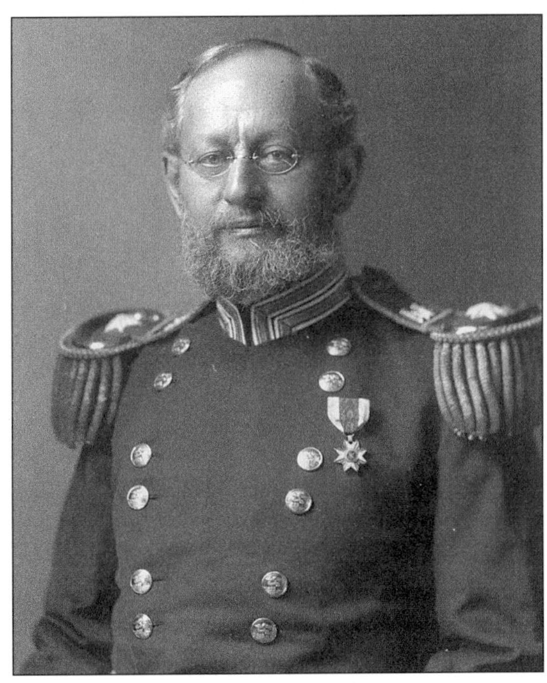

Henry Martyn Robert was a retired army engineer. He is best known for his *Robert's Rules of Order*, which he revised while living in Owego.

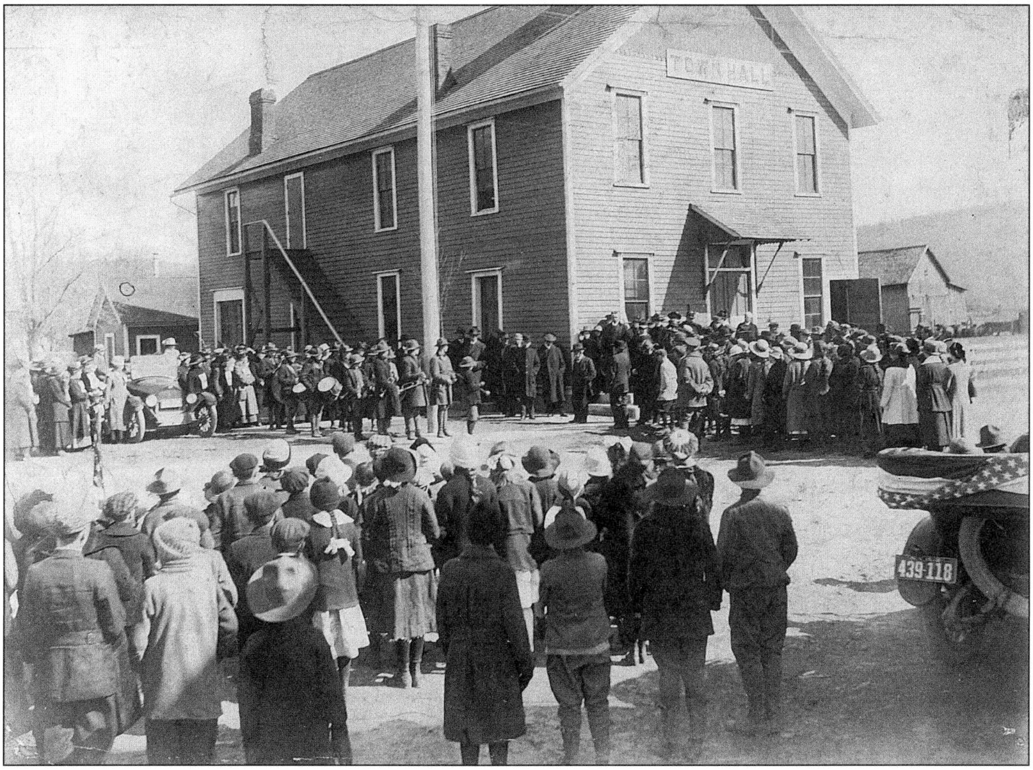

Spencer was the first town in the county to exceed its quota of war bonds during World War I. This flag-raising event celebrated the town's achievement.

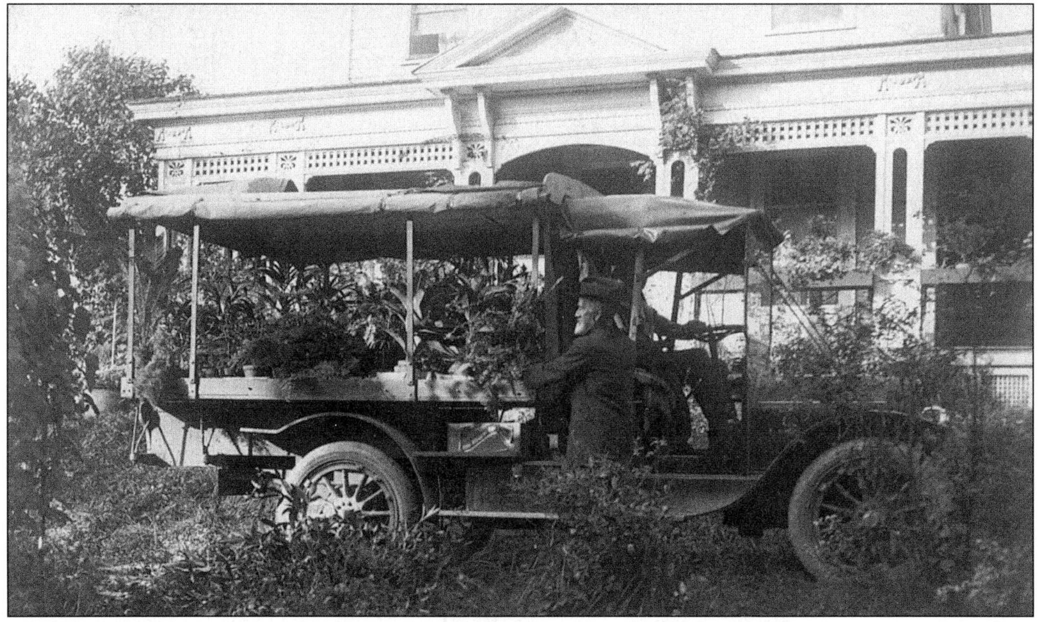

Samuel Loring loads his truck with plants and flowers to be sold house to house. The Loring's had two greenhouses 85 feet in length, in which they grew their plants. This photograph was taken *c.* 1911.

Ransom Pearsall was a descendant of the original settlers of Apalachin. Involved in the lumbering business, he was appointed postmaster of Apalachin in 1893.

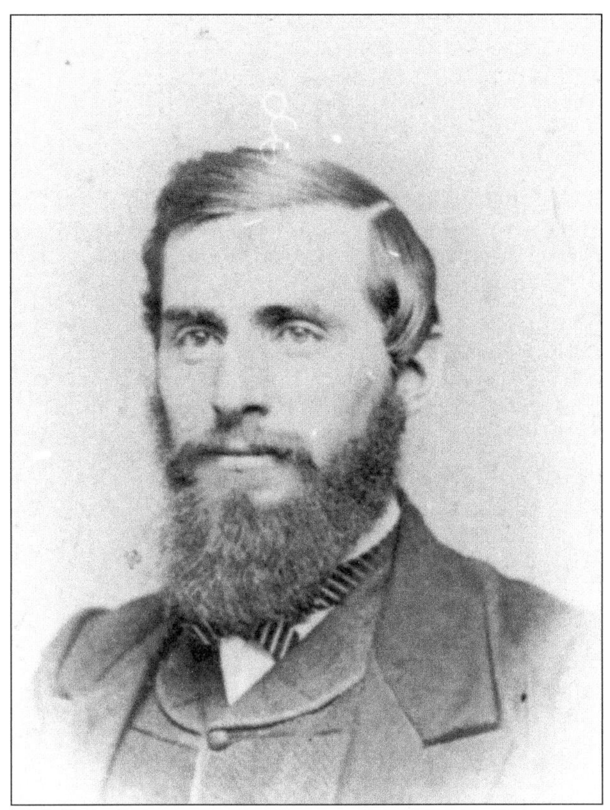

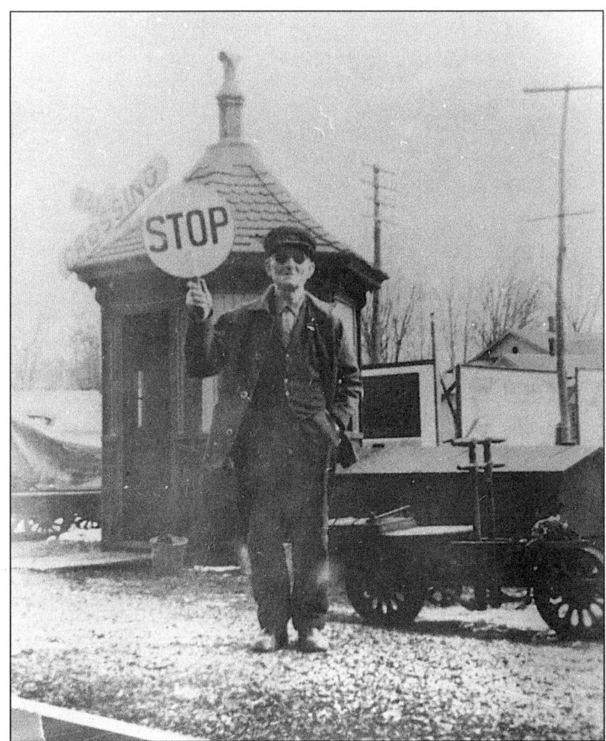

David Warner was a railroad crossing guard for the Delaware, Lackawanna, and Western. This photograph was taken on River Street in Nichols near the Agway Store *c.* 1910.

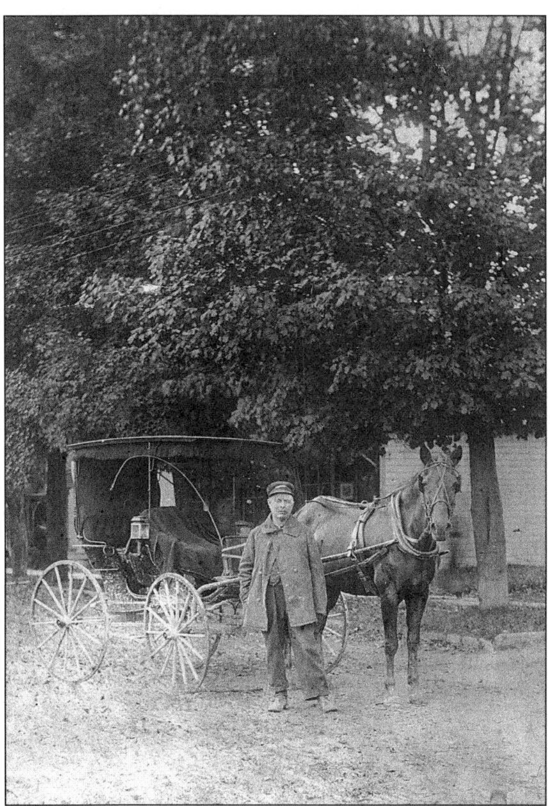

George Montgomery ran an early "bus" line with horse and carriage in Spencer c. 1905.

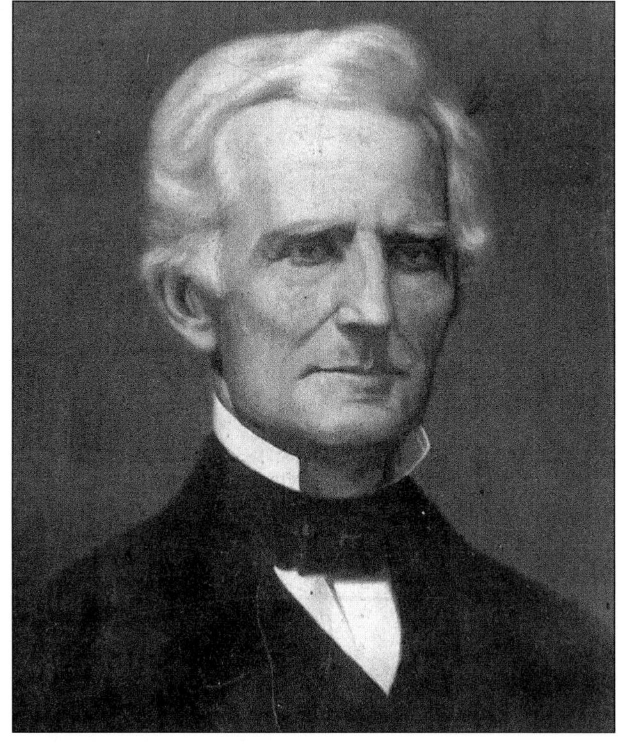

Stephen B. Leonard was born in New York City in 1793. He came to Owego with his family as a young boy. Here, he was apprenticed as a printer, learning his trade in the office of the *American Farmer* newspaper. He bought the office in 1814 and changed the name to the *Owego Gazette*. He established the first mail route from Owego to Bath in 1816 so that he could deliver his newspaper. He was elected to Congress in 1835 and 1837.

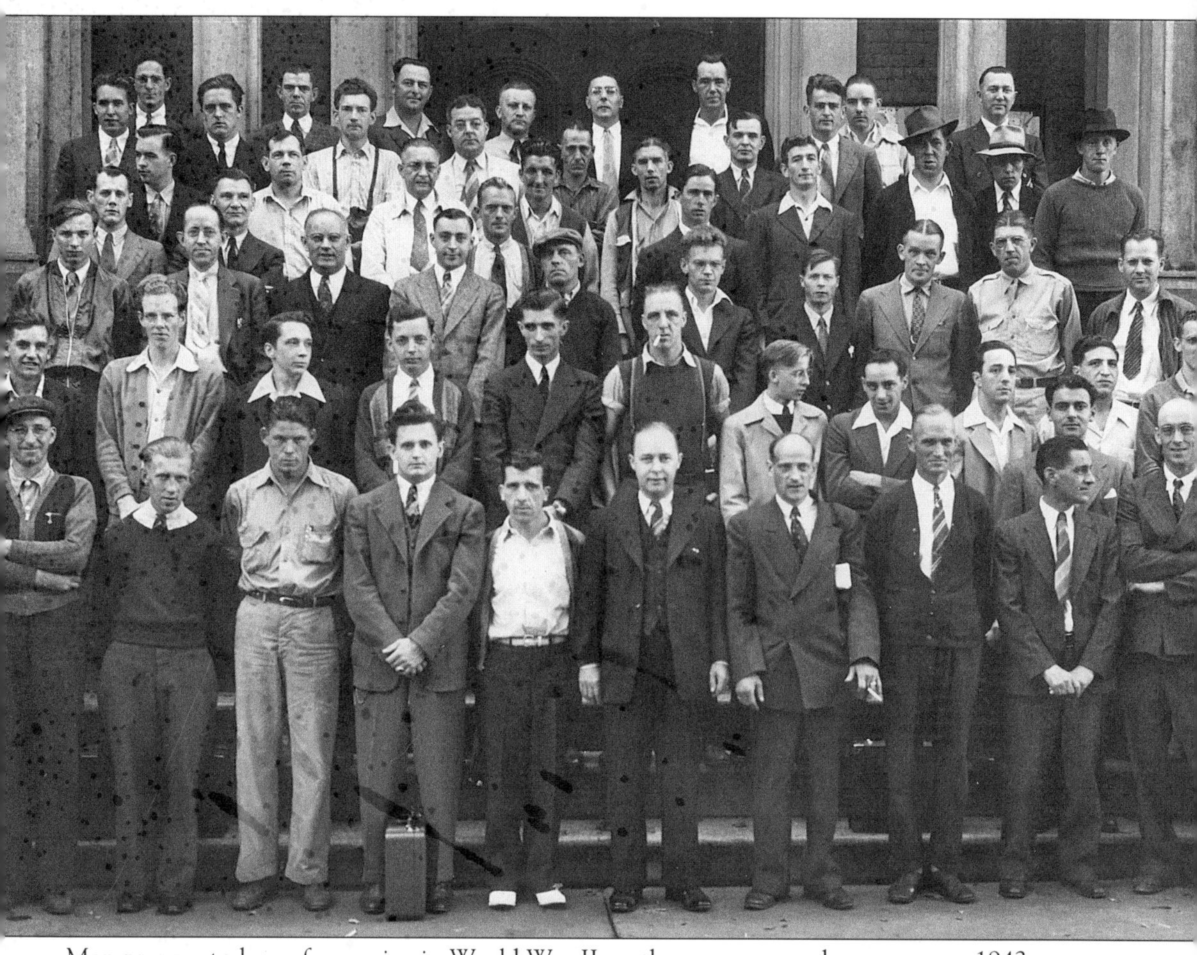

Men prepare to leave for service in World War II on the county courthouse steps *c.* 1942.

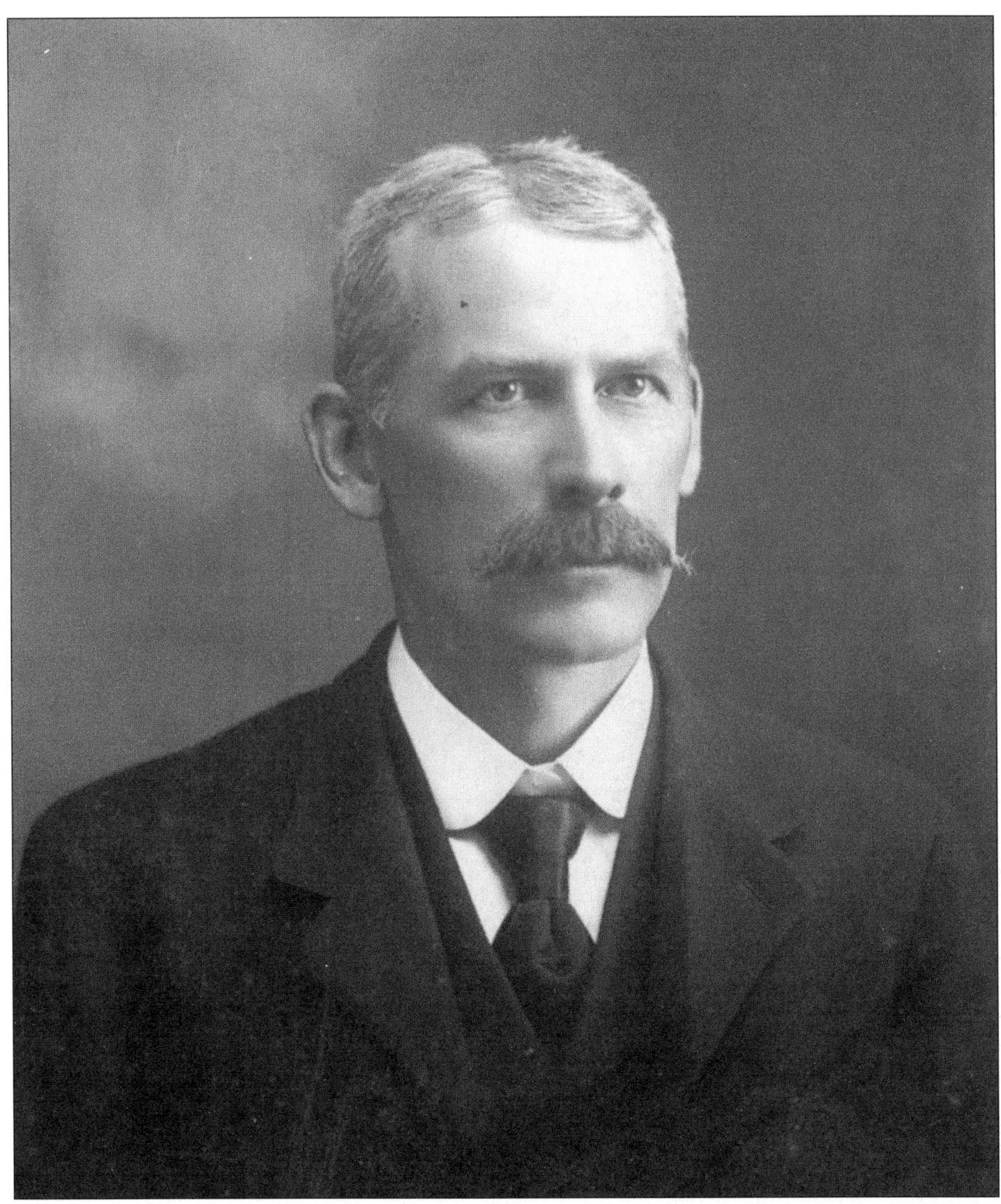

Allen B. Kirby was born April 10, 1857, in Nichols. He worked on the Lackawanna Railroad as station agent from 1881 to 1929. He was the first mayor of the village of Nichols in 1903 and was the director of the Kirby Band for almost 70 years. He died on October 25, 1949, at the age of 93.

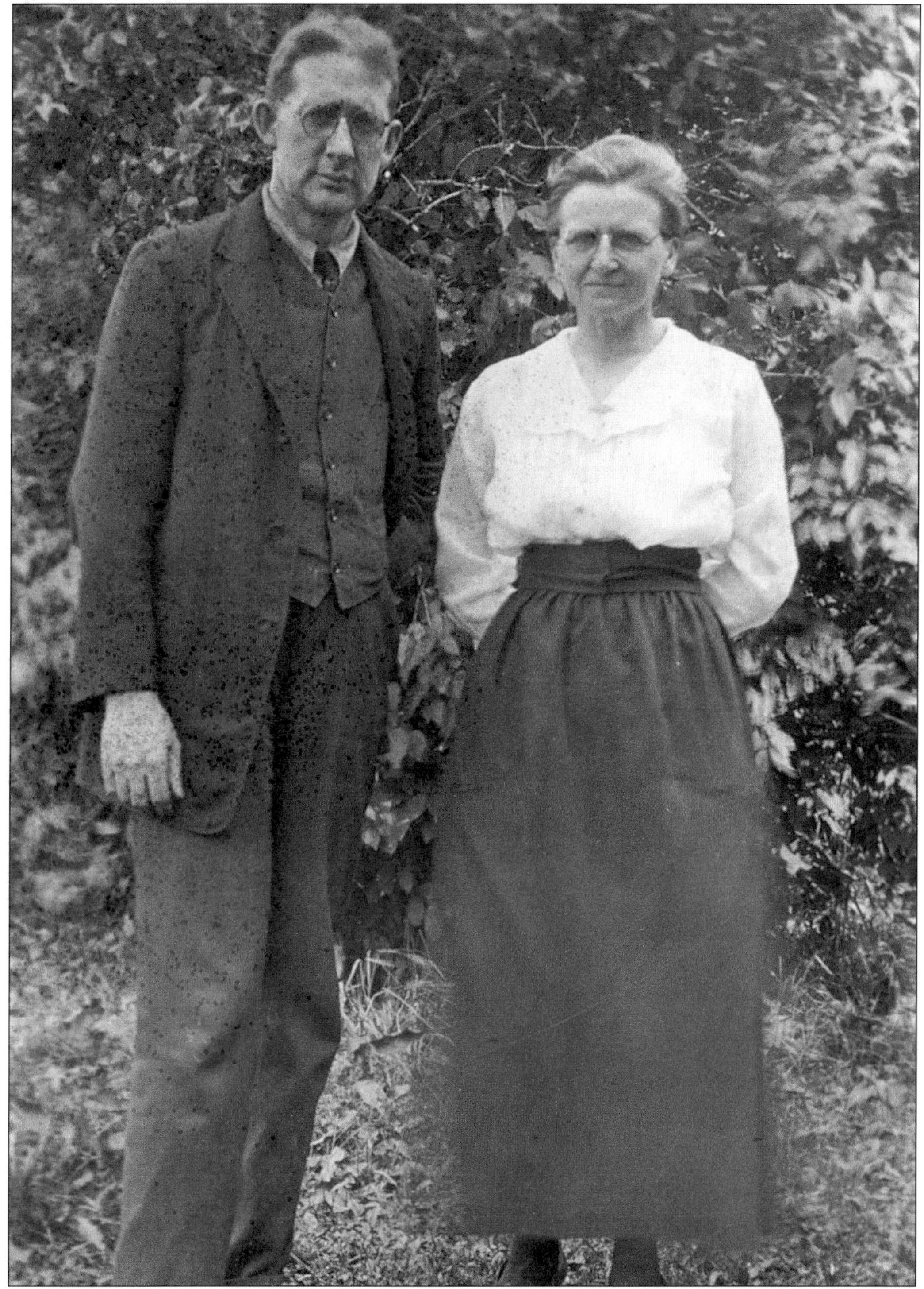

This photograph shows Harry and Anna Swift *c.* 1900. Harry Swift and his brother, Charles Swift, operated the Swift Hardware Store in Richford from 1890 through the 1920s. The town office, where voting took place, was on the second floor.

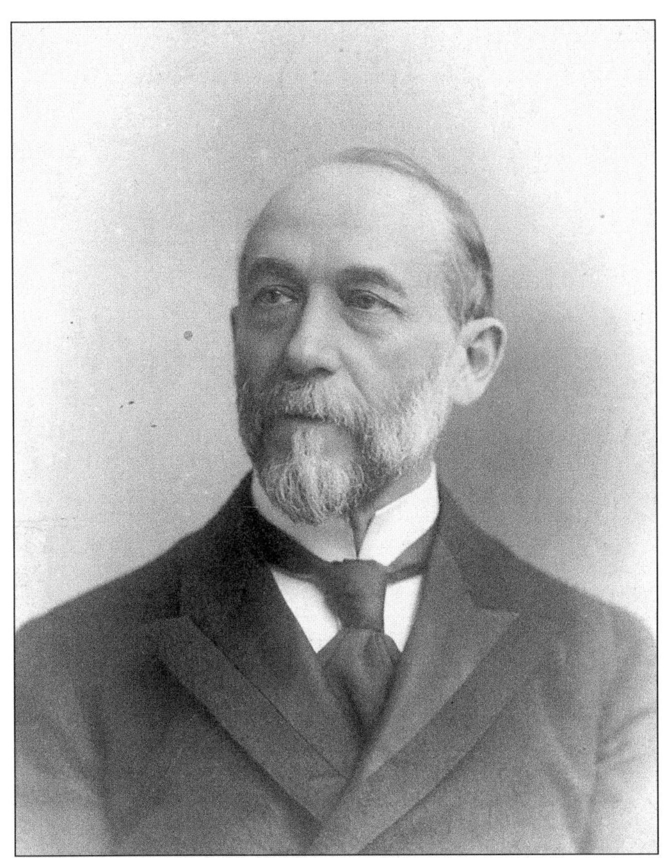

This 1899 photograph is of Thomas Collier Platt. Born in Owego, Platt was elected Tioga county clerk in 1859. He served two terms in Congress, in 1873 and 1875. In 1877, he was chosen chairman of the Republican State Convention in New York. In 1881, he was elected U.S. Senator by the New York State Legislature. Extremely influential in national politics, he virtually ran the Republican party in New York State in the 1890s.

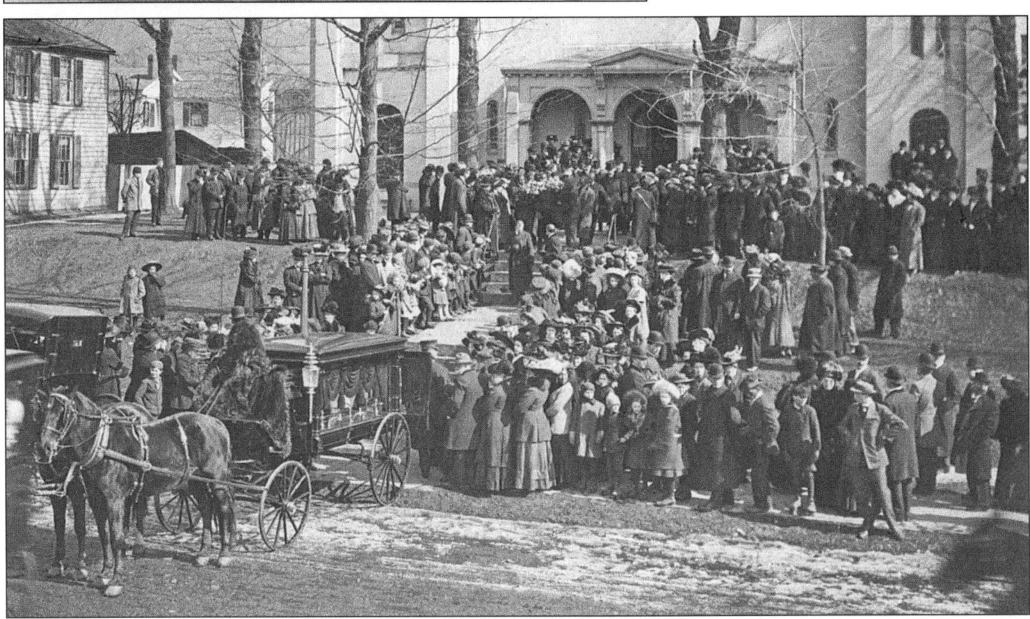

The funeral procession for Thomas Collier Platt emerges from the First Presbyterian Church on North Avenue in Owego on March 9, 1910. The hearse awaits the casket, which is just visible as the pallbearers are about to descend the steps.

Six

Town and Country

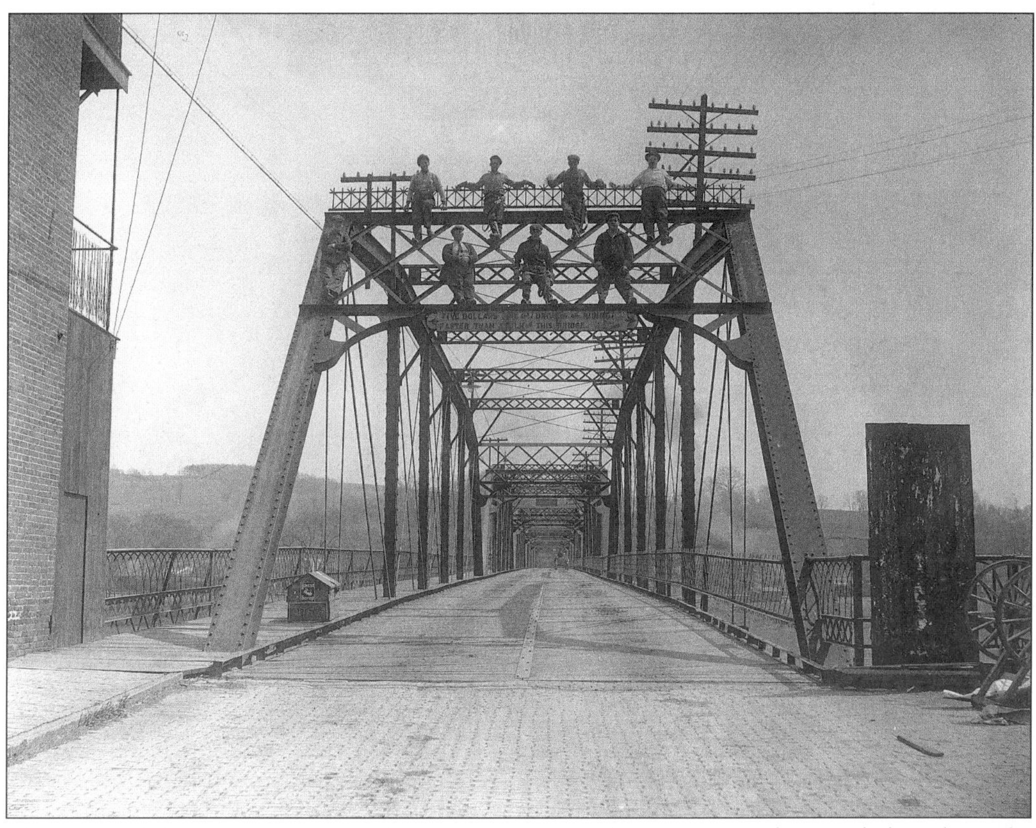

This view of the Court Street Bridge in Owego was taken *c.* 1893. The sign below the eight men on the bridge reads, "Five dollars fine for driving or riding faster than a walk on this bridge. By order Commissioners." This bridge, built by the Owego Bridge Company, was replaced in 1933 with the present Court Street Bridge.

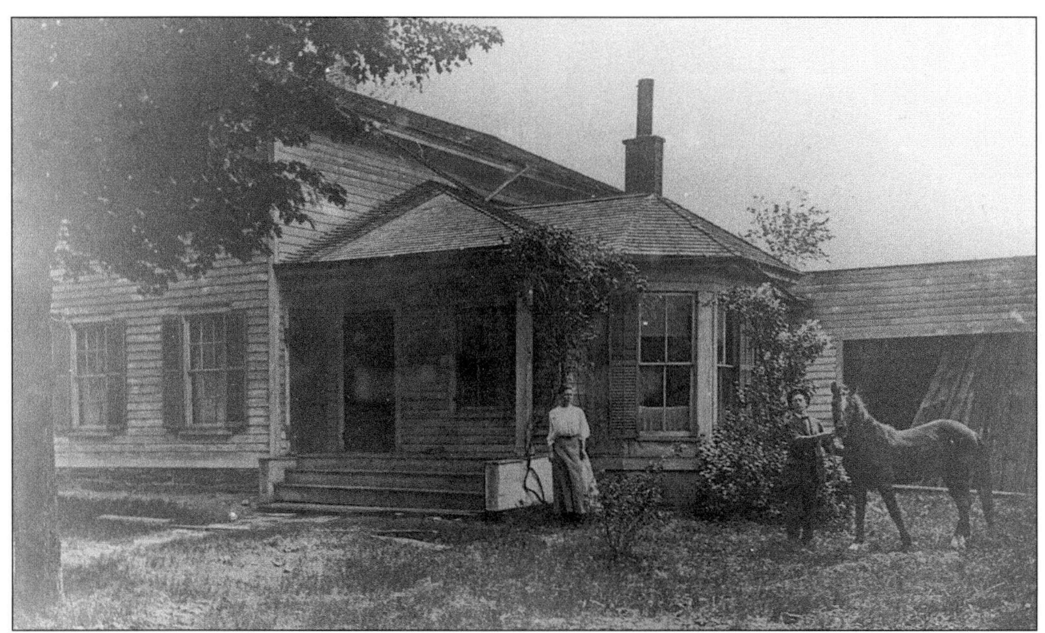

This photograph shows the Elmore Everett house in Nichols *c.* 1910.

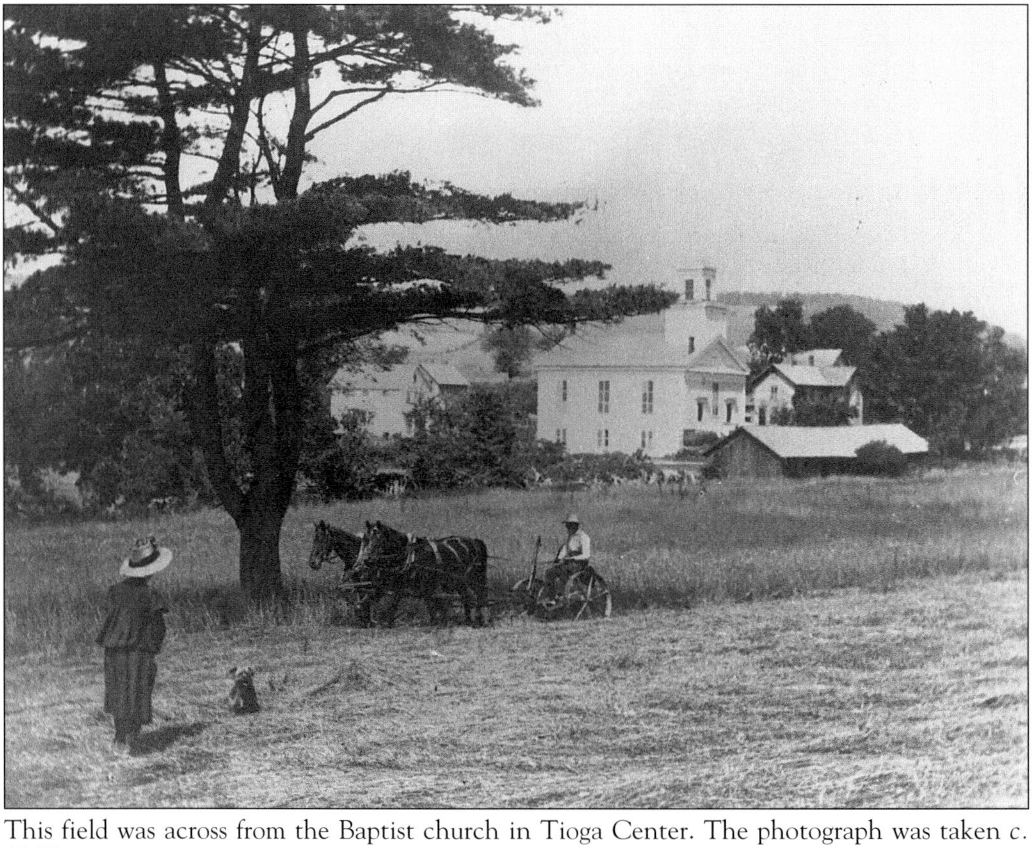

This field was across from the Baptist church in Tioga Center. The photograph was taken *c.* 1895.

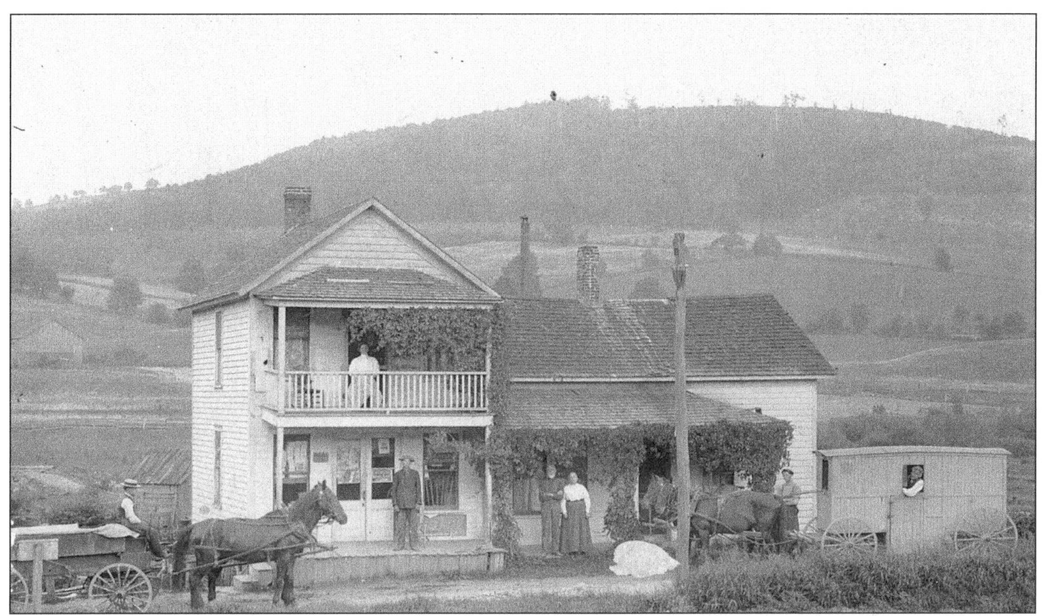

Tuckers Store was located in Prospect Valley in the town of Candor. This photograph was taken *c.* 1900.

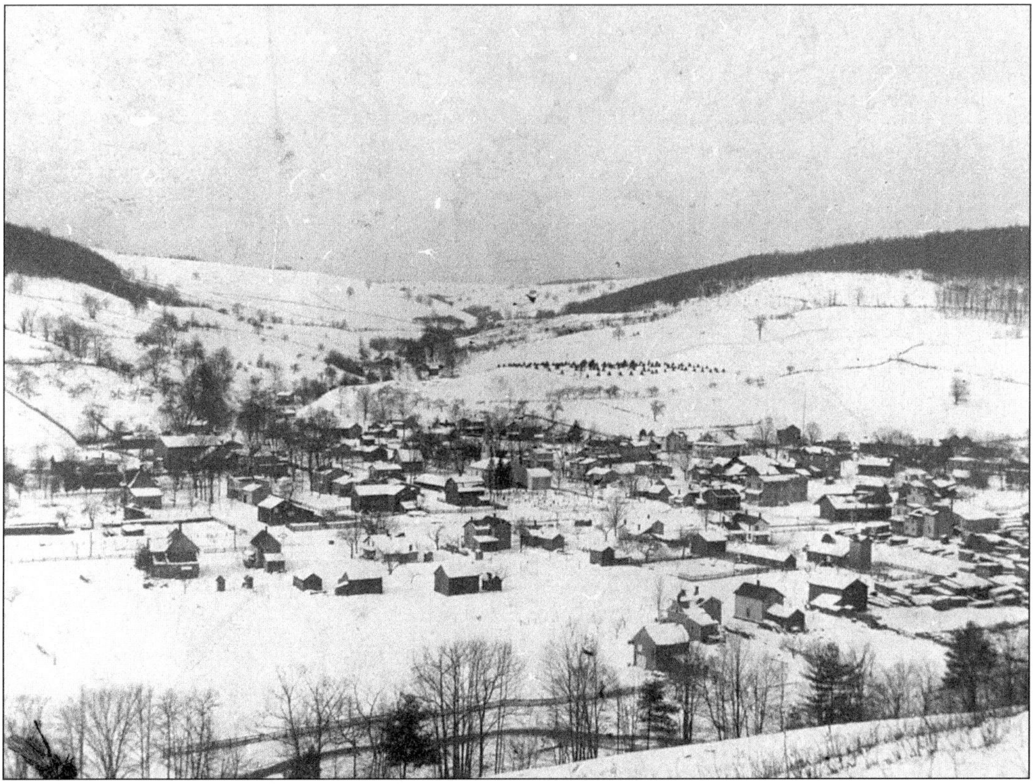

This photograph was taken in 1900 looking west toward Richford. The small pines on the hill mark the cemetery. Finch's Sawmill is at the lower right.

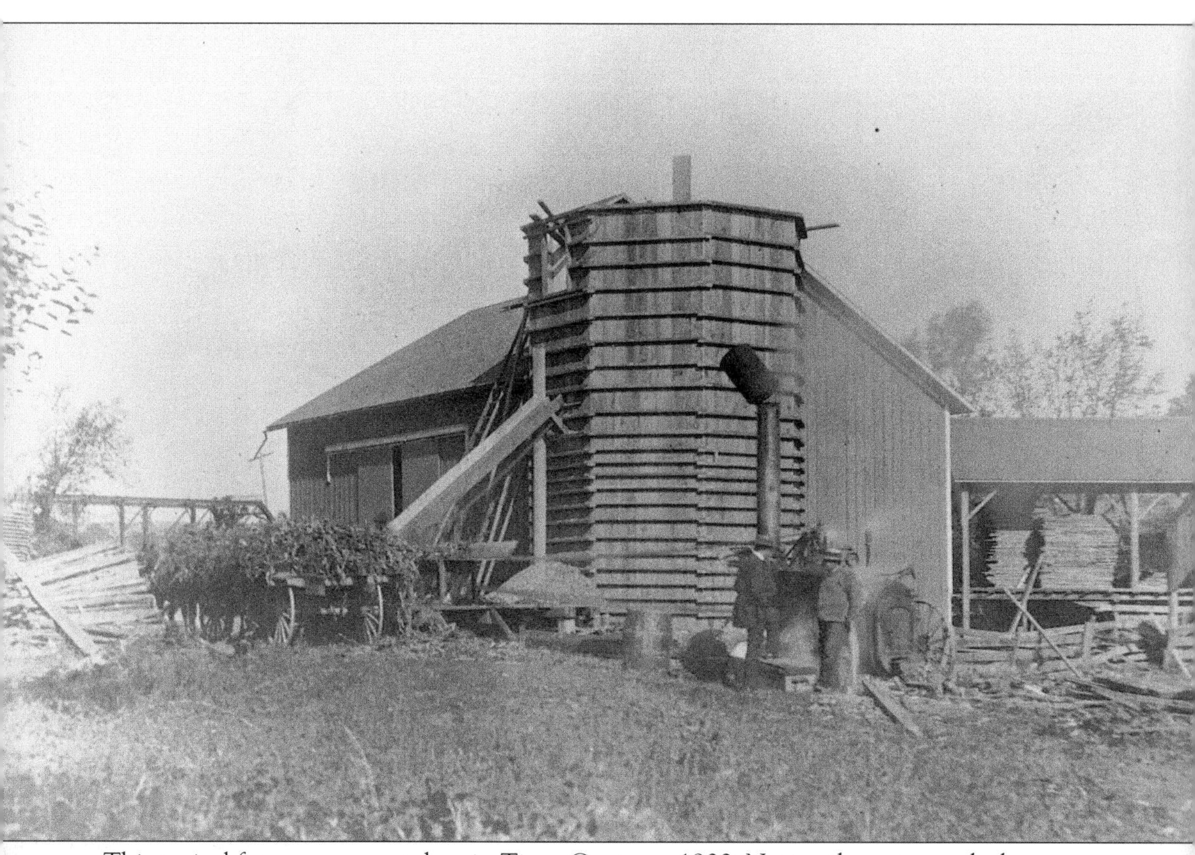

This typical farm scene was taken in Tioga Center *c.* 1900. Notice the octagonal silo.

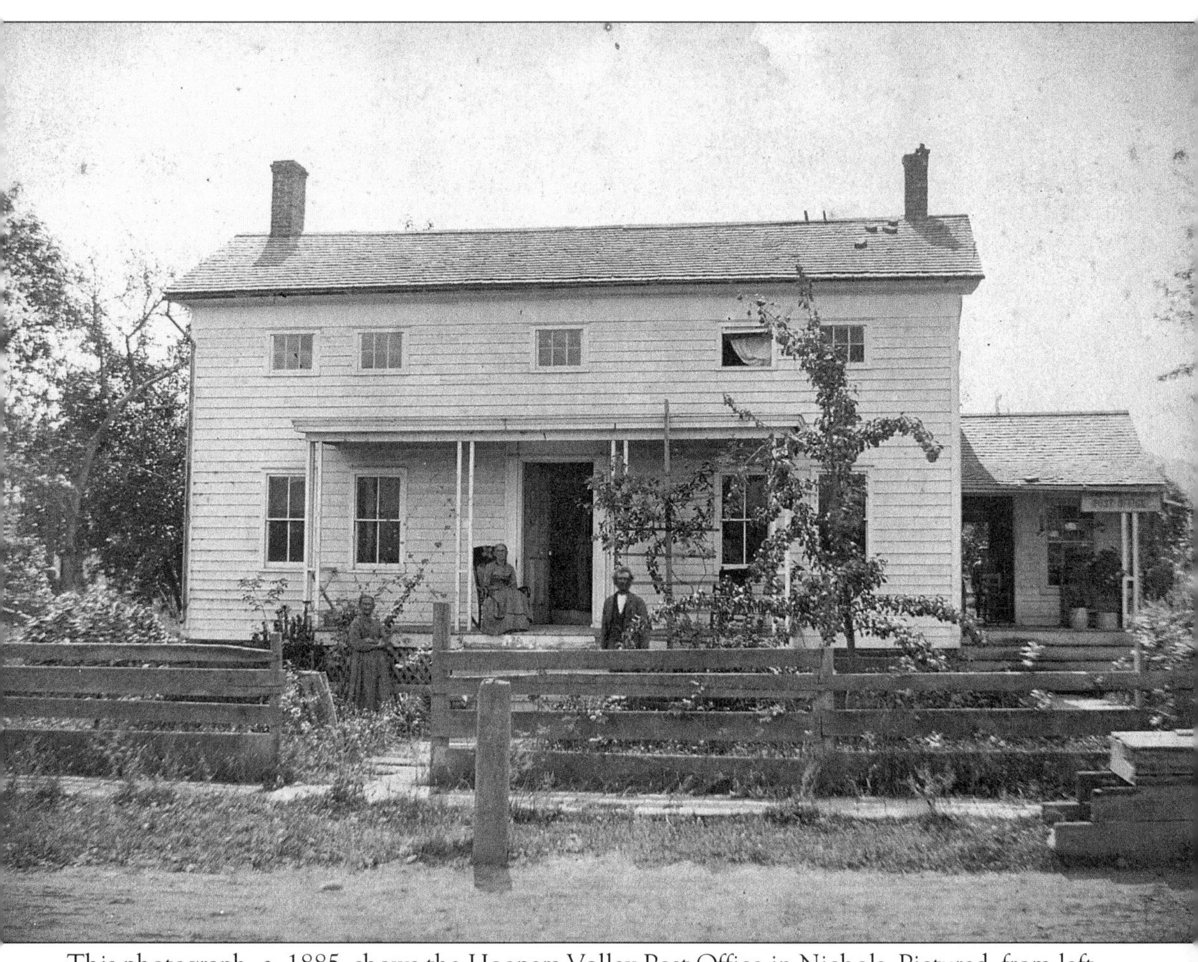

This photograph, *c.* 1885, shows the Hoopers Valley Post Office in Nichols. Pictured, from left to right, are Mrs. Ira J. Parks, Ellen Fox, and postmaster Ira J. Parks.

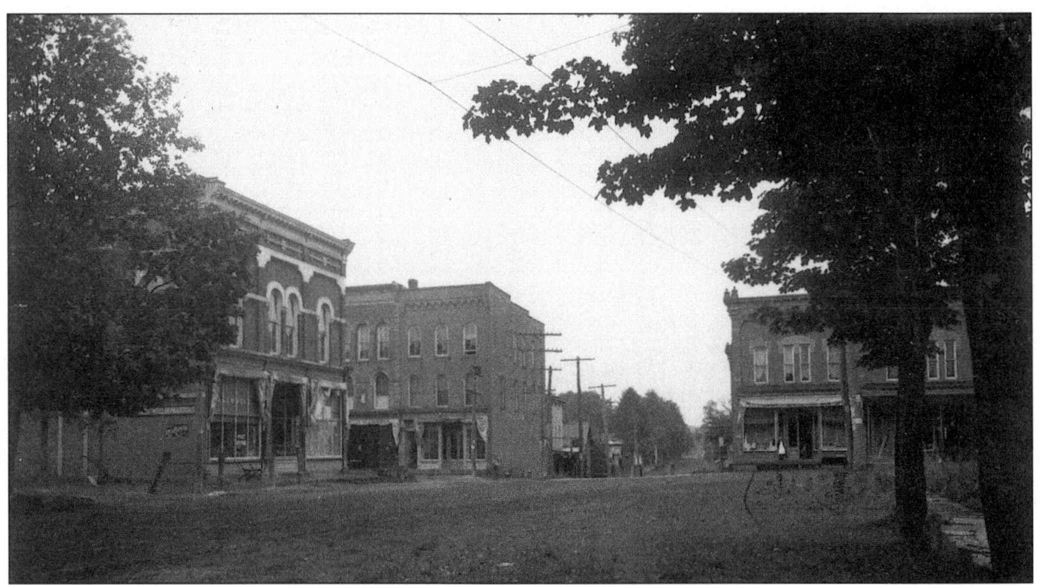

This view of Main and Tioga Streets in Spencer was taken *c.* 1905. Both brick buildings on the left were owned by the Emmons family.

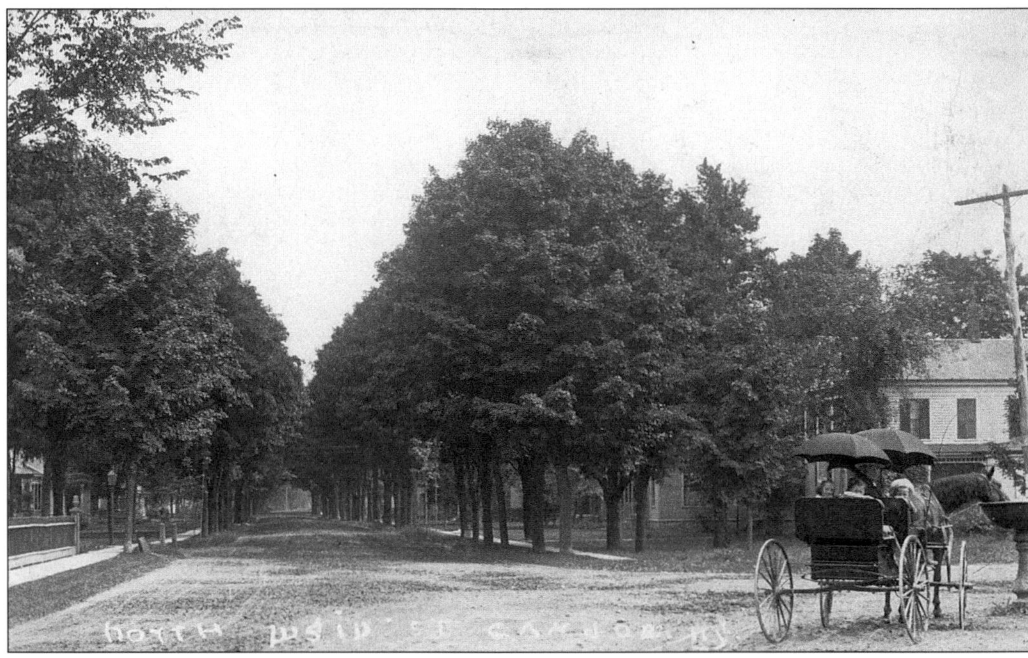

This view of Main Street in Candor was taken *c.* 1900, looking north. The horse is drinking out of the fountain, which was specifically placed there for the watering of horses.

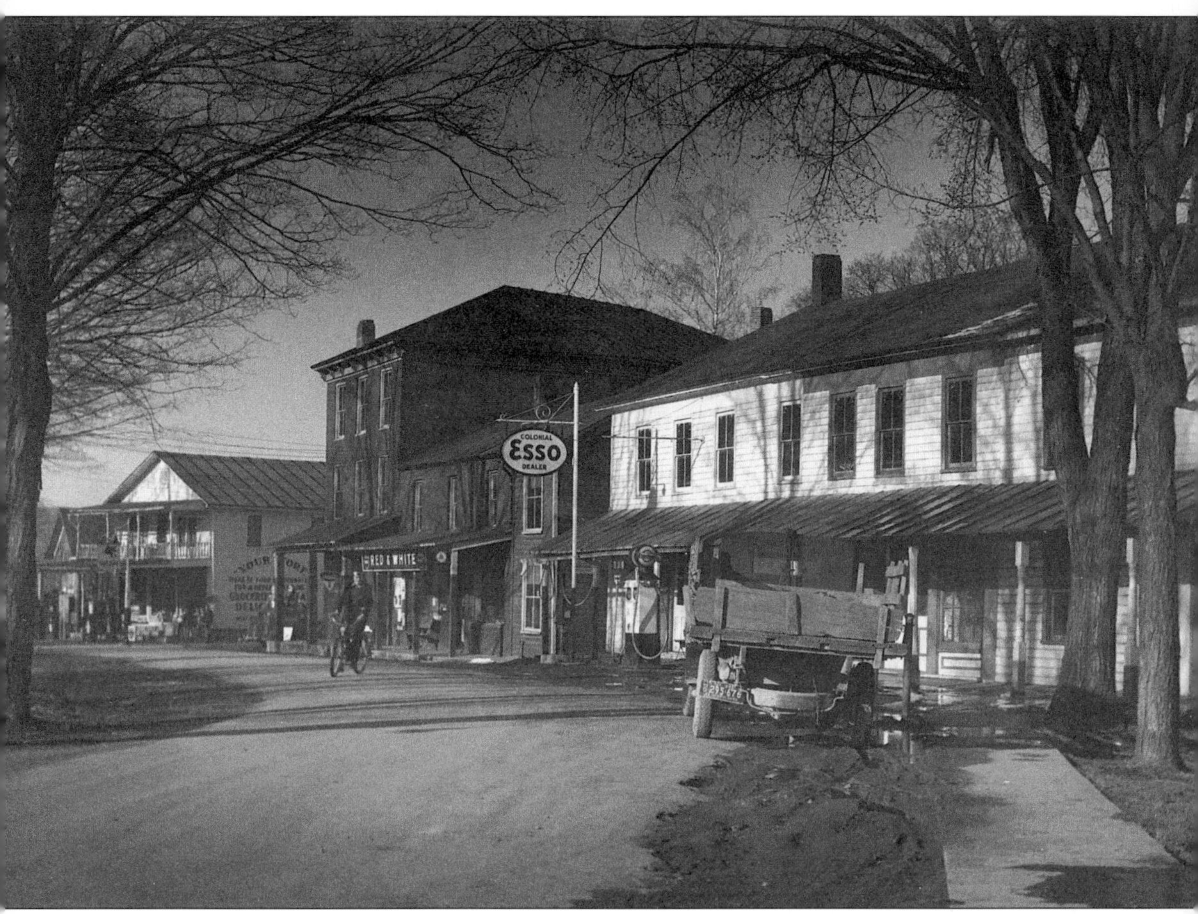

Here is Rawley's Department Store in Richford *c.* 1920. The boy on the bicycle is Russell Rawley.

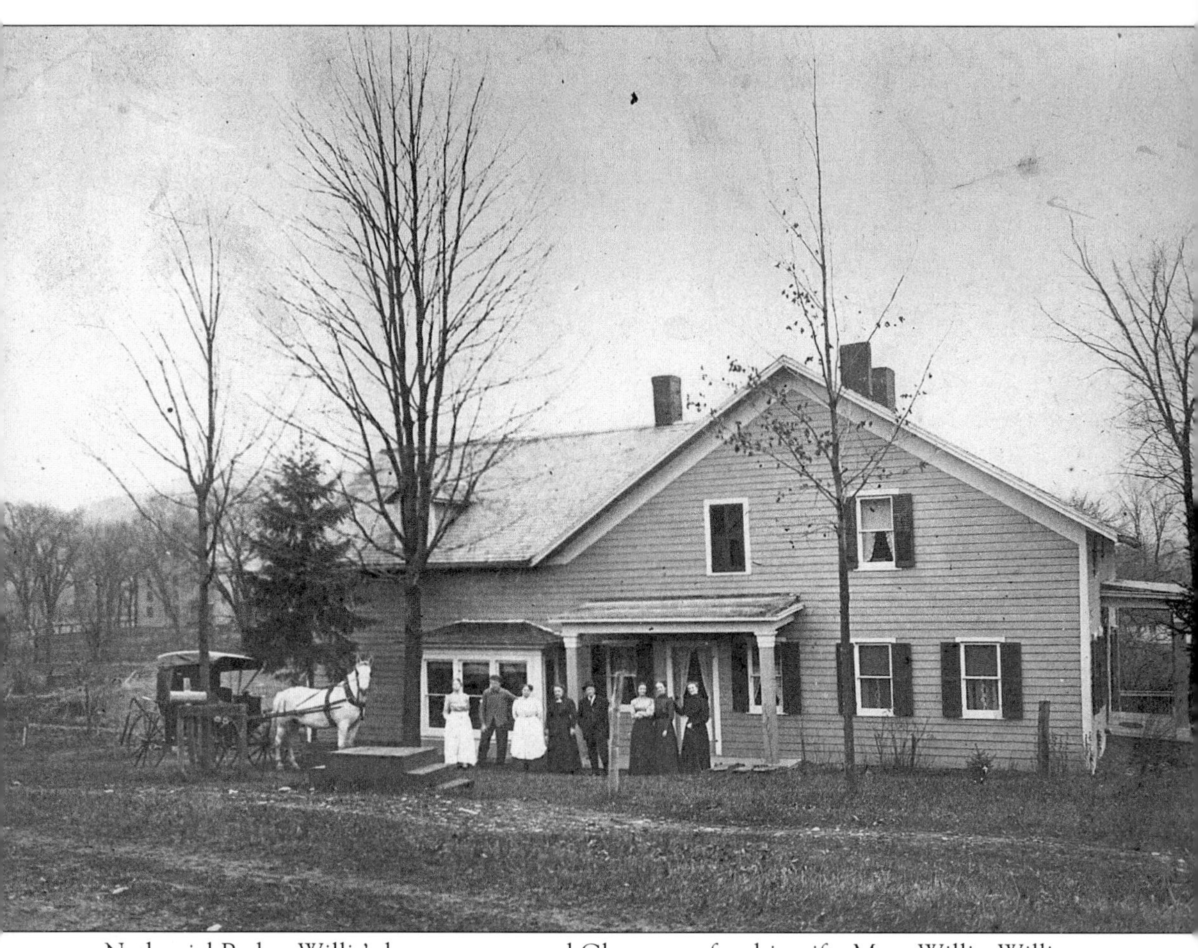

Nathaniel Parker Willis's home was named Glenmary after his wife, Mary Willis. Willis was a nationally famous poet in the mid-19th century. The house is still standing on Glenmary Drive on the west side of the Owego Creek.

This photograph shows the Tioga County clerk's office c. 1910.

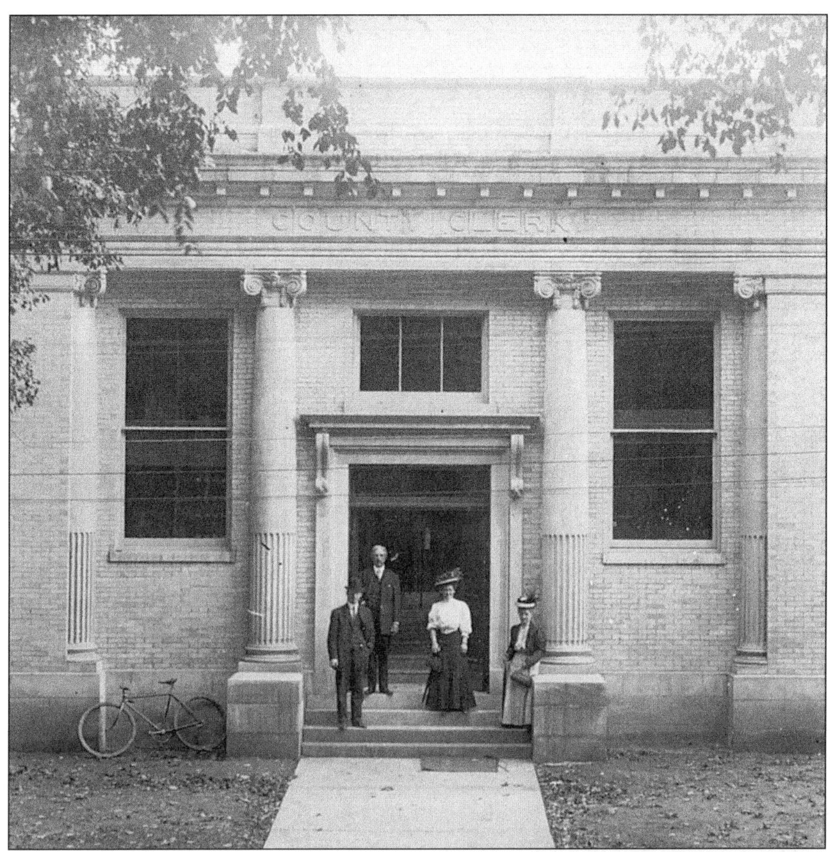

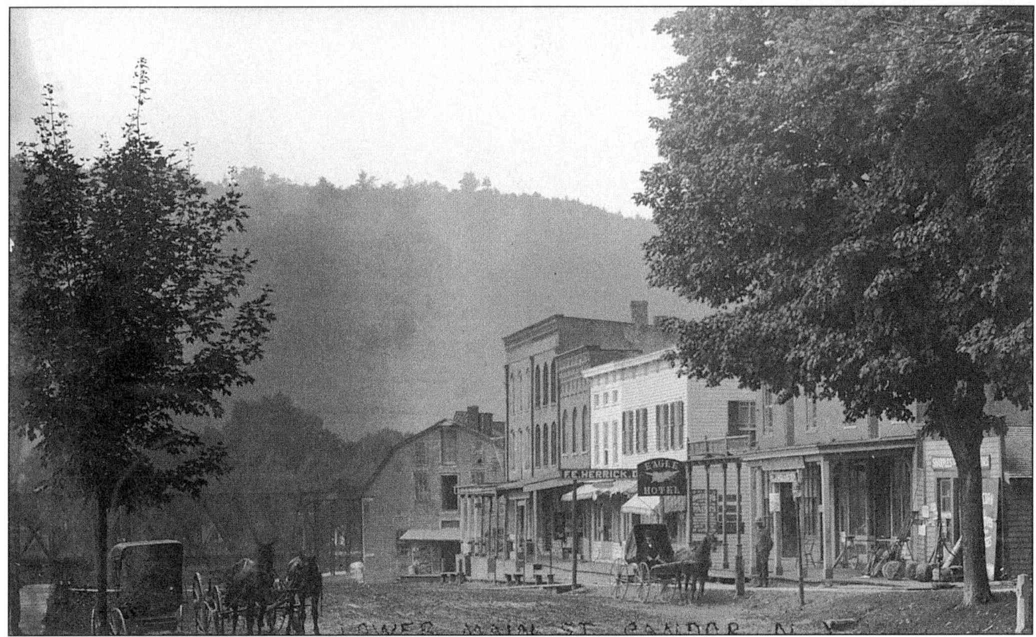

This view of Lower Main Street in Candor shows the Eagle Hotel, F.E. Herricks Optical Office, the old mill at the end of the street, and the old railroad bridge across the Catatonk Creek.

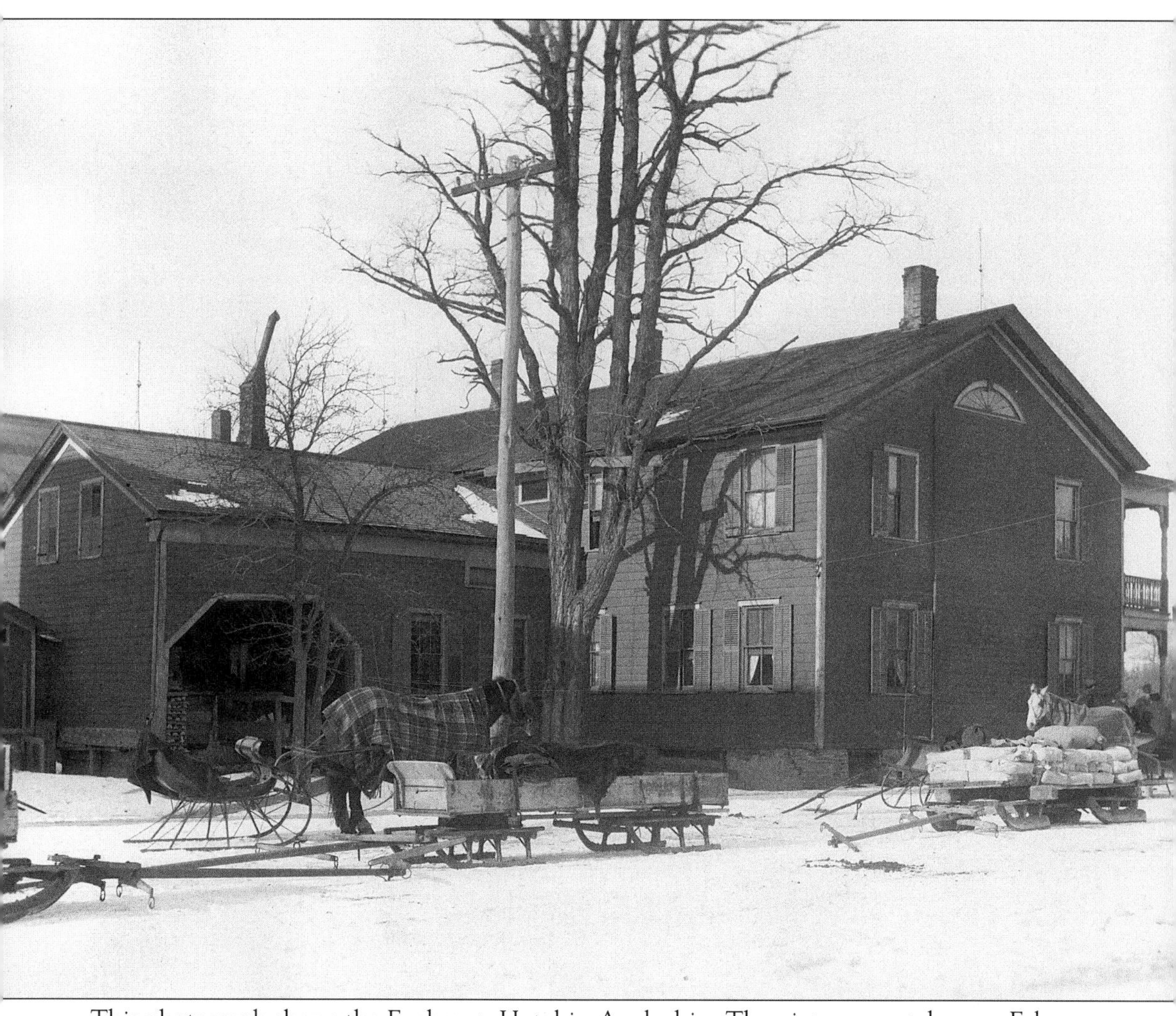

This photograph shows the Exchange Hotel in Apalachin. The picture was taken on February 9, 1915, which was election day. The citizens voted for temperance, making the town dry.

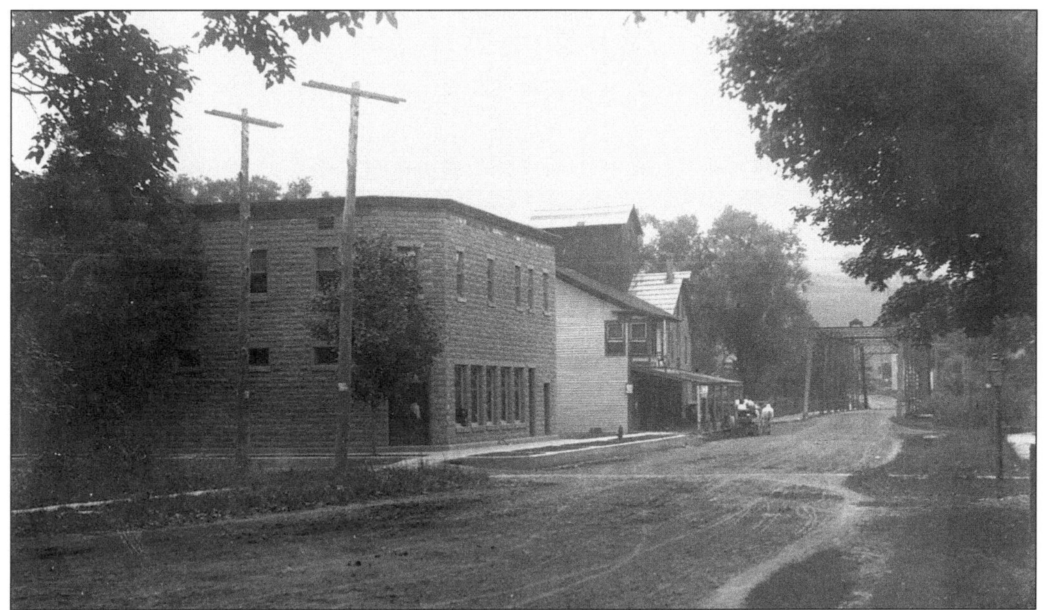

This view shows the Johnson Block in Candor. Notice the gas lamp and hitching post at the right and the high frame bridge in the background.

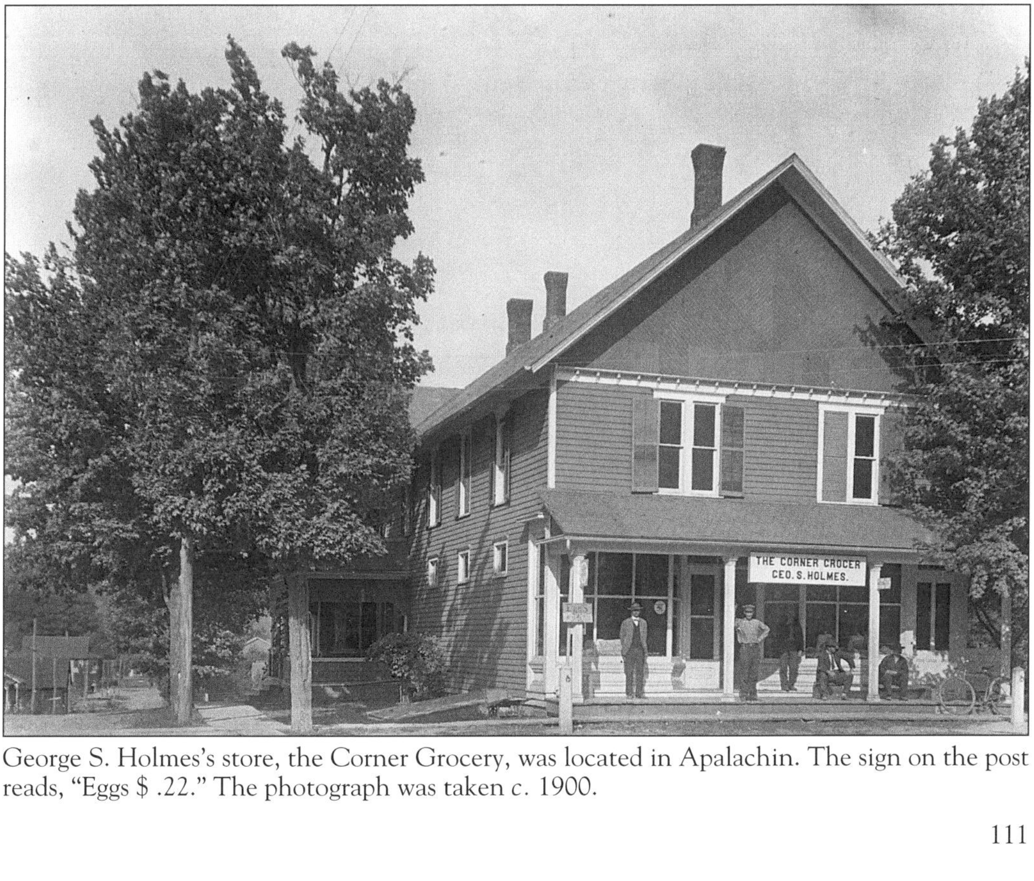

George S. Holmes's store, the Corner Grocery, was located in Apalachin. The sign on the post reads, "Eggs $ .22." The photograph was taken *c.* 1900.

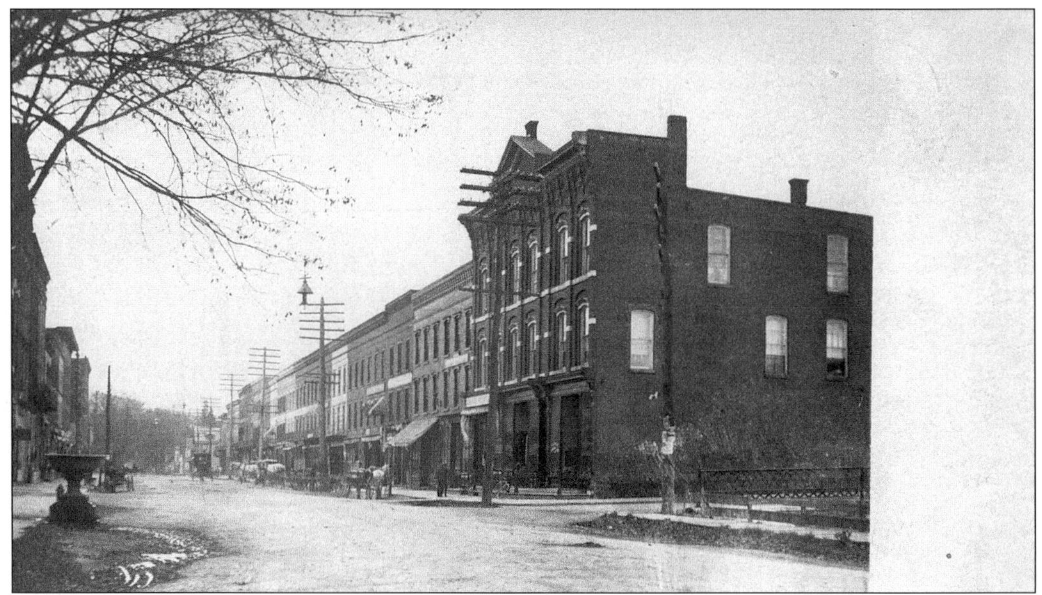

This view of the southeast corner of Court and Front Streets in Owego was taken *c.* 1900. The corner building housed Thurston's Grocery and the *Daily Record*.

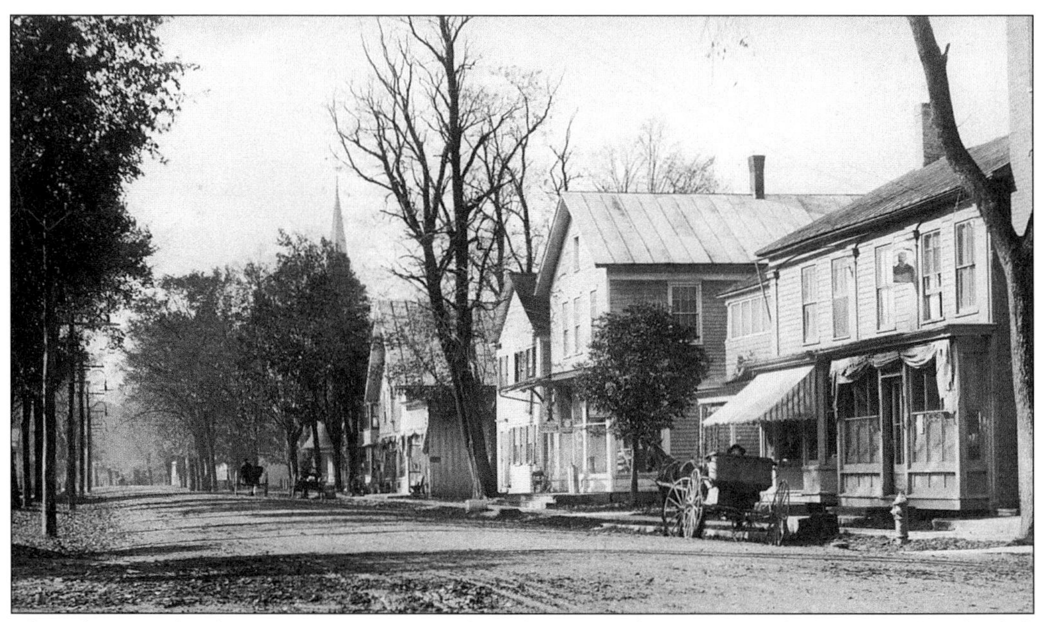

This photograph of Main Street in Newark Valley was taken *c.* 1905, looking south. The left side of the road is lined with electric streetlights. A woman peeks over her shoulder in the carriage at the right.

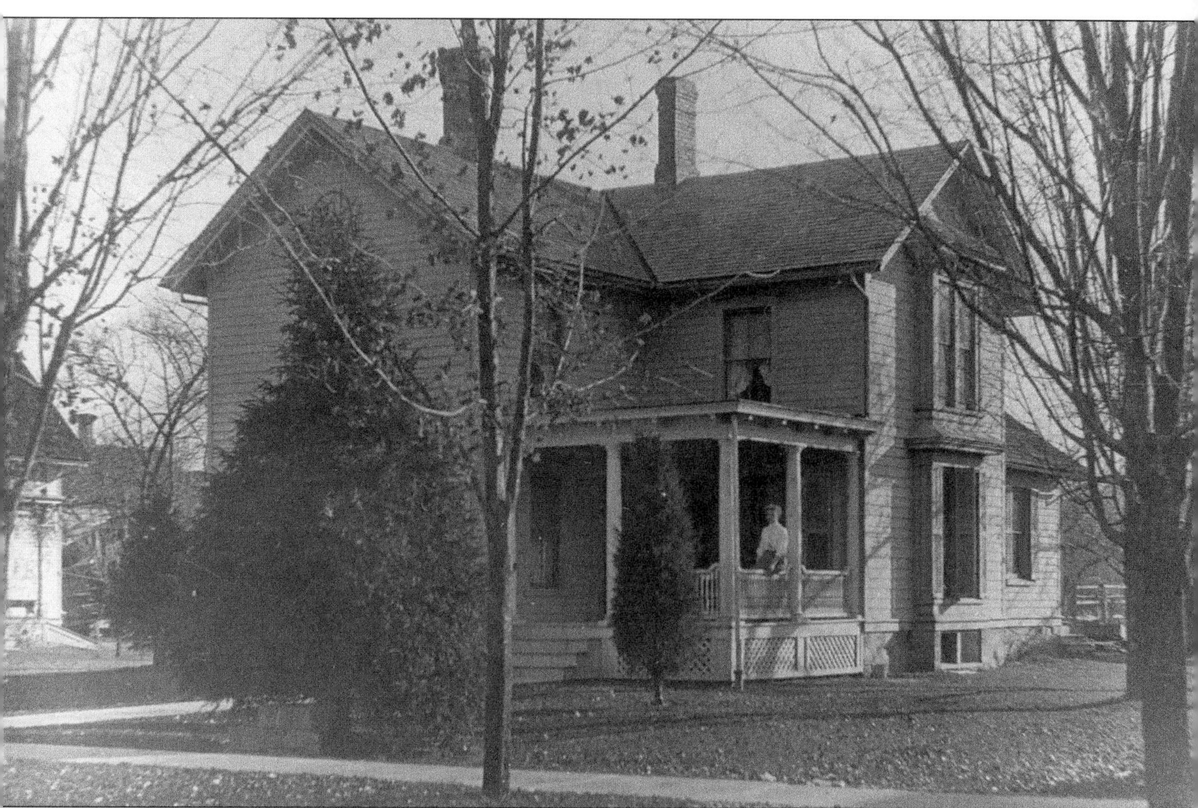

This was the home of Webster Ellsworth, the former mayor of the village of Nichols. The house is located on Cady Avenue in Nichols.

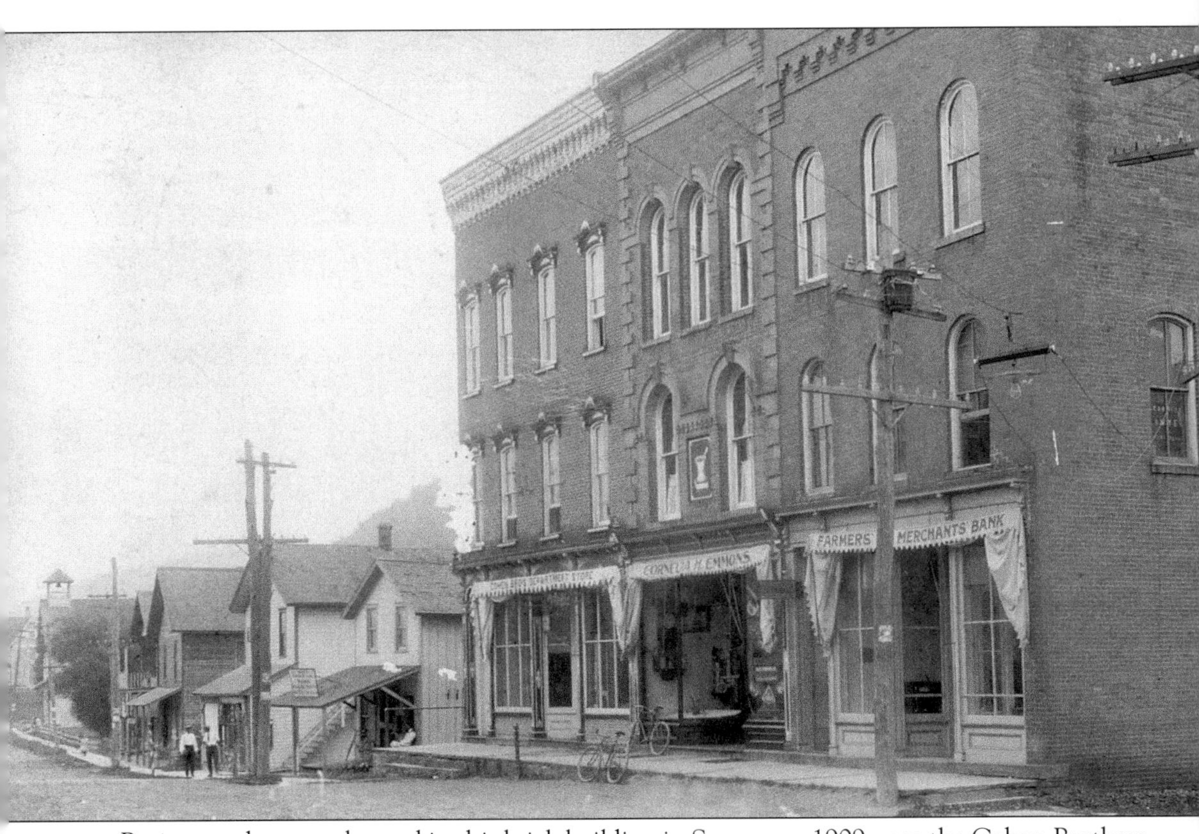

Businesses that were located in this brick building in Spencer *c.* 1909 were the Cohen Brothers Department Store, Cornelia H. Emmons Drugstore, and the Farmers and Merchants Bank.

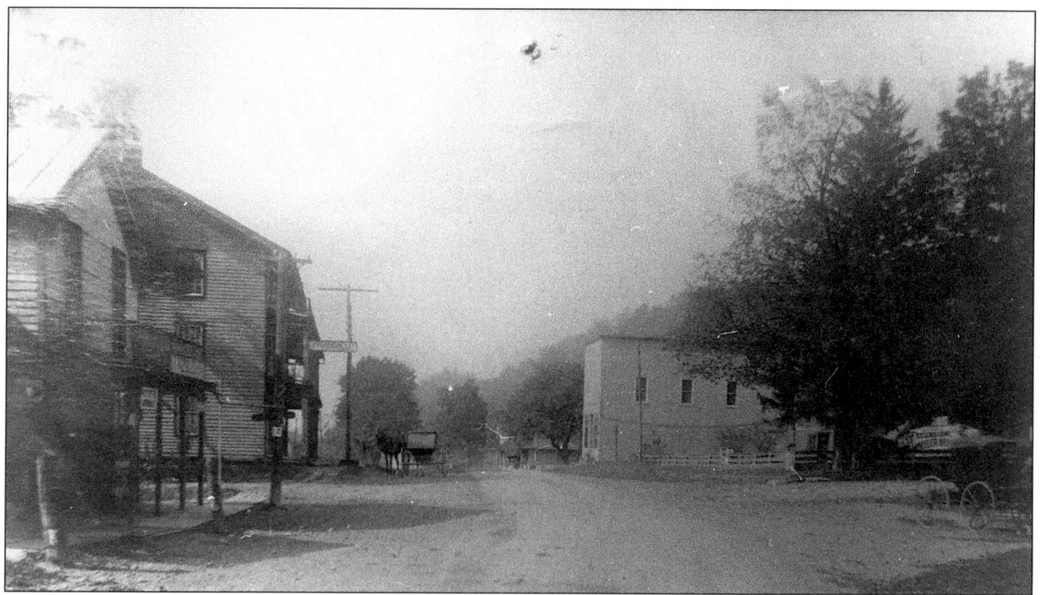

Here is a c. 1900 view of Main Street in Smithboro. Notice the sign at the right advertising Wheeler Brothers Excursions for 15¢.

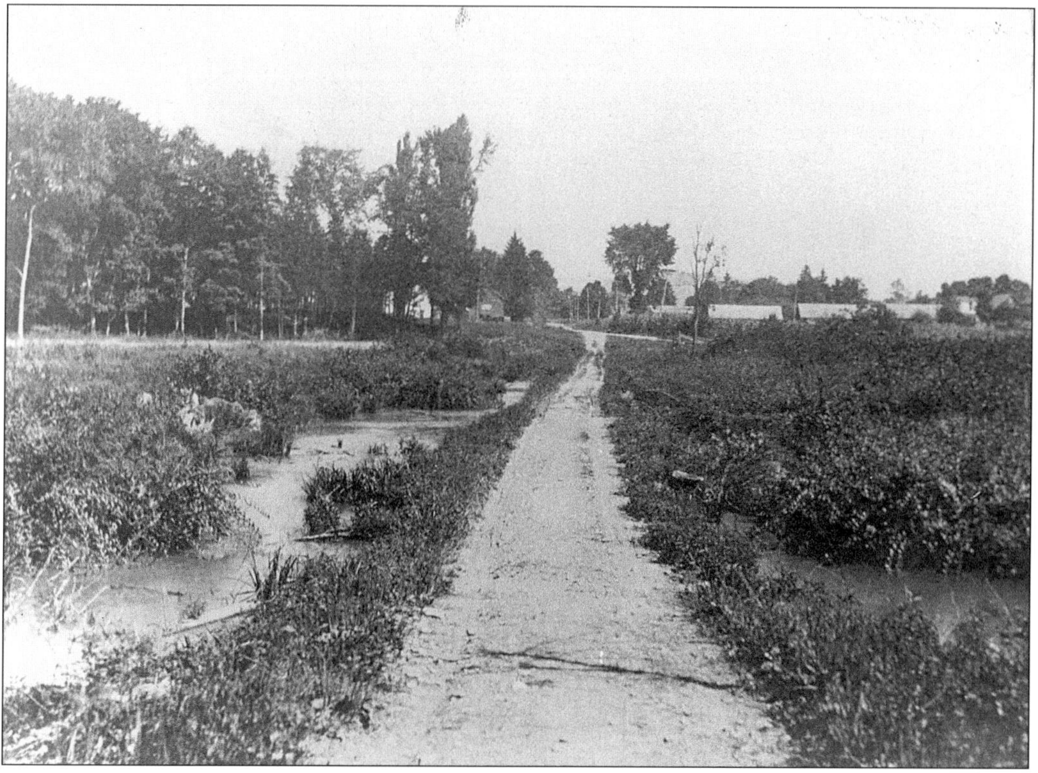

This old floating-log road ran to Nichols Street in Spencer. The view to the north shows a white school on the left and Professor Marsh's chicken farm on the right.

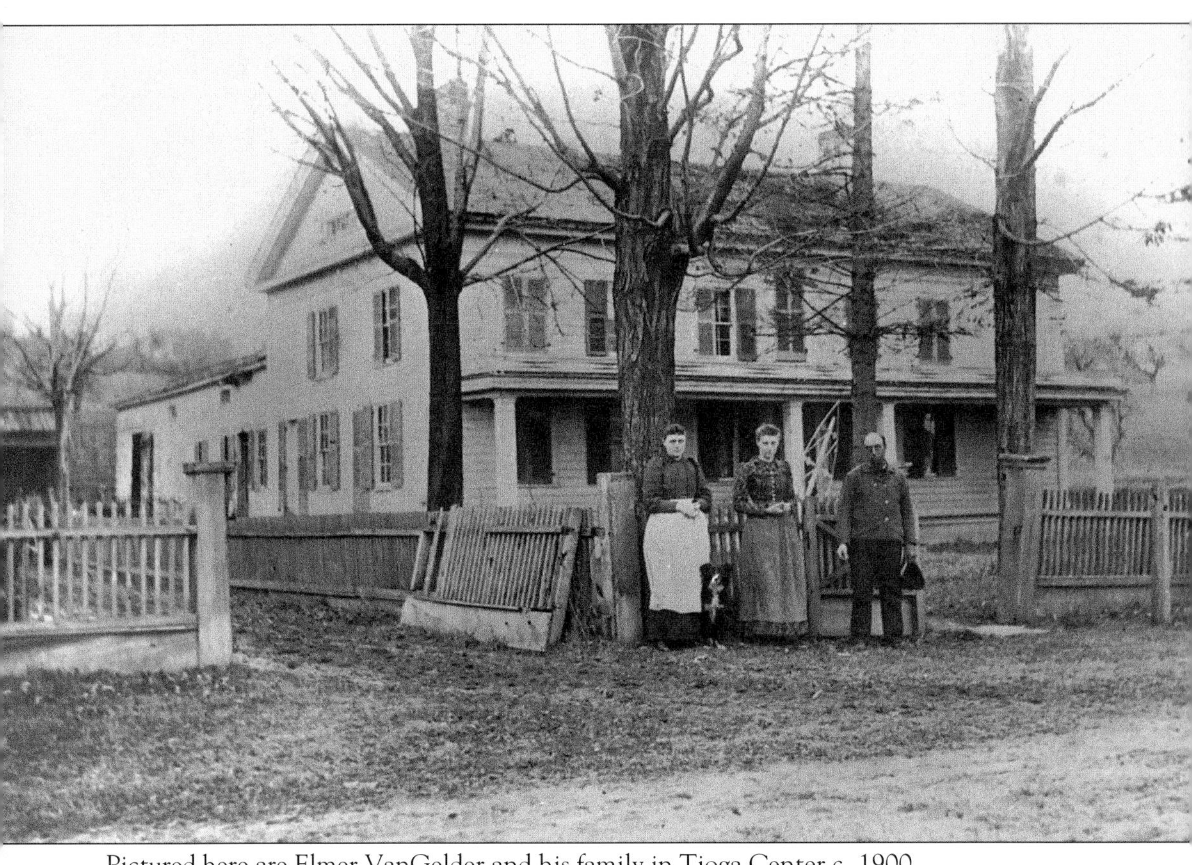

Pictured here are Elmer VanGelder and his family in Tioga Center *c.* 1900.

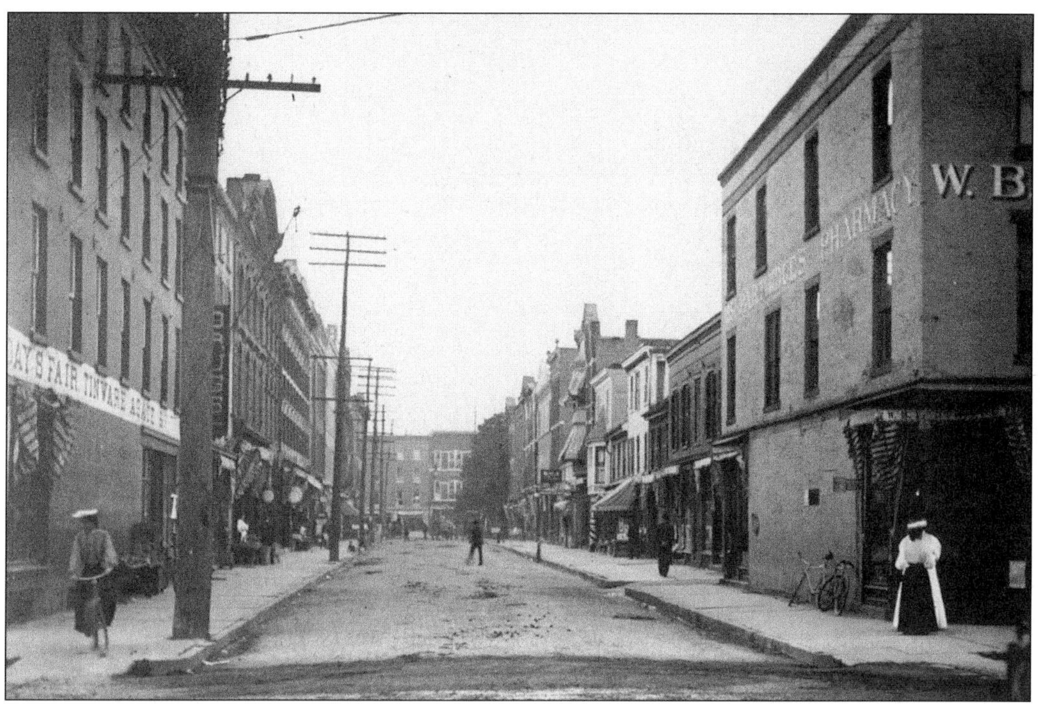

This view of Lake Street in Owego was taken *c.* 1900 looking north. in Owego. On the left, a young lady rides her bicycle.

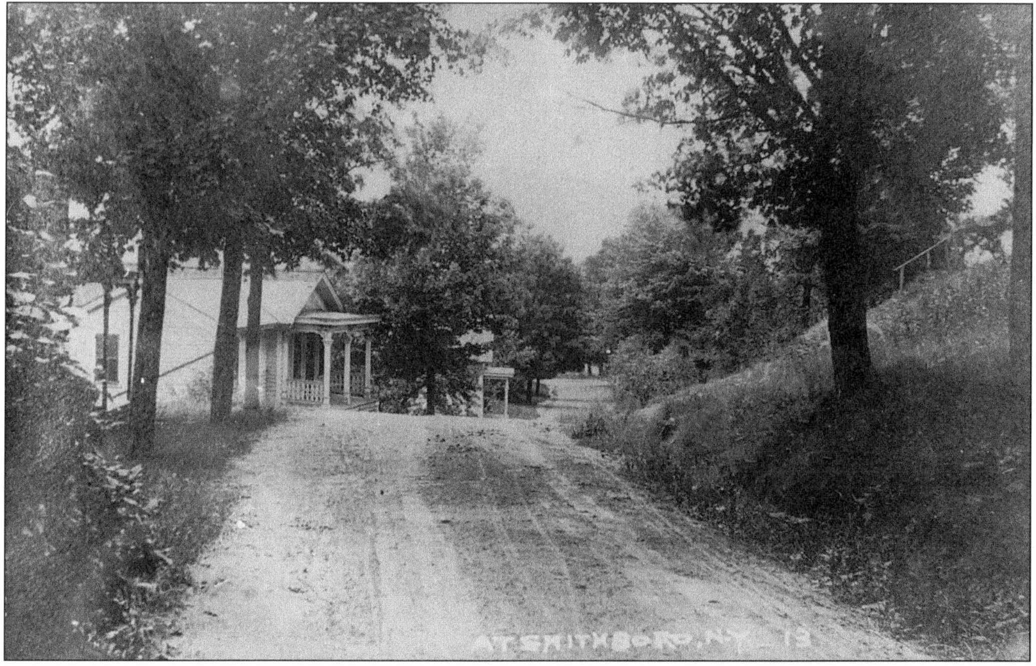

This photograph was taken *c.* 1910. It shows the community of Smithboro.

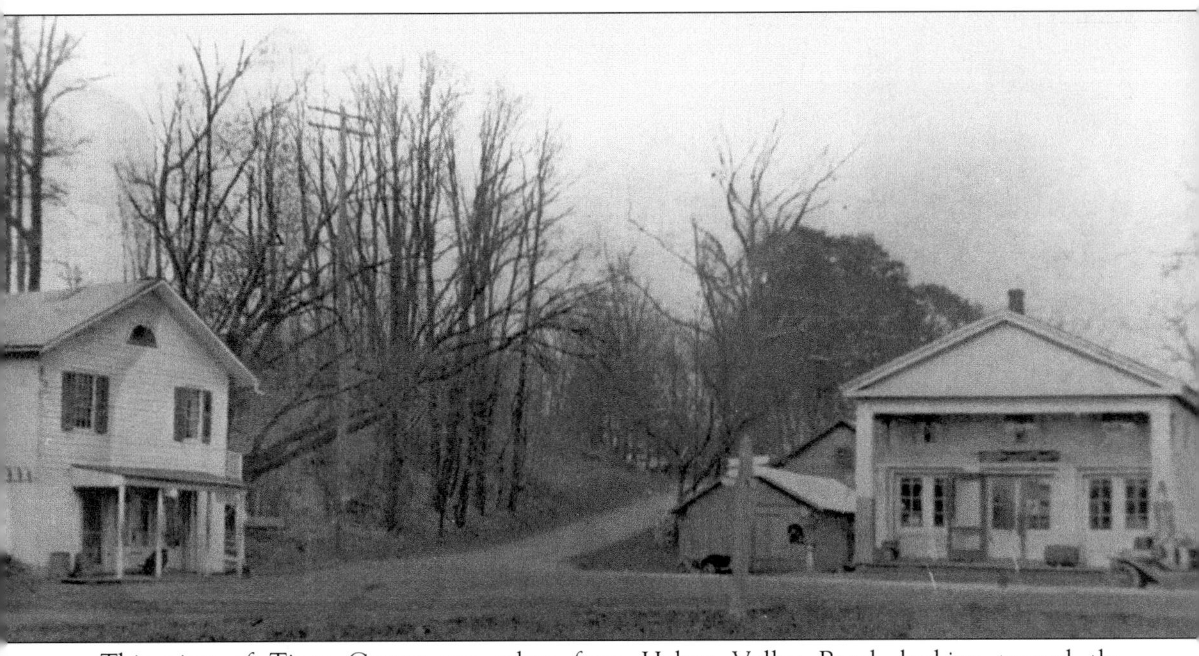

This view of Tioga Center was taken from Halsey Valley Road, looking toward the Susquehanna River.

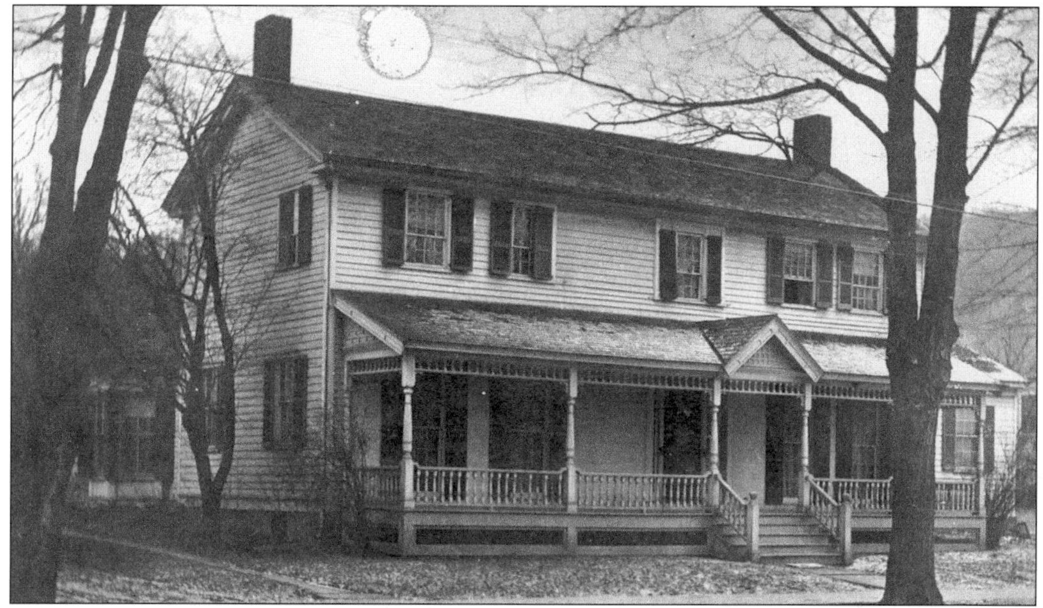

This is the birthplace of Thomas Collier Platt in Owego. The building was moved from its original Main Street location when the Owego Central School was built in 1907.

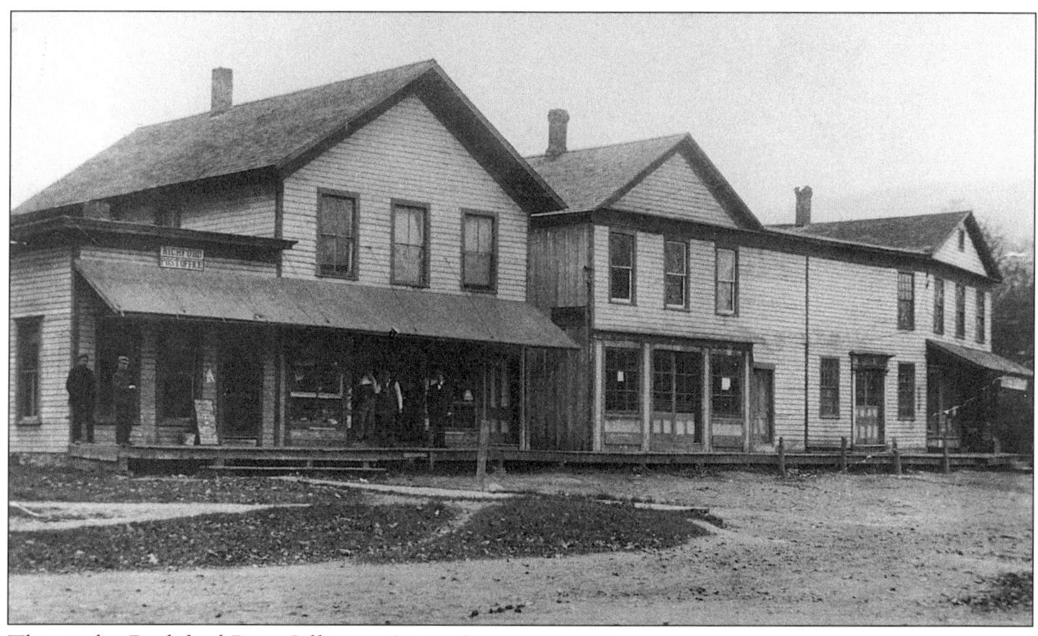

This is the Richford Post Office on Main Street *c.* 1900.

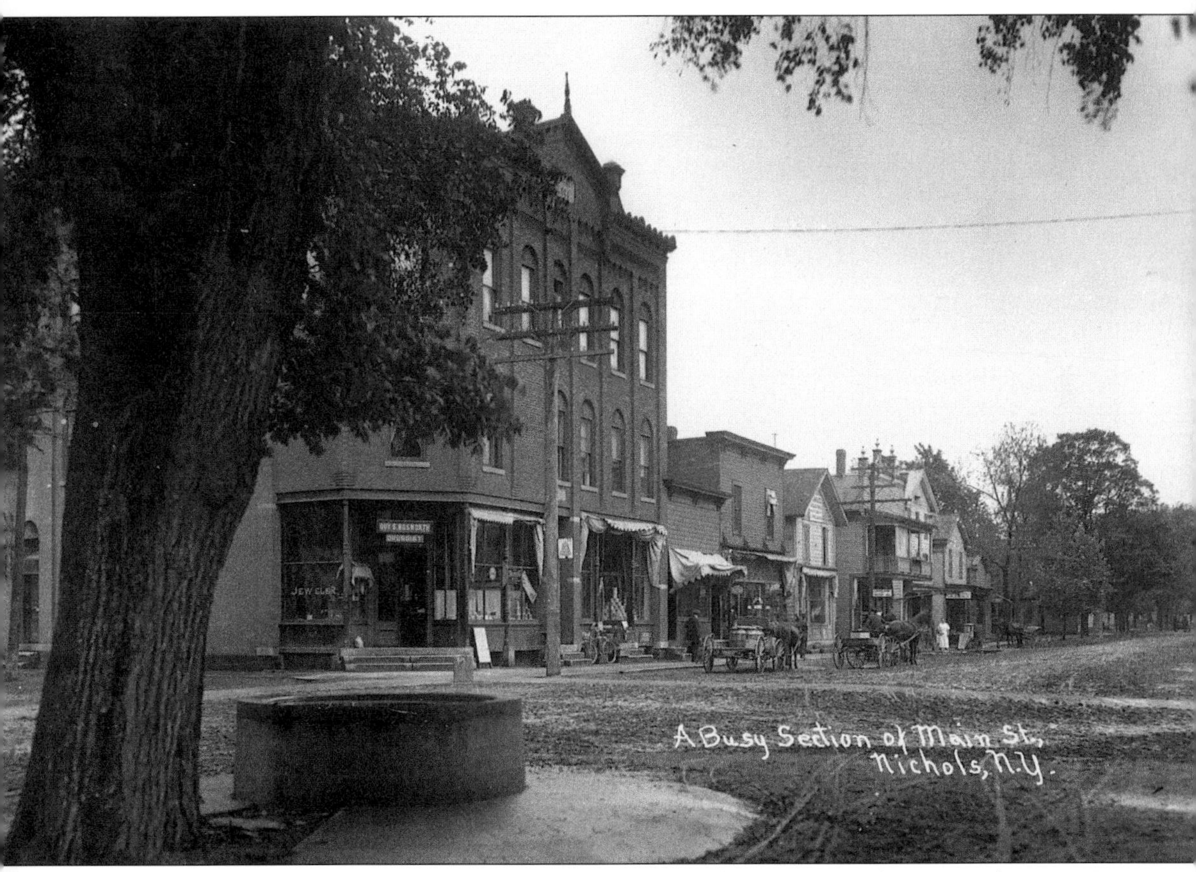

Here is Main Street in Nichols *c.* 1905. Notice the circular water trough next to the tree. Guy S. Bosworth's drugstore is located in the brick building.

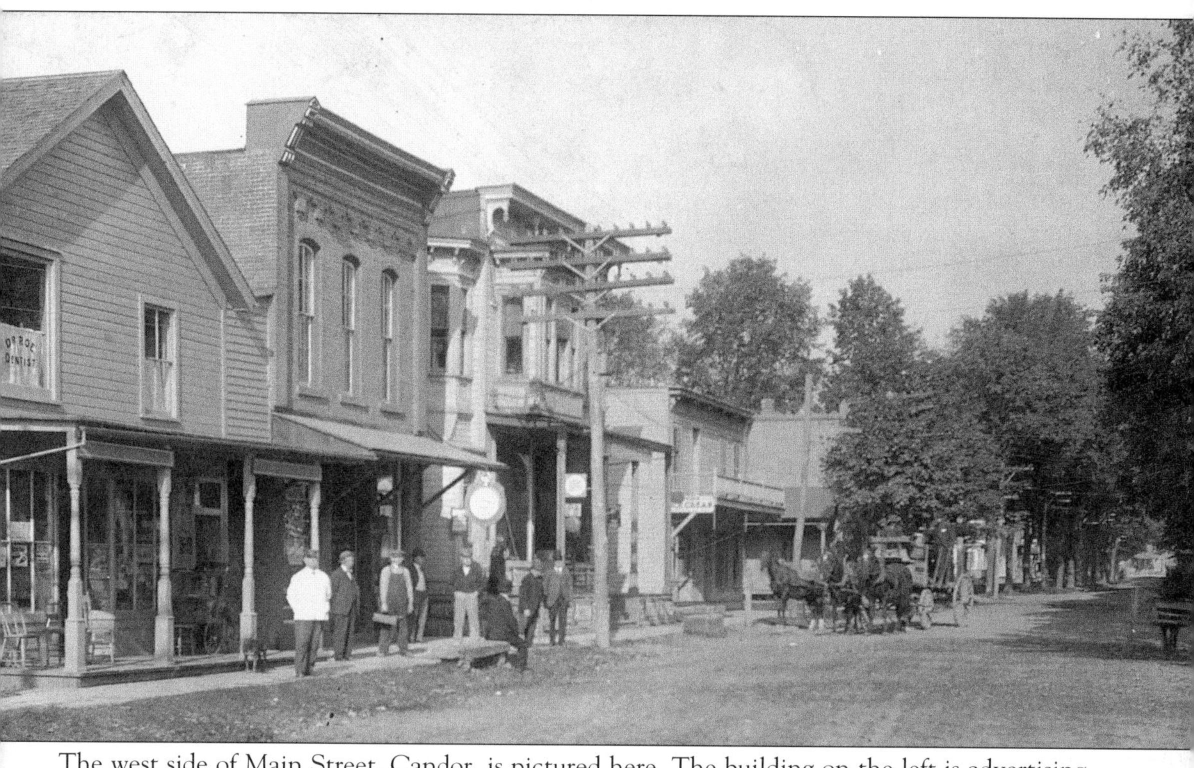

The west side of Main Street, Candor, is pictured here. The building on the left is advertising "Fine and dandy sweet goods." Upstairs, Dr. Roe, a dentist, holds his practice.

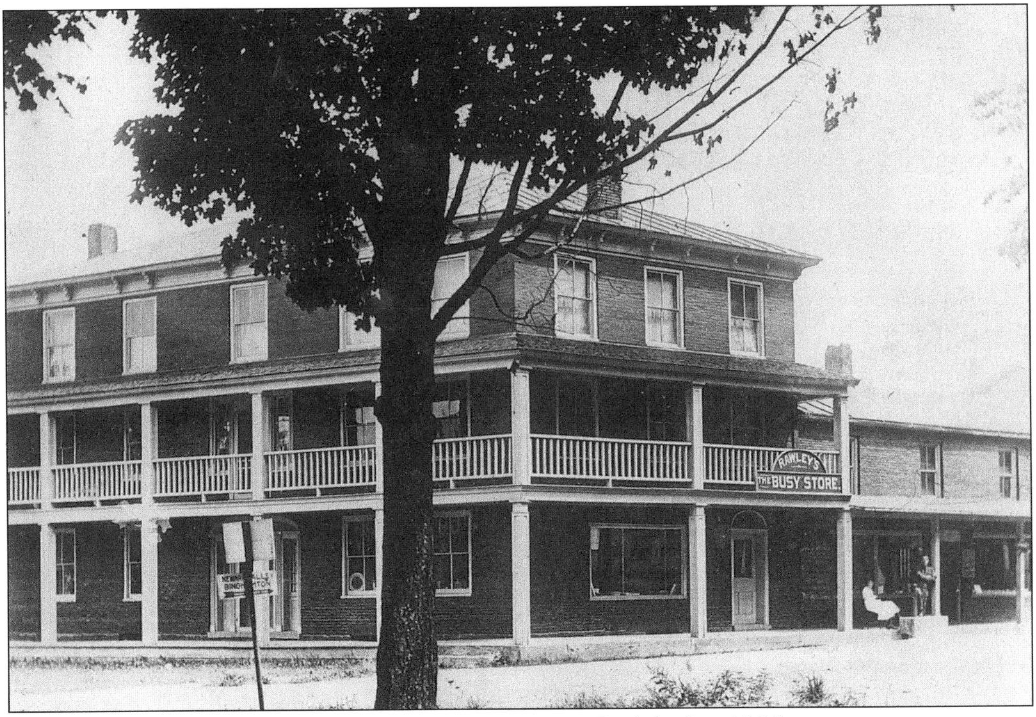

This photograph shows Rawley's Department Store in Richford in 1925.

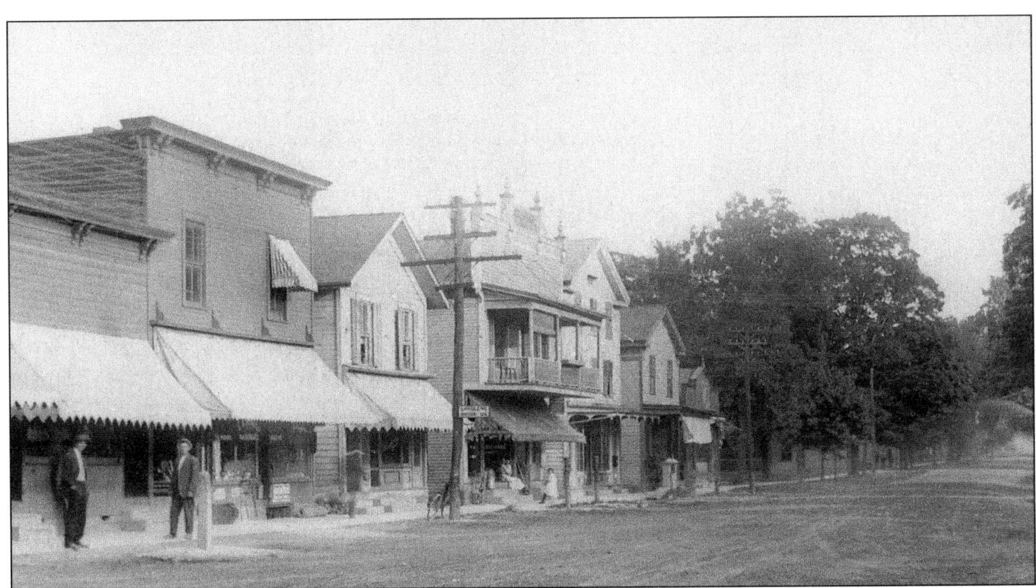

Here is Main Street in Nichols. The second canopy protects the entrance to C.B. Arnold's Hardware Store. The fourth canopy is the entrance to Osborne's Hardware. The sign on the telephone pole advertises "gasolene [sic] and motor oil."

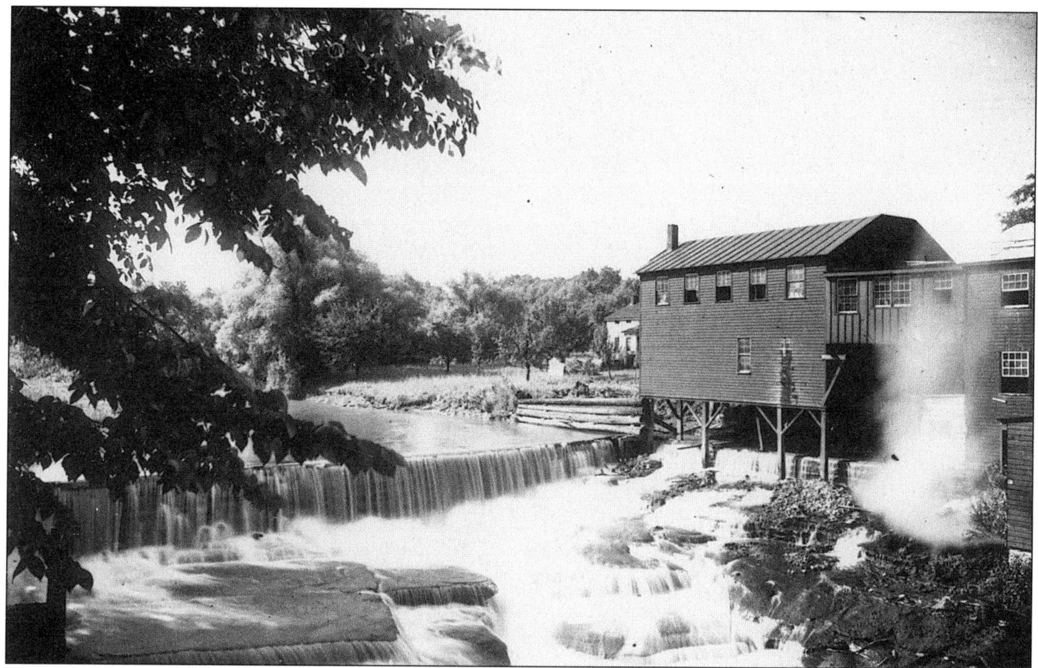

Mills relied on waterpower to produce or manufacture goods. This is a good example of such a mill in Spencer *c.* 1900.

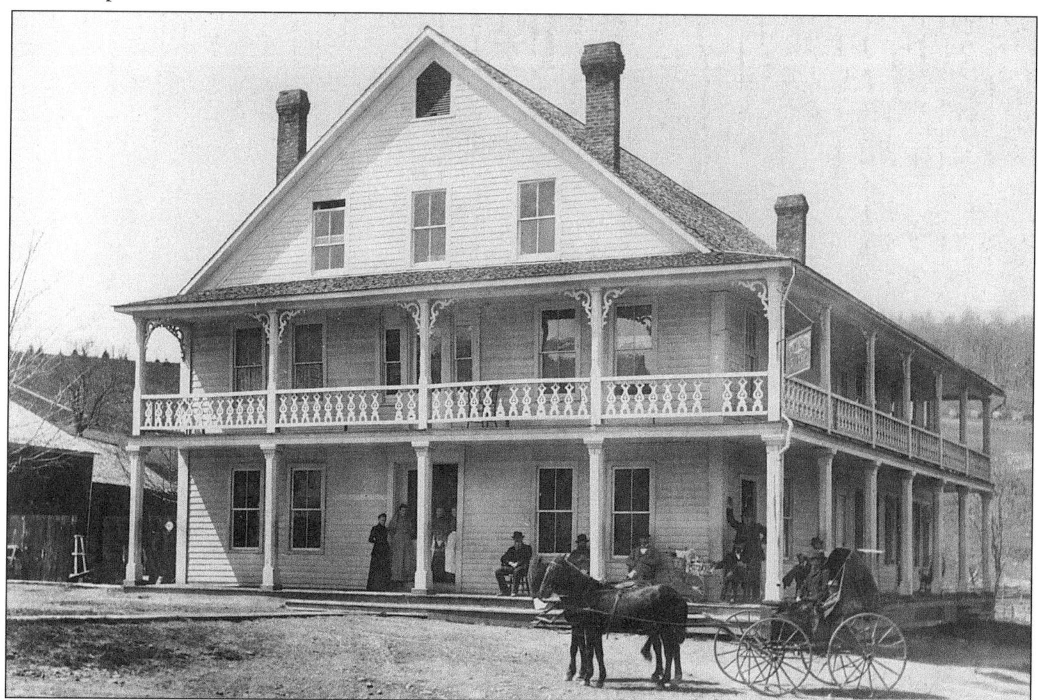

The infamous Richford Hotel is seen here *c.* 1890. Richford was considered, by many citizens living in the surrounding towns, to be "godless" because of the liquor and other activities that were offered here. However, many of those same citizens patronized the hotel late at night. The hotel burned on December 3, 1991.

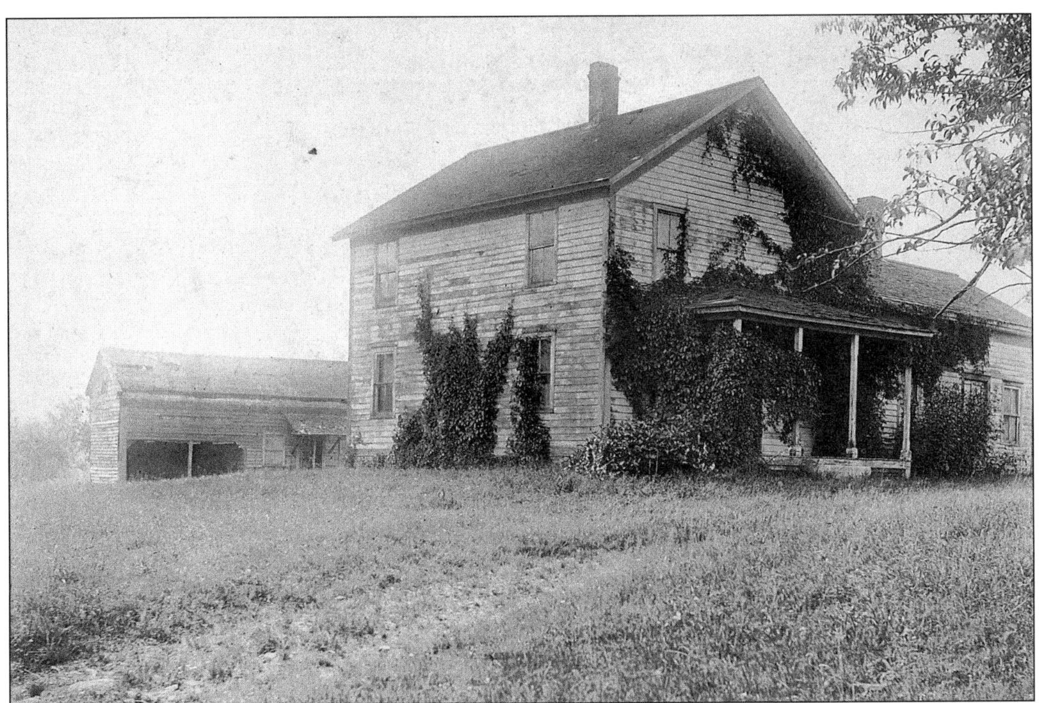

This is the birthplace of John D. Rockefeller in Richford. It was taken apart in the early 1900s, and its whereabouts are unknown today.

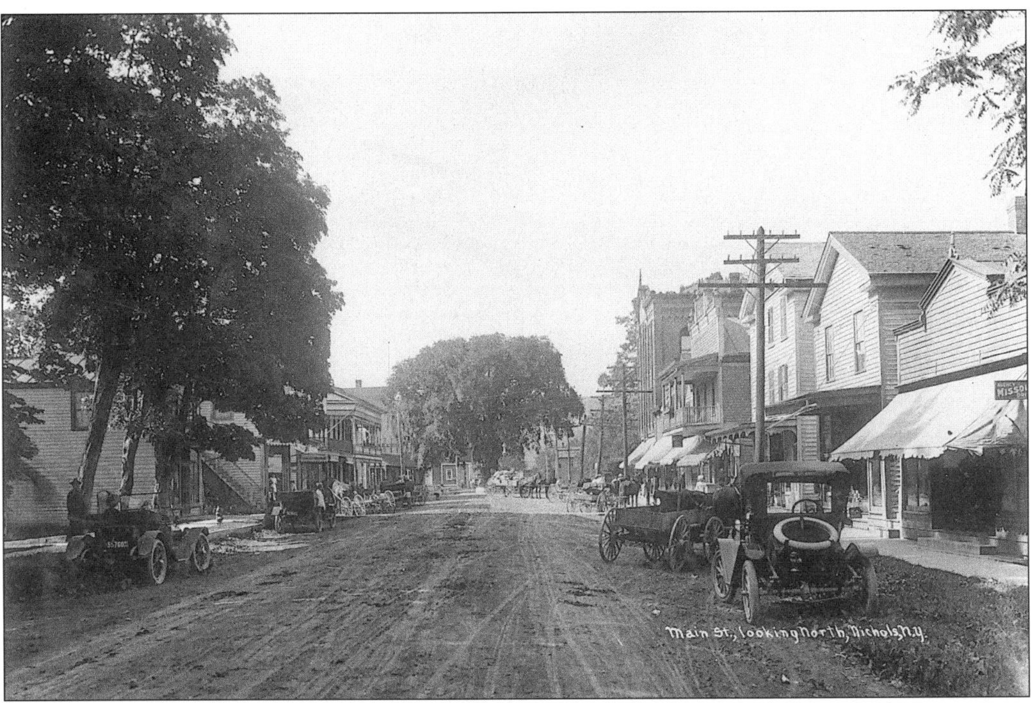

This photograph of Main Street in Nichols was taken looking north *c.* 1910. It shows an interesting mix of automobiles and carriages.

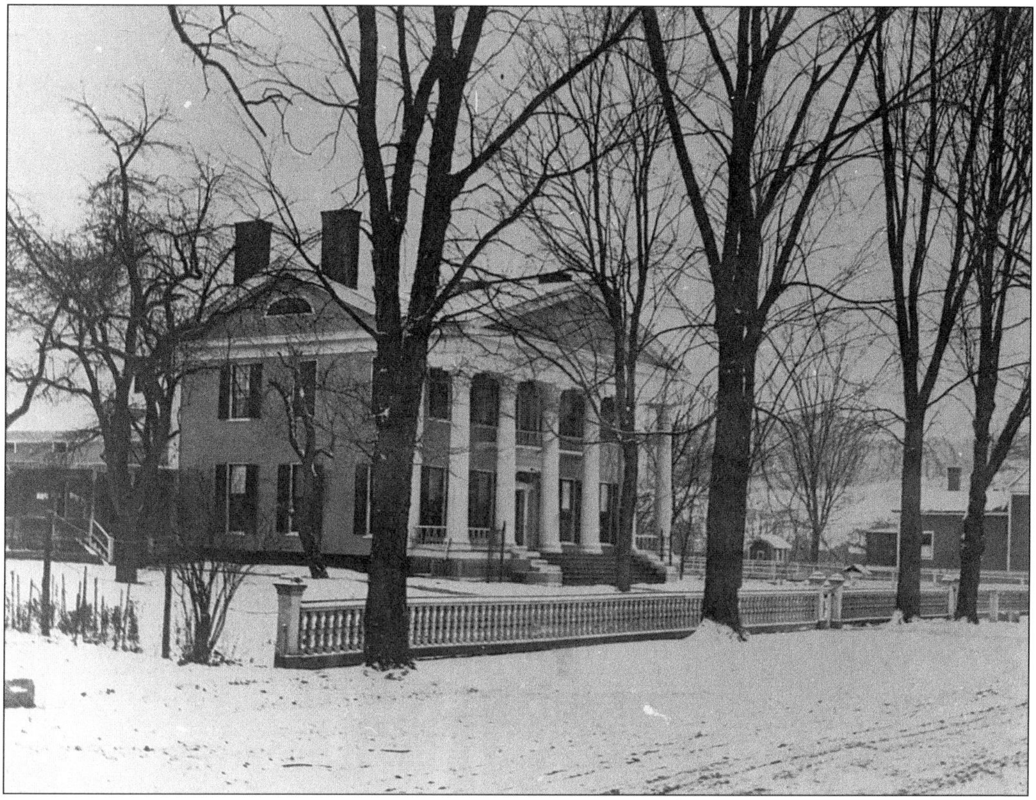

This photograph shows the Cady Mansion in Nichols *c.* 1889.

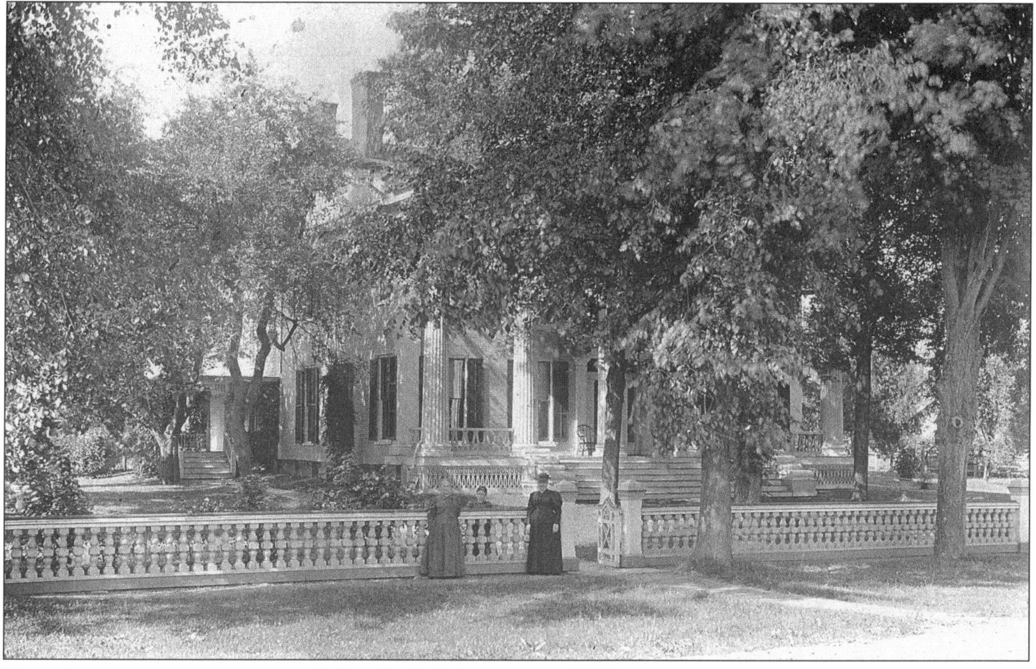

Here is a summertime view of the Cady Mansion *c.* 1890.

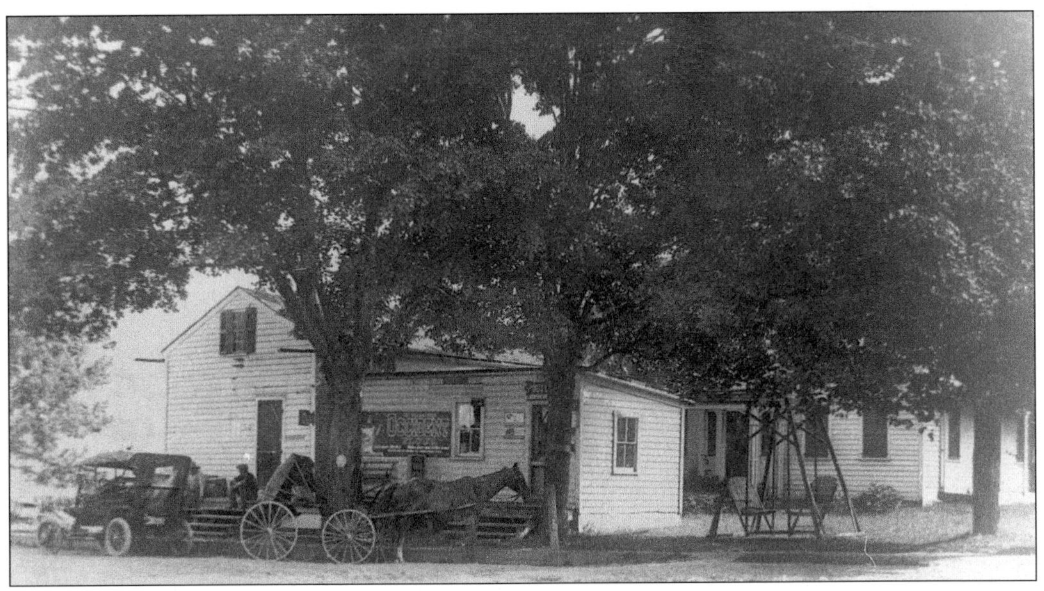

Wheelers General Store was located in Lounsberry. This photograph was taken c 1910.

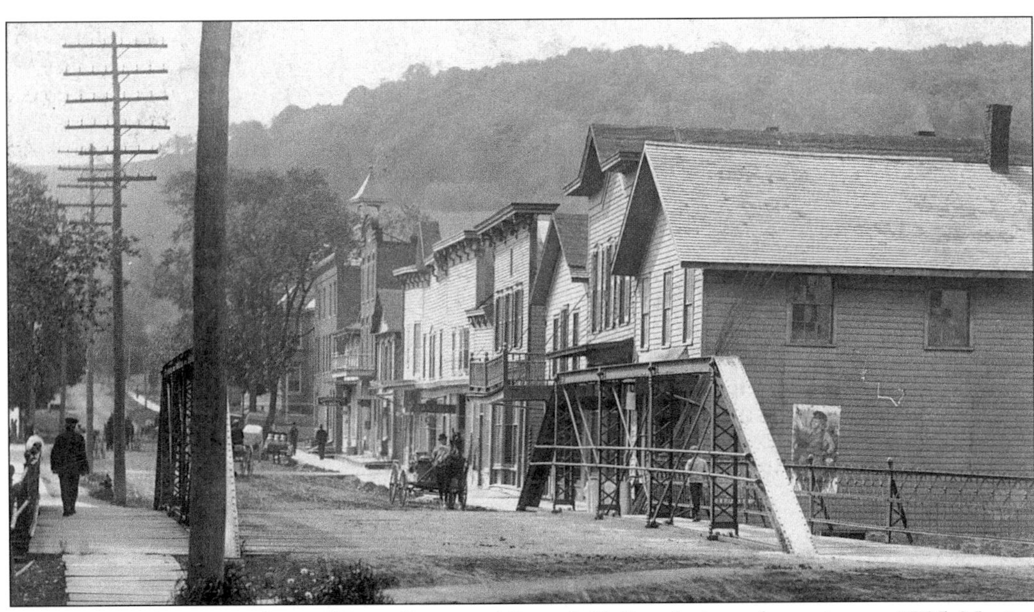

This view looking east shows Water Street in Newark Valley during a busy time c. 1905. Notice N. White's lunchroom, a bakery, and an advertisement for Dutch Boy Paints.

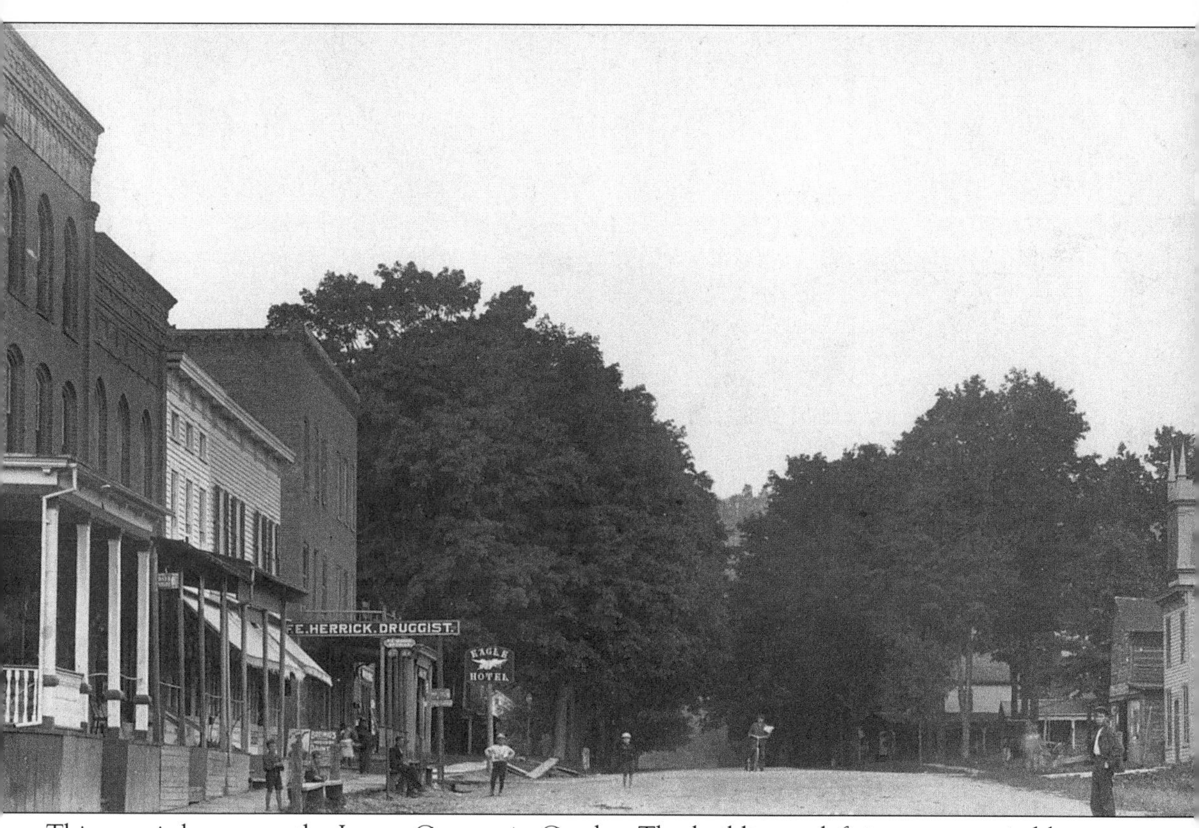

This area is known as the Lower Corners in Candor. The building at left is now occupied by Fitzpatrick's Pub. The Eagle Hotel was destroyed by fire in 1914.

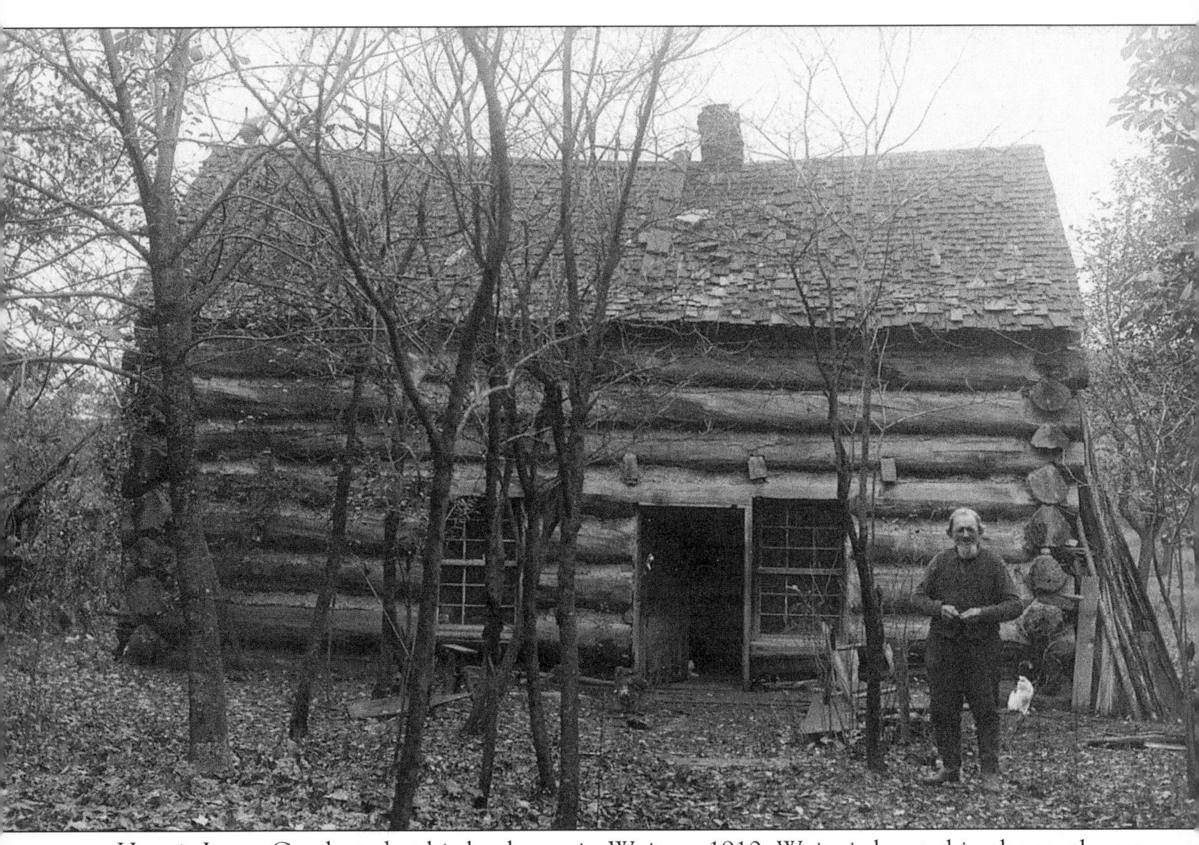

Here is James Goodspeed at his log house in Waits *c.* 1910. Waits is located in the southwest corner of the town of Owego. Except for its glass windows, Goodspeed's cabin is similar to those constructed by early settlers.